Imagining Wholesome Wellbeing of All

About the Author

Jai B.P. Sinha is Professor of Psychology and Management at the ASSERT Institute of Management Studies, Patna, India. Prof. Sinha completed his post-graduation in India and received his Ph.D. from Ohio State University, Columbus, Ohio, USA. He has been a visiting professor at Hunter College of City University of New York, Wake Forest University, Winston-Salem (USA), McGill University, Montreal (Canada) and Copenhagen Business School (Denmark). He has been a National Fellow of the Indian Council of Social Science Research; a National Lecturer of the University Grants Commission, Government of India; and a Senior Fulbright Fellow. He was a member of the Executives of the International Association of Applied Psychology and International Association for Cross-Cultural Psychology and a Vice President of the World Association for Dynamic Psychiatry. He is an Honourary Fellow of the World Association for Dynamic Psychiatry and of the National Academy of Psychology. Prof. Sinha's research focuses on the interface of Indian culture and Western forms of work organizations ranging from small and medium-size enterprises to leading national and foreign multinationals in India. He has published over 150 research articles in national and international journals and has written or co-authored a dozen of books. He has delivered invited addresses and given seminar lectures in most of the countries of North America, Western Europe, former Yugoslavia, the Far East and South-East Asia.

Imagining Wholesome Wellbeing of All

Jai B.P. Sinha, Ph.D.
ASSERT Institute of Management Studies,
Patna 800013

CONCEPT PUBLISHING COMPANY PVT. LTD.
NEW DELHI-110059

ISBN-13: 978-93-88937-85-6

First Published 2021

Published and Printed by

Concept Since 1974

Concept Publishing Company Pvt. Ltd.
A/15-16, Commercial Block, Mohan Garden
New Delhi-110059 (INDIA)
T : 91 11 25351460, 91 11 25351794
E : publishing@conceptpub.com; *W* : www.conceptpub.com

Cataloging in Publication Data--Courtesy: D.K. Agencies (P) Ltd. <docinfo@dkagencies.com>

Sinha, Jai B. P. (Jai Ballabha Prasad), 1936- **author.**
Imagining wholesome wellbeing of all / Jai B.P. Sinha (Ph.D.).
pages cm
Includes bibliographical references and index.
ISBN 9789388937856

1. Economic development—India. 2. Caste—Political aspects—India. 3. Religion and politics—India. 4. Well-being—India. I. Title.

LCC HC433.S56 2021 | DDC 338.954 23

A Pointer

I am concerned about the way India has been developing since the Independence (1947). We started remarkably well. Nehru invited a non-Congress Dalit leader, Dr. Ambedkar, to head the Committee that drafted the Constitution of which we are still proud. Despite the anger and anguish over the Partition, the country opted to become a secular republic prohibiting any discrimination on the basis of caste or religion. And yet, the minorities were allowed to follow their personal laws—reflecting the ethos of Indian tolerance and pluralistic worldview as well as Nehru's assimilative politics. Universal franchise was offered on a platter without being demanded by the people. It, however, led to some unanticipated consequences. Every adult's right to vote made the OBCs (Other Backward Castes) conscious of their numerical superiority. They pressed for the favours and privileges that the Constitution had granted to the SCs (Scheduled Castes) and STs (Scheduled Tribes). Nehru admitted the backwardness of certain classes (not castes). He was also concerned about the lurking communalism; believing that they would disappear with economic development following a socialist model. He was keenly aware of the poverty and the miserable conditions in which common people lived, but was an elitist who subscribed to grandiose: Heavy industries, big dams, world class management and technological institutes, posh science centres, and grand universities, among others. They were meant to build the country from the top and to make it respectable internationally.

The bottom of the pyramid was rather neglected. Priority was not given to build sound institutions for primary and secondary education, rural health care, and stable income generation. In the absence of enabling institutions at the grassroots, a vast majority of young grew up ill-educated, uncertain of livelihood, and unemployable in decent jobs. So, the ambitious among them gravitated to politics, which did not require any formal qualification. All they had to do was to hang around their caste leaders, do their errands, exhort money from the gullible, and get votes for their leader. In no time, they too became leaders wielding power and patronizing and bullying those around them.

However, these were not the villains primarily responsible for degrading the politics. Politics started degenerating from the top immediately after Nehru through infightings among the Congress leaders. As a result, it turned into an unprincipled pursuit of power. Socialism was used actually as a political weapon. Nationalization of banks and other industries and '*garibi hatao*' (alleviate poverty) were its manifestations. Politicians used any means—caste, communalism, corrupt, and criminal—to enhance their hold on power positions. The *license raj* created space for politicians and bureaucrats to collude with the greedy businessmen in order to enrich each other.[1] Internal compulsions of the stressed economy ushered the country into a capitalist mode. Economic growth started accelerating since the 1990s.

The result is that India has one of the fastest growing economies[2]—third largest in the world in terms of purchasing power parity.[3] The country is being catapulted into a global power house.[4] Business and industries in collusion with the State and politics have been cultivating what is alleged to be a highly lucrative "crony capitalism". India is ninth in crony capitalism in the world.[5] Smart and privileged individuals and companies are creating enormous wealth in name of the country, but mostly for themselves, by adopting means that are dubious and exploitative of natural resources. The wealth manifests in the various artifacts, signs, and symbols of an affluent nation.

These wealth creators are the role models for the rest of the people. The bright ones amongst them, even from humble origins, are fired by their ambitions to reach out to the sky. The number of startups is mushrooming, and some of them are growing into unicorns in no time. Less spectacular ones are rising into the huge middle class, mostly from the lower levels.[6] They are still afraid of sliding down into poverty[7]. In order to hedge the fear, they struggle to earn more, compared with others, and find many similar ones getting ahead of them. This leaves them deprived, insecure, and still uncertain of future. They keep running for more money partly to get away from the past, and partly to catch up with those ahead of them[8]. They are more affluent than they used to be earlier, but do not have a stress free, contended, and happy life.

Common to the rich and middle class is their insatiable craving for making money and the material things that money can buy. They use their affluence to show off their superiority over others. Indians have never been averse to earning money and enjoying material comforts. Earning money *(arth)*, according to the ancient Indian dictum, is the first among the four major goals of life, but not the ultimate one. Capitalism has raised it to the level of a *mantra*, a virtue, and the terminal goal. Consequently, it is so engaging that it hardly spares any time, energy, or resources to think of others, sense other's needs, concerns, and interests, or build harmonious communities. It becomes a zero sum game where any investment in relationships (except the calculative ones) means negligence of one's single-minded pursuit of accumulating more money. The craving in fact gets so compelling that it saps the energy for self-care resulting into a number of psycho-somatic problems such as stress, anxiety, depression, and so on.[9] In other words, their material affluence is inimical to both social relationships and harmonious communities as well as to a stress free and happy life.

The vast majority of the neglected and deprived people also crave for money and material possessions that the rich and affluent have. They make some money and the State gives some more cash by way of subsidies. So, many of them are no longer counted as poor. However, opportunity structure is grossly restricted to them allowing the sharks around them to claim their money in no time. They remain marginalized, live in unhygienic conditions, and suffer from serious malnutrition, poor health, little or no education, uncertain income, and even without access to safe drinking water and toilet. They constitute a mass in extreme inequality.

Inequality has always been a harsh reality of the Indian society. But it has increased steeply since the Independence due to the government policies, which favour capitalists and privileged.[10] The billionaires in India are growing at a faster rate than the GDP (Gross

Domestic Product) inviting a view that we have transited from the "British Raj to Billionaire Raj."[11]

Glaring inequality hurts badly particularly the masses of Indians (from lower and lower middle classes) who do not have sufficient human capital (education, skills, health, and productive employment) to mitigate it. They believe that they cannot achieve what they want through fair means. They get impatient and shortsighted, detached from cultural moorings, and devoid of social values. They tend to clutch on any means that holds even a flimsy promise. Vote bank politics takes advantage of it. It plays castes and religion cards to manipulate them. Caste leaders are exploiting it in name of social justice. Hinduism, known for its rich philosophy, pluralistic worldview, and tolerance of other faiths is contrived to Hindutva—an ideology that is exclusive, discriminating, communalizing, and divisive of the culturally diverse Indian society. In sum, casteism and communalism driven by corrupt and self-interested politics along with money making (the capitalist dictum) are diverting the development process away from the wellbeing of most common people.

This is unacceptable. Development process has to be retrieved, reorganized, and directed to enable the *masses of Indians* to realize a *wholesome wellbeing*. A wholesome wellbeing emanates from living a life in harmony with nature and the communities—a life that may be materially modest, but is efficacious, stress free, happy, and worth living. Once masses of Indians have such a wholesome wellbeing, they will not be misguided in name of castes and religion. Caste and religion will still remain a part of their life space, but not the avenues for seeking undue gains.

In order to realize such a wholesome wellbeing for the masses of people, the highest priority has to be given to reshape our primary educational, skills building, health caring, and productive employment generating institutions. They will lay the foundation for self-driven efforts for growth and wellbeing.

The institutions must have adequate resources for building necessary infrastructure and recruiting, training, appraising, and rewarding key and allied personnel. Rules and norms of the institutions have to be well articulated and tightly controlling for the basic functions, while being open, flexible, challenging, and rewarding at the higher, creative, levels. Equally important is to inculcate, through school curriculum, media, and public discourse, a worldview that integrates human development and preservation of environment, without which any development will be empty and useless.

Is it utopian? Not really, but indeed idealistic. The Oxfam pleads that the government must act on behalf of, not only a few, but *all people* for a *human economy*.[12] The Governments (Centre and State) control most of the resources and are the custodian of development. However, the politicians in power and the administrative establishment are unlikely to make a radical change in planning unless strong public pressure is built up. The best way for building public pressure is to call upon the social activists and their organizations who are dedicated to uplift the weak and the marginalized people. Many well intentioned, bright professionals and their organizations are dotting all over the country. They are engaged in giving relief, organizing self-help groups, and preparing the marginalized people to cope with their daily exigency. They are, however, dispersed, unconnected, and constrained by limited resources. These individuals and their collectives have to be organized into the critical forces that can overview the government delivery system, prepare people to demand what they deserve, and pressurize government to allocate resources judiciously. A few already do all these, but that is not enough. There has to have many organized pressure groups to function as catalysts to mobilize government machinery in the right direction. Most important, they have to use their rapport with people and the clout to guide and direct people to cleanse the politics by electing honest, capable, and committed to change individuals.

It is plain and simple. If the major problems of human wellbeing are rooted in politics, they have to be solved politically. Dedicated individuals and their organizations have to get directly involved in politics. If they do, there are well intentioned individuals in politics, business, and government, who are right now subdued, but will rally around. Once they do, a milieu for positive change will be created and many black sheep would also ride on the bandwagon once it gets going. Indians have in their psyche strands of both: vices and virtues, either of which dominates their thought and actions depending on situational demands.[13] A positive milieu will evoke positive responses even in otherwise corrupt politicians, businessmen, and bureaucrats. It is still a difficult and long drawn process. But a beginning has to be made, and sooner the better.

This is the future that is being imagined in the book. It (Chapter 1) shows that economic growth of a country is indeed most efficiently realized by a capitalist mode of development. But such a growth aggravates inequality between a few rich and privileged and the masses which remain largely deprived of the fruits of economic growth. But the rich and the privileged also remain devoid of social and psychological wellbeing. Compensating the deprived masses by subsidies and direct cash transfer are not the substitute of helping them build up their basic capabilities to improve the quality of their life. However, there is a history of why capitalism dominates the development scenario (Chapter 2). More powerful individuals, groups, and nations have invariably defined development for the less powerful ones. Islamic rules and later on the British Raj defined development in their own ways and interests. Gandhi provided an idealistic view that resonated with the Indian cultural ethos and Nehru opted for the Soviet model of socialist development. As they suffered from their own deficiencies, the country was pressed to capitalist mode of development. The masses remained deprived and vulnerable to the politics of caste and communalism. The caste system and religion have their own history (Chapters 3 and 4). Religion tied king's wellbeing with his subjects' wellbeing and thus predisposed the former to remain benign to the latter. The State treated them equitably. Castes originated in guild as a function of occupational differentiation and skills specialization. The State, religions, and castes combined together to lead to pioneering advancements in state-craft, science, arts, technology, and philosophy. They carried the banners of Indian culture, civilization, and religion to all over Asia. However, as State politics deteriorated, religions and castes played dysfunctional roles. The deteriorating process started in the late Hindu regime, through the Muslim rule, to the colonial era. Increasingly getting unprincipled politics has accentuated casteism and communalism to the extremes (Chapter 5). Castes, communalism, corruption, and capitalism are the most serious distracters of right kind of development of the country. The book takes an integrated view (Chapter 6) of these four evils in order to outline a plan of development in which most people will have a state and sense of wellbeing. They won't be burglarized by the politicians nor will they be distracted by the four evils (castes, communalism, corruption, and capitalism). The plan envisions that dedicated individuals and their organizations will initiate the transformative process. They have to get organized into power centres to pressurize government machinery for rebuilding basic educational, health care, and income generating institutions as well as to play politics and get honest and capable individuals elected in important bodies. At the end, the main ideas are recapitulated in a nutshell for those who want to know what the book is all about before start reading the text.

Ideas and information have been sourced from multiple disciples in order to attempt an eclectic narrative of development and wellbeing. Attempts have been made to look beneath the surface descriptions in terms of how the operating mindsets work. Theories and issues in some cases are sliced differently across different chapters often making them appear either repetitive or incomplete in account. However, such instances are meant to examine them either in different perspectives or allow them to converge in order to highlight a point. Where solid evidence was missing, conjectures and personal observations were liberally evoked to fill up the gaps. The purpose was to present as logically cohesive narrative as possible.

I hope the book will interest students, teachers, researchers, and also social activists, and policy makers who are concerned about the wellbeing of the masses of Indians.

NOTES

1. Desai & Bhagwati, 1975.
2. International Monetary Fund (IMF), 2018.
3. World Bank in India, 2018.
4. National Intelligence Council (NIC) Report, 2012.
5. *The Economist's crony-capitalism index,* May 5, 2016 cited in *The Economic Times,* May 8, 2016.
6. Krishnan & Hatekar, 2017.
7. Sinha, 1977.
8. Pandey, 2012.
9. http://www.sustainablescale.org/AttractiveSolutions/Understanding HumanHappinessandWellBeing.aspx on August 25, 2014.
10. Himanshu, 2018.
11. Piketty, & Chanel, 2017.

12. Oxfam Report, January 2017.
13. Sinha, 2014.

REFERENCES

Desai, P. and Bhagwati, J. (1975). Socialism and Indian economic policy. *World Development*, 3(4), 213-221.

Himanshu (2018). India Inequality Report. Oxfam, New Delhi, India. https://www.oxfamindia.org/sites/default/files/himanshu_inequality_Inequality_report_2018.pdf.

International Monetary Fund Report (May, 2018). Asia and Pacific Region Regional Economic Outlook: Asia Pacific. https://www.imf.org/en/Publications/REO/APAC/Issues/2018/04/16/...

Krishnan, Sandhya and Hatekar, Neeraj (2017). Rise of the new middle class in India and its changing structure. *Economic and Political Weekly*, 52 (22), 40-48.

National Intelligence Council (NIC), USA, Report (December 11, 2012). Global Trends 2030. 5th Instalment. Washington, D.C., USA.

Oxfam Report (January 2017). Oxfam Briefing Paper. Oxfam House, John Smith Drive, Cowley, Oxford, OX4 2JY, UK. WWW.Oxfam.org.

Pandey, Madhu (2012). The Middle Class Mentality: A Report. Indian Council of Social Science Research, New Delhi.

Piketty, T. and Chanel, L. (2017). Indian income inequality, 1922-2014: From British Raj to Billionaire Raj? Paper Series, No. 11. In Alvaredo, F., Chancel, L., Piketty, T., Saez, E. and Zucman, G. (Eds.), *World Inequality Report, 2018*. Paris School of Economics, Paris.

Sinha, J.B.P. (1977). The poverty syndrome, power motive, and democratization of work place. *Integrated Management, 12*, 5-8.

Sinha, J.B.P. (2014). *Psycho-social analysis of the Indian mindset*. New Delhi: Springer.

The Economist's crony-capitalism index, May 5, 2016.

http//economictimes.indiatimes.com/articleshow/52175285.cms?utm_source=contentofinterest&utm_medium=text&utm_campaign=cppst.

World Bank in India (October, 2018). India Overtakes Japan as World's Third Largest Economy http://www.worldbank.org/en/country/india/overview.

Contents

List of Boxes, Table and Appendices

LIST OF BOXES

LIST OF TABLE

LIST OF APPENDICES

1
Wealth Without Wellbeing

'Where Wealth Accumulates and Men Decay'.[1]

ECONOMIC GROWTH, GDP, AND INEQUALITY

Economic growth is indeed the foundation for our development in whatever ways we define development. Economic growth is measured in terms of the GDP (Gross Domestic Product) of a country.[2] There are certain advantages in employing the GDP as an index of a country's economic development. An increase in GDP means more products and services available to the people to enrich their consumption basket by building up their capabilities to earn more and more. An increase in GDP also allows government to collect more taxes and ideally spend them more liberally on health, education, livelihood of the poor, infrastructure, social protection, defense, and ventures abroad. It gives a brand image to the country, a sense of power and prestige in the international community, and a clout in diplomatic relationships. However, GDP is notoriously deficient as a true indicator of development. The methods of including and excluding the items of economic transactions as well as the perspectives behind this choice are endlessly controverted. Further, GDP is neutral to the background of the economic players and how they contribute to the GDP. Finally, GDP is a measure of the volume of products and services created and traded. It is blind to their impact on the social and psychological aspects of development, particularly on people's sense of wellbeing. Whatever—products and services—are produced and exchanged by whoever is added to the GDP. Even a crook or criminal producing and servicing something illegally or immorally are contributing to the GDP.

Following this logic, the Eurostat[3] has indeed gone to the extreme. It has made it mandatory for the member states to include prostitution, illegal drugs, and smuggling of alcohol and tobacco in their GDP so long as they are consensual economic transactions. Including illegal drugs and prostitution in the GDP added £10 billion (€12.3 billion or $16.8 billion) to UK economy,[4] which led it to surpass that of France. Prostitution and narcotics, according to the official statistics, constitute nearly $11.5 billion of the total Spanish GDP, which is about one per cent of its total economy.[5] The Bank of Italy estimated in 2012 that the black economy accounted for 10.9 per cent of Italy's GDP. The criminal economy is likely to boost up Italy's GDP by at least 1.3 per cent.[6] The black market transactions of Greece are about 23 per cent of its GDP. In our case, the percentage of black money and the money stacked in foreign banks to our GDP is likely to be much higher. Estimates vary widely. According to the country's top investigating agency, about $500 billion are stashed in foreign banks and the black money amounts to about 50 per cent of our GDP[7]. If we add the economic values of prostitution, illegal drugs, and locally brewed spirit, our GDP will rise steeply to an unimaginable height showing us as much richer than we are officially reported right now and much better in comparison to many other developed countries.

But should that make us feel proud or elevate us to the state of a rapidly developing nation having a greater sense of economic wellbeing? Eurostat argues that GDP is an economic, not a moral, index. But should an economic index, which is devoid of morality, be taken to stand for economic development? Can we promote and flaunt prostitution, drugs, and contraband as a sign of our economic wellbeing? Impact of these illegal and immoral activities on the health, social relationships, and mental wellbeing are doubtlessly devastating. Reports on trafficking of minor girls and boys, mass killing by locally brewed liquor, metal abuse by teens and young adults in India, and smoking by under-age boys and girls are heart-breaking and totally unacceptable as ingredients of our economic prosperity. Obviously, GDP has to be cleansed of immoral economic transactions and economic growth has to be re-conceptualized by taking into account not only how much wealth is being created but also by what—legal and moral—means it is being created.

Even if we extricate GDP from immoral economic transactions, its appropriateness as an index of development is problematic. At best, it is an aggregated estimate of a nation's total wealth without differentiating how many individuals and sectors contributed how much to that wealth. A few may contribute much more than the rest of the population. And, a small part of a country (e.g., West India) or a sector (e.g. IT and IT enabled services) can get so prosperous that they keep the GDP high, despite the pervasive impoverishment around them. Abject miseries of the millions of Indians are indeed covered up so long as we have enough number of millionaires and billionaires to help keep the country high in the GDP ranking. In other words, GDP is sensitive to the volume of wealth being created, but is insensitive to the number of contributors. As a result, some individuals having resources and entrepreneurial skills and orientations rise very high quickly leaving the rest languishing far behind. Similarly, the sectors and the companies, which are privileged in having various resources, attract more privileges and resources and leave the rest far behind. In other words, GDP has built-in scope for enhancing inequality. Long back, Adam Smith[8] admitted that "Wherever there is great property, there is great inequality."

Coexistence of GDP and Inequality

Inequality is ideally distasteful, but inevitable in this imperfect world. Hence, certain degrees of inequality between individuals, groups, and nations are grudgingly accepted as the reality. However, increasing inequality raises eyebrows and the impulse to activate counter-measures; for if it crosses the threshold, it disrupts social relationships, economic activities, and political participation. Socially superiors (*bade log)* denigrate the lesser ones (*chhote log).* Politically heavy weights exclude the weak ones from getting access to power and resources. Similarly, increasing economic inequality excludes the lesser people from participating fully in the economy, restricts their access to resources, and denies employment opportunity to them. As a result, the lesser ones are less productive, their consumption level drops, they have less to save and invest.[9] Hence, there starts a vicious cycle where inequality, if not revered, keeps increasing. In other words, growing GDP is inherently susceptible to increasing inequality. But is it really true?

Simon Kuznets[10] argued that it is true, but only temporarily. As the economic growth of a nation increases, income inequality initially increases because those who spearhead the growth activities gain disproportionally more. But their gains trickle down to the rest of the population. Wages increase, new opportunities are created, new skills are acquired, and talented aspirants climb up hard ways and compete effectively, and so on. Hence, the relationship between increasing GDP and equality has an "inverted-U' shape. The contrary can also be true. Those who are better off economically can consolidate their power and position both socially and politically to exploit the weaker ones and sway policy decisions to keep on hoarding and monopolizing resources and thus increasing their disparity from those below them. Probably, both may happen. Smaller inequality might be challenged and mitigated, but the larger ones tend to increase further. This raises the question whether inequality is good for a country's economic growth.[11]

As a corollary, another question is whether inequality has increased in India in course of its development? Experts differ. Some[12] say, "no, not really" while others[13] vigorously pronounce, "yes, very badly".[14] Among the former group, Bhalla, for example, showed that India's GDP grew from about 3.50 per cent in the first phase of its economic growth (1947 to 1980) to around 5.00 per cent when the economy started opening up (1980 to 1991) to about 8.00 per cent following the liberalization to the year of its acceleration (1991 to 2003). However, the real inequality stayed constant during this whole period of the growing economy. He also calculated that the rural inequality decreased in 15 out of 16 major states of India, and urban inequality declined in 8 of the 17 states between 1993-1994 and 1999-2000 implying that inequality had not worsened in India during the period of economic liberalization.[15] Gehring and Kulkarni substantiated Bhalla that the extent of inequality remained almost the same for 35 years (1966 to 2000) as the Gini coefficient[16] increased from 31.1 to 32.5 only. Bhalla[17] also reported that the improvement in poverty alleviation during the recent period of high growth has been dramatic. The bottom 20 per cent moved towards equality and the poorest achieved higher growth rate than the average as well as the growth among the rich (p. 19). For example, in 1983, more than 80 per cent of the scheduled tribes were poor, the percentage dropped to 45.30 in the year 2007-2008. That is, the poverty in this group declined at 1.4 per cent per annum—the highest for all groups (p. 22). Not all agree to this rosy picture. In fact, the evidence contrary to this rosy picture is overwhelming. Pal and Ghosh,[18] for example, reviewed the findings of a number of scholars to conclude the following:

> ... though the richer sections of the population benefited in the post-liberalization period, there has been a stagnation of incomes for the majority, with the bottom rung of the population severely negatively affected by this process. There is also evidence that, both at the national and the state levels, income disparities between the rural and urban sectors increased during this period. State-level data also showed that not only had the income gap between the poorest and the richest states increased during the 1990s, but urban inequality increased for all the 15 major states in India. Inequality also alarmingly increased in the North-Eastern part of the country, where all the states experienced increased rural and urban poverty during this same period.

For example, on the eve of the take off of the economy (1991), the top one per cent rich had 23 times more income than the half of Indians from the bottom of the demographic pyramid. The ratio has increased to 39 times in the year 2001, and to 73 times in the year 2013.[19] An overbearing face of inequality in India is the number of millionaires and billionaires. Their number increased, in fact faster than the rate of GDP. In mid-nineties, there were only two billionaires having the combined worth of $3.2 billion. By 2012, there were 46 having a total net worth of $176.3 billion.[20] Only three years later in 2015, their number almost doubled to 90. They had the combined net worth of $295 billion. Of them 28 made their appearance for the first time.[21] In the year 2013-2014, the GDP grew by 6.90 per cent that increased to 7.30 per cent the year 2014-2015. However, the number of Indian millionaires increased over three times from 284 to 928.[22] The number of billionaires has increased from 126 in 2016 to 136 in 2017 inviting an observation that India has transited from the *"British Raj to Billionaire Raj"*.[23]

The steep rise in the number of millionaires and billionaires in the post-liberalization period is not unique to India only. According to a survey by the Boston Consulting Group, the number of millionaires in the world grew from 15 million in 2013 to 17 million in 2014. Their control on the world's wealth increased from 40 per cent in the year 2013 to 41 per cent in the year 2014.[24] Oxfam had a similar report disclosing increasing global inequality. It has recorded that since 2015, the richest one per cent has owned more wealth than the rest of the planet; eight super rich now own the same amount of wealth as the poorest half of the world; and the incomes of the poorest 10 per cent of people increased by less than $3 a year between 1988 and 2011, while the incomes of the richest one per cent increased 182 times as much.[25] Rising economic inequality is considered to be a threat to social stability in the world.[26]

Income and Human Development

Following the increase in inequality, a pertinent question is whether income is related to human development. That is, whether the poor suffers while the rich gains on human development corresponding to their deprivation and affluence respectively.

Box 1.1: Economic Inequality and Wellbeing

As growth benefits the richest, the rest of society—especially the poorest—suffers. The very design of our economies and the principles of our economics have taken us to this extreme, unsustainable and unjust point.[27]

Human development is assessed through the Human Development Index (HDI) indicating people's capabilities to have the freedom to live the life that they value.[28] The HDI consists of income, education, and health. Of the three, income is most basic because it can be instrumental to good education and adequate health care. The assumption is that the greater the income, the higher is the human development.

Income of the poor in India has indeed increased over time, although the estimates of poverty reduction vary widely. According to Tendulkar, the percentage of poor has decreased from

58.50 per cent in the year 1983 to 27.90 per cent in the year 2007.[29] Increased income has created a huge middle class of 53.3 million households consisting of 267 million people.[30] However, the scenario at the bottom of the pyramid is still dismal. The monthly income of 74.49 per cent of the highest earning household member is less than Rs. 5,000, the percentage drops to 17.18 per cent earning between Rs. 5,000 to 10,000, and further falls to 8.29 per cent earning more than Rs. 10,000[31], which is still not very much. That is, above 90 per cent of Indians are barely managing themselves, no matter how economists draw the poverty line or boast of realizing the UN millennium goal of reducing absolute poverty.[32] According to another estimate, about 276 million Indians lived below $1.25 per day on purchasing power parity[33] raising concerns about the levels of their human development.

From 1980-1981 to 2013-2014, all Indians' income rose about 45 times, but the HDI during this period increased only marginally by less than 1.6 times (see Table 1.1). Obviously, Indians' human development levels have not been directly benefited by their rapidly increasing gross income. India's HDI ranking of 135 out of 189 countries is still shocking low[34]. Further, inequalities have caused a loss of 28.60 per cent in the Indians' HDI.[35]

Table 1.1: Growth in Indians' Income and Human Development Index (HDI)

Year	*Income (Rs)*	*HDI*
1980	1,784	.369
1990	5,440	.431
2000	16,688	.483
2010	61,564	.554
2013	80,388	.586

Note: Income at the price rate of 2010-2011. Read 1980 as 1980-1981 and so on.

Source: Economic Survey (2010-2011), Central Statistics Office, Government of India (2013-2014), 2014-2015 & The Human Development Report, 2018.

The whole economic scenario of the disproportionately increasing the affluence of the fewer and the miserable life of the rest of Indians depressing their level of human development is the product of the capitalist mode of development.

CAPITALIST MODE OF DEVELOPMENT

Although inequality and GDP coexist in India as elsewhere in the world, GDP is not necessarily directly responsible for inequality. Both—GDP and inequality—are caused by the capitalist mode of development. Capitalism, particularly after the collapse of the Soviet Union and the fall of Berlin Wall in the beginning of the nineties,[36] is now accepted by almost all countries as a sure road for a faster rate of development. *Capitalism is a system of market based exchange of products and services for maximizing one's profit that collectively accumulates into the wealth of a nation.* Profit making has become a virtue.[37] The basic assumption is that human beings are primarily economic creatures and are guided by self-interests. The father of modern capitalism, Adam Smith, made an observation that is often quoted:

> It is not from the benevolence of the butcher, the brewer, or the baker, that we expect our dinner, but from their regard to their own self-interest. We address ourselves, not to their humanity but to their self-love, and never talk to them of our own necessities but of their advantages.

The butcher, the brewer, and the baker are surely concerned about the profit that they make out of the sales of their products to a dinner, but the dinner is also a self-interested person who does not want to pay higher than what he or she must in the market. The dinner explores the market and buys in cost effective ways considering the quality and price of the products. In other words, in a free market there is a competition among the sellers as well as among the buyers and they negotiate out of their self-interests for maximizing their gains and minimizing their costs. Their negotiation results into a deal only if both parties have been able to get what they think is in their best interest. A seller cannot unilaterally raise the price higher lest he or she loses the customers to other sellers in the same line or a buyer cannot insist to pay unreasonably low price lest the seller refuses to sell. They have to understand each other's costs and benefits, safeguard their own interests, but also the interests of the other, and strike a balance that enables them to continue on gainful transactions in future also. It is not a matter of appealing to each other's "benevolence", "humanitarianism", or "needs", but hinting at the "advantages" that each is causing to the other while maximizing his or her own returns. This utilitarian understanding expands, in Adam Smith's schema, the "self-interest' from a narrow groove of being "selfish" in a short term perspective to cultivating "enlightened self-interest" in the long term perspective.[38]

Pursuing profit and thereby creating wealth, the spirit of capitalism, was construed as the Protestant ethic.[39] It has to be accomplished like a religious calling and the success in it is like god's blessing. Those who do so are the privileged ones. However, the profit is not for lavish consumption. Rather, it has to be saved and invested for expanding the business further and for making more profit and creating more wealth. That's how capitalism builds up a nation.

Furthermore, Adam Smith was credited to state that the persons who act to further the interests of others (or the interests of the group or groups to which they belong), ultimately serve their own self-interest. In other words, the striving for profit making has to be steered by simultaneously catering to the interests of others within the rules of the competitive market. Only such profit making is sustainable over time and results in stable growth of GDP.[40] However, the catch is that a market is rarely an 'even playing ground'. Quite often it is rigged by some putting the other at a disadvantage with not much of free choice. The smart, the manipulator, and the powerful get richer faster at the cost of others.

One has to have an entrepreneur mindset in order to outwit others in such a rigged market. Entrepreneurs[41] are intuitively sensitive to their milieu and the people they interact with, the intricacies of market forces, the opportunities they can exploit, and constraints they have to overcome. They set their goals, persistently struggle to achieve them by exploiting existing resources, turning constraints into resources, and creating new resources. They take risk, explore and tread upon unchartered terrains, and opt for high stakes under uncertain conditions. They are unconventional and innovative. They take advantages of the existing systems, rules, and practices so long as they serve their purpose, but do not hesitate to cut corners, deviate from norms, change track, take shortcuts, and disregard popular practices to achieve what they set their eyes on. They are basically utilitarian shifting towards being opportunists if the situation so permits.

Instead of being conscientious or sentimental in cultivating relationships, they use them for achieving their goals. They scan and manage to get close to people who are resourceful and can help them achieve their goals, drop them once the purpose is served, and new ones are sought after for chasing new goals. Their top priority is achieving their goals and maximizing their gains; persons are just like other resources that have to be used so long they are useful. They are the ones who out-smart others, achieve, excel, and make more money disregarding how that affects others. They have high motivation to achieve.

Theory of Achievement Motivation

A psychological theory of national development describes the mindset of entrepreneurs.[42] The theory is centered on achievement motivation (nAchv). Massive evidence from a number of countries was documented to show that if the level of nAchv of the people of a country was high, the country realized rapid economic growth. Achievement motivation in people means that they have a strong need to achieve. A strong need for achievement is reflected in people's constant physical and mental preoccupation with the ways and means of achievement. High nAchv people keep fantasizing about their achievement that mentally prepares them to initiate and sustain creative efforts to achieve what they want. They take reasonably high (but not too high) risks and try hard to keep improving upon their own previous achievements as well as excelling others. They value tangible gains (e.g., money and material things) more than intangible appreciations and compliments. However, there is no reason why others committed to science, arts, music, literature, and so on may not have an entrepreneurial mindset that is driven by an irresistible urge to keep achieving new heights and jealously excelling others in harvesting high reputations, recognitions, and appreciations (besides money if it is a fallout of other achievements).

There are two other competing motivations that human beings have inherited universally.[43] They are the need for affiliation and the need for power. The need for affiliation expresses in a preference for getting close to and relating with others, enjoying their company, cooperating with and sacrificing for and from them, and feeling embedded into social groups. The need for power drives people to influence and control others, make decisions for them, and pressurize them to behave not the way they want, but what the power wielder coerces, rewards, cajoles, or expects them to do. The need for affiliation, according to the theory, dilutes nAchv because the affiliating people prioritize maintaining relationships over achieving their goals in terms of expending their efforts and allocating time to them. Indians are reported to value even working as part of maintaining relationships[44] and if there is a choice between the two, they would prefer the latter than the former. Many Indians, for example, take time out of their work hours to visit ailing friends, participating in social celebrations, or just chatting with friend as their work suffers (How many times and for how long have you been waiting for a person's attention in his office while he was chatting with a friend?).

Unlike the need for affiliation, the need for power enables the high achievers to facilitate their achievements by making a relevant person follow their directives and wishes. But power helps only to a certain extent—so long as achievement remains the master motive and power serves as the facilitator. But if need for power starts dominating, people need not concentrate on making efforts to achieve the goals, they can make others do as they demand or wish. If that happens the less powerful pawns start resenting and resisting, and in subtle ways sabotaging the interests of the powerful. This is probably the reason that the managers who were high on nAchv, low on need for affiliation, and moderate on need for power were found to be more successful in a long term perspective.[45] In the sixties, the theory of achievement seemed so promising to the developing countries including India that they arranged many highly advertised projects for inculcating high need for achievement in their managers,[46] although the impact of which remained largely indeterminate or short-lived.

Part of the reason for the indifferent yield of the training in achievement motivation was that the theory is a product of the Western, particularly American, culture that is not fully shared by many other developing countries. American culture is individualist[47] and a home of the modern capitalism. Many developing countries are largely collectivists and have started embracing capitalism recently and in different forms and degrees. India has a blend of both collectivism and individualism[48] and has a mixed economy that is increasingly getting market driven. In an ndividualist culture individuals are taken to be the basic units of a society. They compete with and surpass each other in order to maximize their individual achievements that add to the national aggregate. That's the way, the USA developed economically—with fewer people, vast land, plenty of natural resources, weak resistance from indigenous people, and rough and tough achieving immigrants. Other countries such as India are different. India, for example, has many more people with less space and a great deal of diversity, less of natural resources, heavy colonial legacy, a long cultural heritage, and a different worldview. Achievement does not always mean making money and profit. It also means being a good, helpful, and affiliative person, obedient to parents, and so on.[49] In cases where achievement is about making money and requires competition, Indians jump in vigorously—*artha* (wealth) is indeed a primary goal of our life. But Indians also have a high need for power and affiliation.[50] So, they use friends, relatives, and other connections as well as power to achieve their goals, which, besides money and material possessions, may also include power and influence upon others or caring for friends and relatives. In the Indian mindset, the needs for three—achievement, power, and affiliation—feed on each other. Thus, high nAchv Indians readily form cliques and groups to acquire, hoard, and monopolize resources, bully others, and deny and restrict other's access to resources in order to maximize their achievement, help and patronize family and friends, and dominate others. Such Indians gain a lot individually, but put the larger collectives at a disadvantage, and worse create acrimonious relationships around them. On the contrary, those Indians who have a strong disposition to cooperate and share scare resources, do not maximize their individual gains, but do maximize their collective achievements while maintaining harmonious relationships.[51]

Here is a dilemma. The inclusive development, where all tend to grow together by cooperating rather than competing, is a better option, particularly in a country like India where resources are limited. But that is not what capitalism or its ancillary, the theory of achievement motivation, aims at. Capitalism aims at boosting up GDP. If there is sufficient number of individuals, though still in tiny minority, having high nAchv and entrepreneurial dispositions and skills to make more and more profit, they push up the GDP. Profit for them is the incentive to remain proactive, agile, and innovative. It is not only the GDP that is increased because of their efforts, but the whole array of inventions, discoveries, varieties of products and services, means of comforts and pleasures, and opportunities for our further development are available to human beings.[52] On the other hand, we have in India an increasing number of social entrepreneurs who have discarded or refused to take lucrative job or business and have started working for the marginalized and disadvantaged people. They employ the best capitalist practices for best results that are not necessarily profit for themselves.[53]

They are, however, still exceptions. In majority of cases, the gains of entrepreneurial efforts are available mostly to the selected few who are better-off. They have greater access than the lesser ones. There is a reinforcing circle. The more entrepreneurial and high achieving you are, the more access you will have to resources that you can use to achieve more and create more resources. Capitalism allows you to privatize and commodify any resource; and once it is a commodity, you can buy, possess, and use it for furthering your profit. For example, the spring water in the mountains of India is abundantly and freely available to the local people. But some enterprising Indians commodify, buy, and bottle or put it tankers and transport it by to a city like Mumbai in order to make huge profit. The local people, who used to have this water free, have now to buy bottled water from them. Similarly, baby care is taken out of the family to daycare centres and is made available at a price—the higher the price the better is the care, but available selectively to those who can afford.

Isn't it ironical that the goods that nature provided, community services, and human transactions that were spontaneously available to the benefit of all people were not counted in the GDP. However, once they are priced commodities, possessed, bought, and sold by a few for profit add to the GDP of the country. The better off can have more of these commodities as they get richer and richer while the lesser and lesser ones have less and less, and hence poorer and poorer—the country gets rich with a few super-rich but lots of people are deprived. This contradiction is succulently highlighted by the Nobel Laureate, Deaton[54], when he commented that "In effect, Indians ...-become poorer because India has become richer".

This is the genesis of inequality, the source of which goes to individual differences in people's needs, abilities, and skills to exploit opportunities, utilize resources, and make profit. Those who are better-off will certainly leave others behind. It is natural. It is not only in economic matters but in all spheres of life, people grade and rank each other on some attributes placing some in the superior and others in the inferior categories. Thus, all societies have inequalities in various degrees and forms and sectors. Often inequalities in one area spreads to other areas as the better-off consolidate their superiority by commodifying and acquiring the scarce resources in other areas. Castes in India are a glaring example of a social inequality that helped the upper castes to gain and retain economic superiority reducing the scheduled castes and tribes to extremely impoverished and ruthlessly discriminated.

What is worrying from the developmental point of view is this unending process of accumulating wealth. It leads to extreme economic inequality that is increasing all over the world. According to a survey of 26 countries by the Oxfam, extreme inequality is "compounding" social and political problems by negatively impacting economic growth, poverty reduction, political participation, social harmony, and so on.[55] These are the domains of which the State is the principal custodian and is expected to collaborate with business to facilitate development. However, in most cases the State fosters business interests and thus entertains cronyism to a certain extent.

It is true also in case of India. There has been a nexus between the State and the business and industry from the British days, although its patterns have been different during colonial, pre- and post-liberalization phases.[56] Liberalization has reduced the State control, allowed greater freedom to the market forces, and greater opportunities to the high aspiring entrepreneurs to collude with powerful persons in government and politics in order to cash on crony capitalism.[57] For example, a systematic analysis[58] of the sources of the wealth of 46 billionaires[59] was quite revealing. Of them, 20 (43%) were the self-made billionaires who had by their own efforts and during the short span of time accumulated more wealth (60%) than the remaining others[60] (53%) who had only 40 per cent of the total wealth of all 46 billionaires. The quick rich billionaires were engaged in sectors such as the real estate, construction, infrastructure or ports, media, cement, and mining. These are sectors where there are numerous opportunities to gain unlawfully through government licenses and contracts and black money. We have numerous reports of undue favours shown to their connected businessmen and industrialists in the allocation of coal mines, government lands, 2-G spectrum, and other natural resources by those in power. There are also reports of fabricating news and views coverage for a price in favour of some rich and powerful political leaders on the eve of their elections. And, real estate is particularly vulnerable to black money and is reported to be the most corrupt activity in India.[61]

Many super-rich businessmen and industrialists tend to sway policy decisions in their favour, grab lucrative contracts, get huge loans from public sector banks with a bad intention not to pay back, evade tax, stash money in foreign banks, and "capture opportunities" by securing the lowest tax rates, the best education for their children, and the best healthcare for the family. In the process, they deprive others of equal opportunity and causes irreversible disadvantages to them that are further aggravated over time and across generations. This is possibly the reason that millionaires and billionaires are increasing fast. And, skeletons of scams and misdeeds are tumbling almost every day from the cupboards of government and industry.[62] There is a recent report based on over six years of rigorous research exploring a deeper and comprehensive perspective on corporate scams and frauds. It is frustrating to see that the corporates, which are seemingly doing well, cheat and commit fraud that risk their reputation which they have built over the years.[63] The story is the same in the West and in India. While the entrepreneurs and their companies are accumulating wealth, the vast majority of Indians are languishing in illiteracy, ill health, livelihood, and other problems. We often lament that while BRAND INDIA waxes the *Bharat* wanes.

Psycho-Dynamics of Achieving

Need for achieving has its own psycho-dynamics. It keeps a constant pressure propelling you to achieve more and more. As you succeed, the success reinforces your need. The need gets stronger; it is insatiable. It presses you harder to put in more efforts to achieve more. There are barriers including others in your way of achievement. You have to overcome the barriers by working hard on them, and if necessary by employing whatever measures you have to adopt in order0 to overcome them. You have to compete with your rivals, outwit them, and remove them from your way, if necessary. The more you achieve the more intense is the competition and the harder it gets to succeed, and greater is the charm of achieving. Achieving is now so engaging and involving that it becomes a compelling force within you. The farther ahead you are from your competitors and the greater control you have over the circumstances, the more sure you are of your capabilities for further achievements. Achieving is now your passion that does not require any excuse or reason for why you are achieving. You strive to climb the Everest because it stands highest in the world and defiantly challenges you.

Achieving something tangible rather than intangible is more compelling, because tangible achievements give more concrete feedback regarding what has been achieved and what is yet to be achieved. Money making, for example, is almost the most attractive single act of achieving. It also directly adds to the GDP, and earn national recognition. The super rich make the country proud of them.

However, money making does not always lead to a greater sense of wellbeing. According to Edward Diener, subjective well-being is reflected in how happy people feel in their life. He and his associates surveyed 8,06,526 people in 135 countries from the years 2005 to 2011 to show that rising income *does* lead to greater happiness, but only to a certain extent.[64] Beyond a point, happiness hits a plateau despite the income increasing further. They called it the "Easterlin Paradox", because Diener's collaborative work with Richard Easterlin convincingly demonstrated this non-linear relationship between income and happiness. Going into the details, Diener and his associates found that income and happiness are positively related in case of poor people. As their income increases, they are able to buy the things that they needed, but could not afford earlier. This makes them happy with a sense of being well economically. However, those who are not so poor already have the basics of everyday life. So, further increases in their income are not that particularly important and hence so crucial for their happiness. For not-so-poor people, other factors are more important. For example, those who are more optimists, have less of unreasonably heightened desires to make money, and have strong ties to friends and family are happier. There are also culture-specific factors. For example, those people whose orientations match the cultural norms are happier.[65] Another study[66], drawing data again from all over the world, confirmed that as national wealth increases, people are happier. However, after a level of income their happiness actually slips back again. This is primarily because the high income is not necessarily converted into people's wellbeing and that people's aspirations tend to rise faster than their income. The study also calculated a critical level of income, most probably for the high income Western countries, that is the watershed between rising and falling of happiness. There is also a report that mindless accumulation of wealth causes physical and mental problems.[67] Furthermore, a number of studies drawing respondents of different age, gender, and other demographics and belonging to many different countries disclosed that those who run after money and material possessions suffer from higher levels of anxiety, depression, low life satisfaction, personality disorders, and difficulties in relating with others meaningfully.[68]

Box 1.2: Materialism Does Not Help

An attitude to life which seeks fulfillment in the single-minded pursuit of wealth—in short, materialism—does not fit into this world, because it contains within itself no limiting principle, while the environment in which it is placed is strictly limited.[69]

On the other hand, a multi-national study[70] claimed that it is not income, but the social capital that make people happy. Social capital manifests in quality network among people who stick together to cope with exigencies, help each other, and cultivates high level of trust. That is, people's embeddedness into their social collectives brings out the best from them and that makes them happier. It is because, the author believes, people are not just 'social' but are 'pro-social', and hence are happier by developing not just from the experience of achieving what they want but achieving both *with* and *for* others. When they do so, they realize *collective wellbeing.*

Weakening Concern for Others

Social capital is not the motivator of development in the capitalist design. The main driving force in capitalism is to provide new and variety of products and services that excite people to strive to own them, and that, in turn, accentuate their desire for newer and more variety of products and services. The market flourishes through these reciprocally stimulating forces of demands and supply. That is the trend in India now. There is an ad by a famous Indian film star urging people not to remain satisfied with a particular brand of a product, but to ask for more and for better. The Indian cultural heritage, on the contrary, values austerity, containing desires, and sharing whatever meagre resources we have with others because the whole world is our family[71] (we shall return to them later in the book). There are indeed individuals who espouse such values in varying degrees. They are, however, exceptions. The majority are now engaged in endless striving for money and material possessions. Not that the values are unknown to the ideal Indian values, but the values are buried in the backyard of their mindset. Once a while they might be brought out and enacted in the flashes of pro-social behaviour. The dominant trend is of money-making that shape and colour the whole social milieu of people from varied walks of life. They all want to get rich, and rather quickly.

The rich have this insatiable urge for money and material possessions that is highly consuming. It leaves very little space for cultivating relationships, except for utilitarian purposes. Whatever energy, skills, experiences, and insights the highly aspiring individuals have are invested into achieving what they are hankering after. Other people, friends, relatives, and in extreme cases even family members are secondary. Their needs, problems, and expectations are not that salient, they have to be sidelined. However, they may be useful now or in future and therefore have to be kept in good humour and used as and when necessary. Once used, they are redundant and disposable. That is, other people are at best the means and have only functional values. They are like money and materials that have to be possessed to have a sense of competence, self-esteem, and control not only over their own life events but also on the life events of many others. The rich feel confident that they can buy anything and anyone, provided they set the price right. That turns into an arrogance resulting often in subtle, but at times not quite subtle, denigration of lesser people. In other words, too much wealth dehumanizes the rich. They lose their sensitivity to others, and thus emotionally get cut off from others. They feel glamourous and accomplished outside, but lonely and alienated inside. Their sense of wellbeing suffers.

Rest of the people see only their glamour, are enamoured, and emulate them. Hence, they tend to acquire most of the same syndrome. Indians are known for their mythic orientation whereby they tend to introject the attributes of mythological characters and behave or rationalize their behaviour accordingly.[72] The rich are the *bade log* (superiors), they are like mythological characters. Indians identify with them, try to get closer to them if possible, acquire their attributes, and become like them.[73] Hence, the insatiable urge for money making and material possessions of the rich, accompanied by their lack of sensitivity to others, spills all over the Indian society. However, the urge and the insensitivity manifest differently at different economic levels because of their different circumstances.

The middle class too have an insatiable urge for money and material possessions. They distaste the poor and distance from them, but are extra-sensitive to the people of their own class, not to their feelings, needs, and expectations, but to their achievements. They continuously scan and compare with each other being jealous of those who are surging ahead and suspicious of those who are lagging behind but catching them up. They do not have enough money to have an air of arrogance to buy anyone or anything. They still have to watch every rupee that they spend, save for rainy days, but show off for their superiority over others. They cannot be playful with their money like the rich. They have to maintain a delicate balance between their private expenditure, and the public display of their affluence in order to keep their face up in social encounters.

The middle class has tremendous impact on the country's development because of its size that is expanding fast. Estimates of their size vary. According to one, less than 15 per cent of the population belonged to the middle class in 1993 when the liberalization of the economy was initiated in a big way. After a decade (in 2004), 26.20 per cent of the population was in the middle class. It almost doubled to 47.10 per cent only in five years (in 2009), and was projected to reach 70.20 per cent by 2014.[74] According to another estimate, 113.8 million households or 547 million individuals are likely to belong to the middle class in the year 2015.[75] Yet another estimate in the year 2012 fixes the size only to 70 million.[76] These estimates vary because of different ways of operationalizing the middle class, but they all recognize its fast growth. Income, of course, is the most basic to identify the middle class. It affects the consumption level that raises the standard of living. Related to income is a shift towards quality food, better housing, good education, and adequate health care. Quality food means more of proteins than calories and more of fruits, milk, and vegetables than cereals. All these precondition a large and open market. So, the middle class press of liberalization of economy where they expect to improve the quality of their life. Middle class also signify a relatively high social status derived from the socially desirable ways of earning livelihood. That is, *how* people earn, not only how much they make. A street vendor, for example, might collect more money than a school teacher, but the latter has an edge over the former in the social hierarchy. In other words, middle class consists of white colour job holders, professionals, and those who have inherited property and have a good standard of living. Middle class is also identified by the values they hold. Traditionally, they were the custodians of cultural values and norms (we shall return to the details later in the book), which are now subdued by the capitalist values, norms, and practices. Money and material possessions become the prime value. Money makes it easy to recognize the middle class. It consists of those who have less money and material possessions than the rich and more than the poor. But that is over-simplification. The demarcation lines are not quite clear. The upper echelon of the middle class seamlessly mixes with the rich and the lower boundary is indeterminate depending on how the poverty line is drawn. This is precisely the reason that the upper middle class readily identifies with the rich and behave like rich to the extent that they can afford to by indulging in show off. On the other hand, the lower middle class has an identity problem in the sense that others might still consider them belonging to the lower class. They avoid such a situation by maintaining as much distance as they can from the poor—both in their lifestyle as well as in their thought and disliking for the poor.

Part of the tiny middle class of the pre-liberalization days had inherited wealth and reasonably high social status. Along with the wealth, they also inherited traditional values of caste and class hierarchy, conformity to social norms, and so on. On the other hand, the overwhelming majority of the new middle class is the first generation that has varied demographics and humble beginning. They are the ones who have struggled hard, overrode economic constraints, and cope with social discriminations to raise their income, gain professional positions, and claim social status to enter into the middle class.[77] Their memories of living in scarcity and suffering denigration in the hands of socially superiors are still fresh. Their parents and relatives still carry the scars. And, the pervasive poverty around them triggers the fear of poverty that they have just been able to escape. The threat is too strong to afford any compassionate stance to the poor: "Right in front of its door, there is so much poverty and misery, so much suffering, and yet they [middle class] do not react. It's as if this misery simply does not exist".[78] So, they want to forget the poor: "They teach themselves to see only what they want to see [not the poor], yet the senses must stay in the subconscious, suppressed but not all together, to emerge in self-remembered dreams ... [thus,] they live in fear of poverty for themselves, regarding it as a personal threat".[79]

In order to hedge their fear, they distance from the poor, dissociate from less affluent friends and relatives, and seek the company of more affluent ones in order to make-believe that poverty is too far behind to touch them. They do not subscribe to traditional values of hierarchy, but value achievements, particularly accumulating more and more money and material possessions. They pitch their aspirations high and higher and then make all out efforts to realize them. When aspirations fly high, achievements have a hard time to catch up, and the result is a sense of dissatisfaction about what they have achieved already.[80] The middle class suffers from a sense of insecurity, apprehensions about their job prospects, social acceptance, their health, concern for their and their children's future, and whether the children will take care of them when they will get old.[81] They think that whatever they have achieved are not enough. The struggle is still on, and so is the persistence of dissatisfaction, scarcity, anxiety, and insecurity fueled by rising aspirations. They are hardly at peace with themselves.

There is an additional concern that adds fuel to the fire in the mindset of the middle class: Many others with similar background and merit are surpassing them. Human beings have a natural tendency to compare with others.[82] They compare their merit, background, and experiences in order to judge whether their achievements are disproportionately larger or smaller than others; larger make them feel accomplished while smaller let them down. They feel relatively deprived. Relative deprivation is "the conscious experience of a negative discrepancy between legitimate expectations and present actualities".[83] It makes people jealous. While comparing with others is a universal phenomenon, there is a cultural difference. People in many other cultures tend to compare with similar-others and feel elevated or deprived if their achievements and rewards do not commensurate with what they think they deserve. On the other hand, Indians compare not only with **similar-others**, but also with persons of dissimilar merit and background if their achievements have any, even remote, relevance to them. We have the 'Lord Indra Syndrome'. Lord Indra is the supreme god—the king of gods and goddesses. But, his throne starts wobbling whenever a mortal continues doing *tapasya* (asceticism) for a prolonged period, lest the latter claim his throne. He sees to it that the latter is distracted and his asceticism is disrupted.

Indian middle class have inherited similar sensitive antennae about the people around them. They boast of their own achievements and suspect that others are jealous of them, and are trying to pull them down. But they are themselves jealous of those who are surpassing them. Others, they think, must be using unfair means. They feel they too have to employ the same (unfair) rules if they have to compete in the game. Power naturally comes to their mind. They need power to add to their merit to counterbalance and outwit their rivals. Power can also neutralize the risk in employing unfair means. Power can help make more money. Power and money are the twins that can reinforce each other to create and expand a culture of corruption. Power also lies in networking with powerful persons. But they must be very careful because there are other powerful persons who are also competing in the same line. They have to play the game delicately by colluding as well as competing, maintaining a façade of trusting relationship while keeping their gunpowder dry, and scanning for alternative alliances in case the current one fails. In such a game, they can trust only their family members and those who have proven to be trustworthy beyond any doubt. Those who trust other than family and friends are considered to be gullible—readily available for taken advantage of. They too start mistrusting others. And yet, trust is an espoused social value and trusting is indispensable in India where majority of social transactions are made out of legally valid contracts. Thus, Indian middle class intuitively cultivates a cleaver strategy of hiding their intentions, posing to trust others and maintaining a collectivistic stance while guarding their own interests, and making a quick move to surpass others as soon as a situation permits.[84] This of course costs in terms of peace and happiness in the mind.

The poor are fully exposed to such a middle class, the most of which has risen from poverty. The poor naturally tend to emulate them, but their own limitations make them worse. Not that poverty in India is a post-Independence phenomenon. Poverty has been endemic to our people. If there were *daanbir* Karna (a mythological character) and emperors like Kanisk who used to give away everything including their clothes to the needy, there must be poor and needy ones to take them. The poverty got only worse from the ancient to the medieval to the British days. It is now more stigmatic and painful because of others from them getting affluent over night. Further, it continues to refuse to get eradicated despite the schemes of the government, cash transfer, and aid by donor national and international agencies.

Poverty, however, is not an affliction unique to India only. There are countries, which are worse than India, and there are miserably poor even in rich countries. Poverty is part of human existence because there are people and countries that have acquired disproportionately more wealth by fair or foul means putting other people and countries at prolonged and grave disadvantages. There are differences in degrees of poverty; nevertheless it casts a dark shadow wherever it exists.

Poverty does not only restrict the poor's access to resources necessary to live comfortably and to seek ways and means of improving their prospects, but also cultivates a culture of poverty—the way people think, feel, behave, and relate with others. The poor in Mexico City, for example, were characterized by, among other attributes, excessive dependency, helplessness, powerlessness, inferiority complex, and a self-perception of personal unworthiness.[85] Poor Indians too were found to have a strong tendency to over depend on government and other development agencies for all sorts of help. They were enthused so long as external assistance kept inflowing, but drifted in to passivity as soon as it dried up.[86] Poverty was reported to dehumanize Indians, restrict their access to resources, diminish their self-esteem and retard their capability to cope with their day-to-day problems, causing a sense of helplessness and powerlessness.[87] The poor also suffered from nutritional deficiency, weak self-efficacy, and retarded perceptual skills, which prevented them to access to legitimate means to achieve their goals. Consequently, they were found to drift to crimes and other socially deviant behaviour. The poor, as if, were trapped in a vicious circle where their incapability led to pathological ways of behaviour that further compromised their capabilities resulting into the loss of their sense of wellbeing.[88]

Elsewhere in the world, poverty was found to dent the family and distort parental behaviour. It caused stress to the family members, reduced their sense of well-being, and lowered their mental health.[89] The poor did not have appropriate and adequate access to health care services. They got sick very often and sought emergency services at advanced stages of disease increasing the risk of morbidity and mortality.[90] There were numerous pressures in the family that often resulted into conflicts and loss of emotional warmth for each other. The members suffered from depression and other forms of psychological distress, which constrained their interactions with the children.[91] They were erratic in behaving with their children—praising and rebuking the children at their whims rather than what the children did, and often kept aloof from and indifferent to them.[92] Children too suffered from poorer health, maladjustment, and lack of motivation for achievement.[93] There is no end to the numerous ways poverty afflicts people and compounds their disadvantages that are transmitted to the next generations. Poverty tends to perpetuate, unless it is deliberately overcome.

Social Protection of the Poor

Because of the endless, widespread, and cruel effects of poverty, the concern to eradicate it has also got a long history. *Protecting the poor is an older concern than the discourse on development.* The former was part of the age-old values of compassion and decency while development is rather the modern imperative to improve the quality of life of even non-poor. However, the two streams of thought—social protection and development—have converged presuming that there cannot be a satisfactory development without taking the poor out of poverty and putting them, along the main stream, on an upward trajectory. The shift is highlighted when the concept of "social protection" was redefined by the World Bank not only as the "safety net" for coping with sufferings but the "spring board" for jumping out of poverty into a flight for development.[94]

The social protection was defined as a "set of policies and programmes designed to reduce poverty and vulnerability by promoting efficient labour markets, diminishing people's exposure to risks, and enhancing their capacity to protect themselves against hazards and interruption/loss of income;"[95] by adopting a three legged—social insurance, social assistance, and market – support to the poor as well as those who were marginally non-poor.[96] Social insurance schemes are contributory and designed to help both poor and non-poor to cope with risks of illness, old age, and unemployment. Social assistance was meant only for poor in terms of cash transfers, subsidies, child welfare and assistance to the elderly, health assistance, disability benefits, and disaster relief. The market programmes include employment and livelihood measures that help people make some regular income. An index was developed that consisted of social insurance, social assistance, and employment considering the cost, coverage, poverty targeting, and impact of the measures of social protection.[97] A review of the status of social protection in 35 Asian and Pacific countries by analyzing comprehensive (the year 2009) data on government social protection programmes revealed that India was well below the most of the countries in providing social protection. It spent only 1.70 per cent of its GDP on social protection getting the score of just 0.051 while Japan was at the top spending 19.20 per cent of the GDP and earning 0.416 score.[98] In fact, most of the Asia Pacific countries, according to another review, were still not providing equitable benefits to their poor. The poor received less social insurance benefits than the non-poor and the quantum of social assistance to the poor and the non-poor was similar. The coverage of labour market programmes was also similar for both the poor and non-poor.[99] In other words, whatever social protections were available to the Asia-Pacific countries, the poor often got less than or as much as the non-poor resulting probably in the widening of the gap between the poor and the non-poor.

The World Bank made a strategic shift, while re-defining social protection as the "spring board", by emphasizing the importance of *building capabilities* of the poor to come out of poverty. Earlier poverty was conceptualized as absence of assets. Those who have enough to consume now and in future were considered to be non-poor. So, the poverty reduction efforts were simple: To give money and material assets to the poor in order to make them non-poor. By the same token, the idea of development was confined to giving monetary and material assistance to the undeveloped countries in order to get them out of poverty. It was proved to be not so simple and straight forward solution. The economic conditions have been complex and have turned into more turbulent by globalization. Dumping of money and material resources did not ensure that the poor will become and remain non-poor in future also. Globalization opened up more opportunities. But it has also increased competition to exploit opportunities. Because the poor are less competent to compete they are often worse off. The crucial concern is the *capabilities* to so manage efforts and activities that the poor do get out of poverty, but do not risk falling back into poverty again. Hence, the emphasis in social protection shifted to the *social risk management*, its operationalization, identification and the extent of vulnerability of different disadvantaged groups. It was argued that "assisting individuals, households, and communities in dealing with diverse risks is needed for accelerated poverty reduction, and sustained economic and social development".[100] Social risk management included getting rid of unproductive decisions and behaviour of households (e.g., taking children out of schools, delaying health care, selling livestock) that are made more problematic by natural disasters (e.g., drought, cyclones, floods, etc.), social conflicts, and unfavourable economic events and forces (e.g., policy reforms, increasing unemployment, etc.). Three sets of interventions were delineated for building up the risk management capabilities:

1. **Informal assistance** from the family, friends, relatives, and neighbours, which can help only to the extent of social harmony and the norms of reciprocal cooperation in the society. It has, however, limited potential and may not

work adequately in serious exigencies; particularly as social sensitivity is decreasing in the capitalist mode of development.

2. **Market driven support** that can be derived from banks, companies, and other financial agencies. The evidence is that the more disadvantaged a group is, the less access it has to the market based resources that are competitively made available to relatively better off.
3. **Government interventions** are the only most crucial instrument available to the needy. There are a number of schemes that cover the eligible groups and implement them in cost-effective ways with minimum leakages.

Poverty Alleviation Efforts in India

In fact, poverty alleviation has been a major concern of the Indian Government since the Independence (1947), although the achievements have been far from satisfactory. Out of ideological enthusiasm, a variety of programmes were initiated in the early years of Independence. Soon, the concern got caught up in the politics of poverty where a added aim was to gain political mileage. The 20-points programme for *Garibi Hatao* (alleviate poverty)—a slogan—was a potentially powerful instrument for socio-economic transformation as well as a sure triumph card to win over the hearts and minds of not only the poor of the country but also those non-poor who were sympathetic to the poor. Since then, the 20-points programme has been the basic structure for aligning government policies and practices to their changing priorities and political considerations. It was restructured in 1982, in 1986, and again in 2006 containing 64 schemes designed to address specific problems being faced by the poor as well as marginally non-poor.[101] Even the subsequent government refurbished it to suit its new mission of socio-economic transformation of the society. In this political process of alleviating poverty, the old schemes were refined, replaced, duplicated, differentiated to target specific groups and sections of the poor, and proliferated to a great extent.[102] They covered such a variety of issues that it is difficult to locate them all. A sample of them includes consumer protection, drinking water, employment to unskilled landless labour, empowerment of weaker sections, food security, housing for poor, forestry, improvement of slums, minor irrigation, land reforms, pension, rural electricity, rural roads, self-help for income generation, urban rejuvenation, women and child welfare, and so on. Obviously, they are targeted both to the poor as well as non-poor.

Despite such a prolonged and wide-spread assault, the poverty has managed to continue afflicting millions of Indians. A survey of caste and class document revealed a pathetic scenario both in rural and urban areas.[103] Some of the statistics of the wretched conditions in which millions of Indians live have been quoted earlier. The reasons are well-known and fully documented. There is, for example, hardly any agreement where to draw the line of poverty. So, we do not know who are poor and who are not or how many of Indians are really poor. Statistics vary widely, while government estimates[104] are conservative documenting smaller percentage of poor than other estimates which showed higher percentage of poor in the country. In such a muddled milieu, the non-poor manage to pose as poor and claim benefits meant for the poor. They have manipulated to procure the BPL (Below Poverty Line) cards meant for giving social assistance to the poor. It was found that about 40 per cent of the BPL cards are misappropriated by the non-poor.[105] The Public Distribution System (PDS) was found to be so ineffective that 58 per cent of the subsidized grains did not reach the targeted group and almost a third of it found its way into the market.[106] On the other hand, the really poor having no skills or connections with the locally resourceful politicians or government functionaries and are, therefore, deprived of such facilities. Similarly, the policy decision to provide reservations in education and jobs for the traditionally socially and economically disadvantaged—the scheduled castes (SCs), scheduled tribes (STs), and backward castes—are usurped by the creamy layers in them who are rather politically active and economically affluent. The worse are those with disabilities. The government statistics about them are grossly underestimated (2.13%).[107] Even the National Sample Survey estimated that 8.40 per cent of rural households and 6.1 per cent of urban ones have a disabled member.[108] According to the WHO (World Health Organization), the global estimate is around 15 per cent. India cannot be that better off. Not only the size of disabled is underestimated, more than 70 per cent of those who are identified having disabilities could not get government support because they could not handle the bureaucratic procedures.[109] They need several documents and must visit government offices several times, which is expensive particularly if the disabled lives in a village. The logistics of claiming benefits, the paper work, and the attitude of government functionaries are too much to handle for the disabled.

Besides the problems in identifying the target groups, there are problems in finding adequate money and resources for allocation, streamlining the delivering process, and sealing leakages. The funds are just for firefighting (meeting the urgent and immediate needs) but not enough for capability building for future shocks or springing out of poverty. Prime Minister Rajiv Gandhi reviewed with the top bureaucrats in 1985 that led to the conclusion that only about 15 per cent of a rupee of assistance reaches the poor.[110] Further, the costs of delivery were reported to be so high that the government had to spend Rs. 3.65 for transferring R 1.00 to the poor.[111] The two most ambitious programmes, the *Indira Awaas Yojana* (Indira Housing Scheme) and the Mahatma Gandhi National Rural Employment Guarantee Act, 2005 (MGNREGA) were crippled by many factors. The *Indira Awaas Yojana*, with a budget allocation of some US$ 6 billion over the five years 2007-12, was meant to address the shortage of housing suffered because of the amalgamation by state governments of the central government funds into own favourite programmes, imposition of additional terms and conditions by State governments often raising beneficiary contribution that they were not able to make, MPs (Members of Parliament) and MLAs (Members of Legislative Assemblies) directing funds to their own supporters, petty corruptions by government functionaries, and unavailability of land for constructing a house.[112] The MGNREGA was meant to provide assured 100 days of employment to the rural unskilled labour. It indeed helped many poor both economically and socially, but was crippled by many factors. There was no foolproof way to distinguish poor from non-poor. Many non-poor took undue advantages by manipulating records in collusion with government functionaries and *panchayat* members. There were reports of rampant corruption. The labour was not paid fully and had to bribe to get assigned work. There was no provision to build up new abilities and skills for future. The measurement of work was faulty. There were fake job card holders even in the names of one or two years old child, dual muster rolls, and so on.[113] Similar reports are available about other government schemes. A sample account of them is as follows:

> In his 1994 study, Kirit Parikh found that, based on the 1986-87 NSS [National Sample Survey], "cereals distribution in the states is not particularly targeted to the poor. In fact, in almost all the states, persons belonging to the bottom 70 per cent of the population get more or less the same amount...For every rupee spent less than 22 per cent reach the poor in all states, excepting in Goa, Daman and Diu where 28 paisa reach the poor" (pp. 14-15). Some fifteen years later, there is not much improvement. According to the large 1999/2000 NSS, the proportion of poor households who actually accessed rice from the PDS was only 11.3 per cent. In other words, of the eligible poor population, only 11 per cent was able to buy the subsidized rice. For wheat, the proportion was even smaller—only 5.7 per cent. Further, only 29 per cent of the wheat and rice that the government claims it distributed via the public distribution system was actually distributed. This low fraction means that 70 per cent of the food is unaccounted for—not accruing to either the poor or the rich.[114]

Aapka Paisa, Aapke Haath (It's Your Money, Have It)

Being fed up with the inefficiency, corruption, and costs of giving subsidiaries, a Direct Benefit Transfer (DBT) scheme was launched by the Government of India (January 1st, 2013). The professed ideology[115] was that poverty has been perpetuated because a section of people have been wrongfully deprived of societal resources. Therefore, it is an obligation of the government to return back what is legitimately due to them: *Aapka paisa, aapke haath* (It's your money, have it). It is not a charity but an effort to pay back the debt and thus restore social justice. Additionally, the DBT scheme aimed to reduce leakages, cut down corruption, eliminate middlemen, target beneficiaries better and speed up transfer of benefits to eligible individuals in a cost effective way. The scheme hit a serious barrier at the outset: How to reach out to the needy directly? Earlier the State governments through State functionaries used to identify the beneficiaries. For reaching out to them directly, the solution[116] suggested was to issue a unique identification card, *Aadhaar*, with the biometric measures that can distinguish one Indian from another to the extent that no one can manipulate to have more than one card (thus eliminating the chance of collecting multiple benefits). The next government emphatically kicked start the process of issuing *Aadhaar* cards and decided to use it from April 15, 2015 for direct cash transfer of benefits under all Central Government's schemes having a financial component. There was another barrier: How to transfer cash in a situation where a large number of poor did not have a bank account. It was taken care of by another scheme, *Jan Dhan Yojana* (Planning for People's Wealth), which too was vigorously launched to entitle everyone, including the poorest to open a bank account in any of the banks on the basis of the *Aadhaar*.[117] A problem, however, still exist. *Aadhaar* identifies individuals, but does not distinguish who is poor and who is not, nor does it identify the family as a unit that is generally the target of social protection. The government aims to transfer about Rs. 4.0 trillion (Rs. 4,00,000 crore) a year to the deserving beneficiaries of its subsidy schemes and welfare programmes. Food, fuel, and fertilizer constitute a major part of them. They are not meant only for the poor, but will also cover the lower middle class. Probably, the information from the Census[118] will be used for the purpose.

The scheme of the direct cash transfer (DCT) has a strong international support. The idea germinated in Mexico in 1997 and flourished in Brazil in 2007 where the Bolsa Familia Plan[119] led to transfer money directly to all poor families on the conditions that they regularly send their children to school, take nutritional food, allow pre-natal and post-natal medical check-up of their children, and so on. The Plan was a great success because it was managed through efficient targeting, disbursement, and regular monitoring of the disbursed funds. Soon it caught up like a wild fire and spread to 45 countries ranging from Latin America, Africa, South Asia, Europe, to the USA and reaching out to millions of poor people. It was labeled as a 'silent revolution' of 'elegant southern [Latin American] initiative' that bypassed governments and NGOs (non-government organizations), challenged the aid-industry and its experts who invariably complicated and mystified aid giving programmes, and let the poor themselves decide how to use their money.[120]

The Direct Cash Transfer schemes come in many forms and varying emphases serving variety of purposes. It is often meant for social protection or productive investment, providing relief and resources for rehabilitation during post-emergency situations or incentive for building capabilities for coping with future exigencies and improving quality of life. It is given in small recurring instalments or relatively in large lump sum amounts either unconditionally or conditionally, in form of vouchers, or cash payment against the amount of work performed.[121] The options are not always mutually exclusive and can be chosen in various combinations and sequences. GiveDirectly[122], for example, is a famous Cambridge (MASS, USA) initiative since 2008 helping extremely poor people in Kenya and Uganda. It directly transfers lump sum unconditional cash to them via mobile phone—giving out millions of dollars and claiming that 90 per cent the funds actually reach the poor and only 10 per cent are spent as transaction costs. The Bolsa Familia Plan of Brazil was a conditional cash transfer. The Indira *Awaas Yojana* (Indira Housing Scheme) is an example of the conditional cash transfer and the Mahatma Gandhi National Rural Employment Guarantee Act (MGNREGA) is an example of cash for work.

The idea of Direct Cash Transfer has a highly attractive face. It is politically expedient and helpful in getting votes; it satisfies the humanitarian concerns of those involved in the transferring process; technology has made the transfer easy and accountable, the recipient feels being empowered instantly by having cash in hand, and the statistics regarding poverty alleviation (increased income and expenditure of the poor) improves instantly.

But is it effective in alleviating poverty by building up capabilities?

The answer depends on whom you ask. Both the providers and the beneficiaries are very positive, although the providers lament that, they wish, they had more to give and the beneficiaries grumble that they really need more. Their faith is based on the assumption that the cash allows flexibility to use the money and that the beneficiaries are capable of and are really using it wisely. Others have reservations. They indeed concede that it is a powerful instrument for both social protection and development, but only if certain conditions are met. The conditions are capsuled in the following statement, "... cash transfers are far from a panacea, and questions around the *appropriateness* and *feasibility* of cash transfers in different *contexts* are important and urgent."[123] The Overseas Development Institute (London) has systematically examined such conditions.[124] Resources available to a country for social protection and development investment at the grassroots are an important consideration. The reality is that most of the developing country governments have been able to allocate not more than one percent of their GDP to cash-based social assistance programmes while the oil exporting OECD (Organisation for Economic Co-operation and Development) countries allocated an average of eight percent of their GDP for the purpose.[125]

Targeting the genuine needy ones is another ticklish problem. We have seen how difficult it is to decide who fall below the poverty line and who stand above it. Considering the inadequacy of resources, one can argue to bypass the complications of drawing the poverty line and advocate to identify the extremely poor people and target the benefits to them. It is easier; but there is still a dilemma. Should the benefits of a government programme be restricted only to the extremely poor? What about the marginal groups of people who are vulnerable not in economic terms but on other important criteria (low castes, disabled, sick, elderly, etc.). Poverty is now considered to be a multi-dimensional malady and there exists a large advocacy group that asks that the benefits should be based on the criteria of deprivations and should be available to all those who fit in those criteria. The cash subsidy for the cooking gas, for example, has been given to all consumers on the ground that its actual cost is too high, and it is politically unacceptable and socially divisive to withdraw them from the non-poor even if the government finds a way to identify them. Food security is another complicated issue. The poor of course should get priority. But should the cash for food be unconditional to its nutritional values? Many marginalized people are likely to have money for buying cereals, but not vegetables and fruits. Should the government meet such needs under the food security scheme? Health care poses a similar problem. Such issues lead to another complication: How to devise a basket of schemes differentiated for different groups of needy, decide the amount of cash for them, timings, monitoring, and evaluation of impacts on the beneficiaries. Inadequate cash for constructing a house, for example, does not serve the purpose and is likely to be spent on some other needs that could be more pressing at the time. Too much of cash is, on the other hand, likely to result in adventurous enterprises or spent lavishly. Similarly, a poor person, who has just bought a livestock with the large lump sum cash transfer, might be forced to sell it unless followed by small, regular and time bound payments for livelihood protection. The provision of large lump sum cash transfer attracts the local godfathers as well as the petty government functionaries to chip parts off the grant. These are, however, the nuts and bolts of the direct cash transfer that can be taken care of at least to a reasonable extent, if not perfectly, by correctly targeting the beneficiaries, designing the amount and sequence of transfer, streamlining monitoring and supervising procedures, and putting in place a fair and firm administrative regime. However, the most *critical conditions* for the effectiveness of the direct cash transfer are (a) the availability of appropriate institutions and (b) the poor's capabilities to access them (c) for utilizing the transferred cash judiciously.[126] Let me elaborate.

Cash in hands indeed gives an instant sense of empowerment. Even the extremely poor and totally illiterate people have an intuitive inclination to use it first of all for feeding the family, getting medical treatment of the sick, sending children to school, buying essential things, arranging for a shelter (*Roti, Kapada & Makaan,)* and if there is still any surplus, investing it for future income. But complications arise because of the variety in the baskets of goods and services that are available at different prices and of different qualities. Consumption pattern is of course more crucial than income for assessing the poor people's quality of life[127]. For example, some of them emulate the middle class and as their income rises consume tastier but not necessarily more nutritious food.[128] Nobel Laureate, Deaton[129], rightly emphasized the crucial role of household surveys for generating data for assessing the quality of life of the poor. But, he could not go beyond the items of consumption by seeking information about the prices that the poor have to pay for the quality of products and services that they get. The poor do not always have sufficient skills and knowledge to see through the cunning ways and manipulative practices of the sharks they have to deal with. They often end up with underweight spuriously priced commodities, particularly whenever they venture to buy non-basic fashion items (e.g., chips, biscuits, *kurkure,* soap, cosmetics, etc.). Medical treatment is rigged with malpractices. The doctor-pathologist-medical shopkeeper have such a nexus that they have to go through unnecessary tests and over medication of (often) expired or spurious drugs and unnecessary procedures. The same medical store that keeps the standard medicines has a rack full of fake and expired medicines that they sell to the poor and illiterate patients. The poor, like the middle class people, are quite keen to send their children to a school. But there has to be a viable school for them. The government primary schools, we all know too well, are in a mess. They are good enough for attracting children to get the mid-day meal and to leave immediately thereafter. They are enrolled, but hardly get any education and are likely to drop out. The trend among the poor is to send their children to the so-called English medium schools. The good ones are highly priced and so unaffordable. But the nominal ones have mushroomed not only in urban but also rural areas. It is ridiculous sight to see small toddlers oozing out of these schools in dirty dresses, often without shoes, but having a long loosely hanging ties along with unkept faces. Move above the primary level, you will find many virtual middle and high schools that do not exist physically, have no teachers, or teaching schedules, but enroll large number of students who pay the fees to them but go to a nearby coaching factory to acquire some information that might help them in passing examinations. The virtual schools manage to get them registered at some recognized schools to appear at the final school examinations. Quite often there are substitutes who take the exams on their behalf or there are helpers hanging around the examination centers to guide them in writing answers. Without having the foundation learning, most of these students are incapable of getting any job or doing any productive work. The situation at the ground level, except for some exceptions, is Alarming.

Integrative Thought

The direct cash transfer does improve income and expenditure statistics and to that extent reduce the documented percentage of population below the poverty line, but life of those who are now no longer counted as poor goes on as usual. The sense of empowerment that they had for the moment by having the cash in hand evaporates like the morning dew. It is just like the political empowerment granted by the universal franchise on the eve of an election. What is left is a long hangover of resentment with a foggy feeling of being cheated.

A deeper damaging impact of the direct, particularly unconditional, cash transfer, is the erosion of their potentials to build basic capabilities to override the odds. Building capabilities is basic to human development.[130] Little children build up their capabilities by causing an impact. They try and try and are able to stand up, and then walk a few steps, pick up their toys and throw them, and so on. That gives them the confidence that they can do things. Later on they try and are able to do more challenging things. The more challenging things they do, the more they are appreciated. As they grow, they compare themselves with others, feel good if they are better off, try hard to excel if consider themselves to be equal, and harder if they are lagging behind others. This process is basic to self-development and has to be engaged in throughout the life. As a result, people establish *effort-outcome linkage* and the motivation to make persistent efforts expecting to achieve positive outcome. This is self-efficacy[131] that leads to the experience of self-confidence and self-esteem, which are the core components of one's wellbeing.

The poor lack this self-efficacy except the knack to survive in day-to-day existence. They do not have either expectancy or skills or opportunities to turnaround their disabling conditions. So, they give up to their destiny, run after government reliefs and subsidiaries, and prostrate in front of the powerful affluents to give them some crumbs. They are impatient and short sighted and can be enthused by even flimsy promises. Politics exploit their weaknesses. As caste and religion are central to the life of people, politics fan their casteism and communalism to use them as vote banks. Cash, subsidies, or reliefs only perpetuate their miserable life.

In order to jerk them out of their pessimism and helplessness, some tangible, direct cash, or incentives are necessary. However, they should be directed to take initiative and as soon as they start taking the initiative, the incentives must be reframed and made contingent on their making further efforts. In this respect, conditional cash transfer is more scientific than the unconditional one. However, the critical consideration is *the rewards are contingent on making efforts*, and have to be calibrated *to higher and higher levels of efforts*. For example, sending children to school is the lowest level of efforts that should be rewarded only initially; thereafter further rewards must be contingent on the parents' efforts to see that the children really learn. Seed money for starting a small shop may be necessary, but the shopkeeper must work hard to generate surplus, procure credit, pay debt, and build up the business. Spending money on medical treatment is of course important, but the emphasis has to be shifted to cost-effective healthcare. Cash for food is fine, but the condition should be to improve nutritional values rather than imitating the affluent people in buying junk food. For such a design for conditionality, they need first of all sound institutions such as good primary schools, effective health care centres, training institutes for skills, and development administration, which can facilitate their access to opportunities to improve their lot by working hard and diligently.

Institutions right now are in bad shape and there is not enough incentive to work hard except for survival. Work is available only irregularly and payments do not only commensurate with the amount of work. Hence, expectancy to earn more by working hard remains weak. At the top of it, now they get cash either unconditionally or nominally conditionally. This gives a wrong signal. Earlier, they knew that they cannot earn more by working hard. Now they know that they do not have to work hard to earn money. Earlier they were not positive to work because it was not paid proportionately, now they think that they get money because they are poor. The work in case of conditional transfer (for example, in the Mahatma Gandhi National Rural Employment Guarantee programme) is taken for an excuse to give them money. It is now also an excuse to ask for more money. Neither quality nor quantity of work is relevant. Further, the government and donor agencies are believed to be obliged to keep giving relief so long they are miserable. So, they must keep displaying and exaggerating their miserable conditions in order to morally oblige the donors to give money more generously.

Displaying their miserable condition disables them further. First, they start believing that this is the best way to cope with their adversities and to make some gains. Their helpless and hopelessness assume instrumental value. They earnestly believe that they have to depend on others for improving their living conditions. The more they depend the more they lose their sense of self-efficacy. Making serious efforts to improve their lot makes less and less sense. So, the poverty perpetuates, despite the cash, subsidies, or relief that they get. A Study at the Overseas Development Institute (London) points out the risk of creating dependency.[132] Rather, transfers of tools, sewing machines, or agricultural inputs were more useful for the recipients. Similarly, Julia Kurnia, director of the direct person-to-person microfinance lending platform Zidisha+, observed that the GiveDirectly's direct cash might lead to over-dependency in the recipients.[133]

The idea of giving cash in order to help poor come out of poverty is part of the old paradigm that under-developed countries can be developed by the aid from developed countries. The paradigm has been subject to criticism from many quarters. In Mexico, for example, foreign aid was found to waken self-assertion and cause self-denigrating tendencies in people.[134] Similarly, African people are reported to get so addicted to receiving aid that they seem to have lost their cultural identities, motivation to try hard on their, sense of common purpose, and have drifted into passive inertia and demoralization. The result is endemic poverty, corruption, and even civil wars.[135] Foreign aid is again reported to foster dependency, encourage corruption, promote poor governance, perpetuate poverty, and hinders the possibility of economic growth by the people themselves.[136] The direct cash transfer is likely to have similarly negative consequences for the poor in India.

CONCLUSIONS

Despite the high sounding rhetoric such as inclusive development and sustainable development floating around, development has been equated to economic growth measured in terms of gross domestic product (GDP). The GDP indicates how much wealth has been created in a nation, irrespective of who—crooks, criminals, or virtuous—created by what—fair or foul—means. As fewer and more gifted and privileged create more wealth, growth in GDP is invariably associated with increasing inequality among the people. GDP is not perfectly related to human development either. They both—GDP and inequality—are caused by the capitalist mode of development that has been gaining ground in the world including India. The driving force in this mode is the insatiable hunger for making profit by competing and superseding others, by being creative and innovative, smart, manipulative, and exploitative. The urge to make more and more money dehumanizes the rich and causes social, physical, and mental stress without adding to life satisfaction. The same urge in many from the humble background propels them into the middle class, but keeps them comparing and competing with others without being sensitive to other's needs and concerns. It leaves them relatively deprived and dissatisfied and hence susceptible to use any means that hold promise to get them ahead of others. The low class is worse, because they emulate the worldview of those above them, but do not have capabilities to improve the quality of their life. They both—middle and lower classes—are vulnerable to politics, which evoke casteism and fan communalism to mobilize them with an eye on their vote banks. Development discourse has been focused on poverty alleviation, which was earlier attempted by various forms of aid and subsidies, but now favours direct (earned or unearned) cash transfer to the poor. Direct cash transfer is politically expedient, technologically efficient, and instantly pleasing to the poor, but is likely to defeat its purpose by instilling excess dependency in the poor and depleting their self-efficacy to make self-reliant efforts. In sum, the whole approach to realize human development through economic growth favouring a few is misdirected and needs to be examined in order to direct it to the development of all ensuring their state and sense of wellbeing.

Notes

1. Oliver Goldsmith,1770/1907.
2. The concept of GDP was introduced by Adam Smith (1776) as the measure of a nation's wealth and it also stands for national income (Gehring & Kulkarni, 2006).
3. European System of Accounts, 2010, June.
4. Abramsky, & Drew, 2014; alao http://www.dailymail.co.uk/news/article-2888416/Who-said-crime-doesn-t-pay-Counting-prostitution-drugs-GDP-figure-seen-UK-s-economy-overtake-France-fifth-largest-world
5. http://www.thelocal.es/20140925/sex-and-drugs-add-9-billion-to-spains-gdp
6. http://www.abc.net.au/news/2014-05-23/drugs-prostitution-set-to-boost-italy-gdp-result/5473548

7. The Central Bureau of Investigation (CBI) Report quoted by the BBC on February 13, 2012
8. Adam Smith, 1776
9. Gehring&Kulkarni, 2006
10. Kuznets, 1955
11. Persson & Tabellini, 1994
12. Bhalla, 2011; Gajwani, Kanbur, & Zang, 2006; Gehring & Kulkarni, 2006
13. Boston Consulting Group, 2015; Pal & Ghosh, 2007; OXFAM, 2014
14. Bandyopadhyay, 2013
15. Bhalla, 2003
16. Gini coefficient is a measure of inequality, although it does not sufficiently explain the overall variation in income distribution in a country (Gehring & Kulkarni, 2006, p.7).
17. Bhalla, 2011
18. Pal & Ghosh, 2007, p. 25
19. The Times of India, Patna, February 2, 2018, p. 8
20. Gandhi & Walton, 2012
21. Forbes illionaires List of 2015. http://www.forbes.com/sites/naazneenkarmali/2015/03/03/
22. Survey by Boston Consulting Group reported in **The Economic Times,** New Delhi, May 30, 2015.
23. Piketty, & Chanel, 2017
24. Global Wealth, 2015; TheEconomic Times, New Delhi, May 30, 2015. 23 Oxfam Briefing Paper, January, 2017.
26. World Economic Forum, 2012
27. Oxfam Briefing Paper, January, 2017
28. Sen, 1999
29. Bhalla, 2011, Table 4a, p. 21
30. The National Council for Applied EconomicResearch's (NCAER) Report, 2015.
31. The Socio-Economic Caste Census, 2011/2015.
32. Bhalla, 2011, p. 2. "The Millennium Development Goals of below 15 percent absolute poverty set for 2015 have been achieved a full decade earlier."
33. The World Bank, 2015
34. The Human Development Report, 2018
35. The Human Development Report, 2018.
36. The Soviet Union formally collapsed on December 26, 1991. The demolition of Berlin Wall started in the summer of 1990 and was completed in 1992.
37. Friedman, 1970
38. David Larson, Spectrum, 23 January 2009. http://spectrummagazine.org/node/1368
39. Weber, Max (1905/2002)

40. Kinsey, 2008
41. See profile of entrepreneurs in Sinha, 2014, pp. 124-126
42. McClelland, 1961, 1965
43. McLelland, 1985
44. Kakar, 1978; Sinha, 1990 among others
45. McClelland, 1982
46. McClelland & Winter, 1969
47. Kim et al., 1994; Triandis, 1994; Hofstede, 1980; among others
48. Sinha, 2014
49. Misra, & Agarwal, 1985
50. Pareek, 1968
51. Sinha, 1968; Sinha & Pandey, 1970
52. Muller, 2013
53. See details in Sinha, 2014, pp. 140-143
54. Deaton, 2010, p.16
55. Oxfam, 2014
56. Details will appear later in the book.
57. Mazumdar, 2008
58. Gandhi & Walton, 2012
59. Forbes Annual List of Billionaires
60. Most of them had built upon inherited wealth
61. KPMG, 2011
62. KPMG, 2011
63. Banerjee, 2015
64. Diener, 2013; Diener & Diener, 1995; Diener et al., 2010; Diener, Tay, & Oishi, 2013; Oishi, et al., 1999; Tov & Diener, 2007, among others.
65. Fulmer et al., 2010
66. Proto & Rustichini, 2013
67. Kasser, 2002
68. http://www.sustainablescale.org/AttractiveSolutions/UnderstandingHuman HappinessandWellBeing.aspx on August 25, 2014.
69. Schumacher, 1973
70. Helliwell, 2013
71. *basudhaiva kutumbakam*
72. Roland, 1988
73. Sinha, 2014
74. *Bhalla*, 2011
75. The NCAER Report retrieved fromhttps://en.wikipedia.org/wiki/Standard_of_living_in_India
76. Meyer, & Birdsall, 2012
77. Pandey, 2012
78. Grass 1999, p. 2
79. Mehta 1967, p. 565
80. Proto & Rustichini, 2013

81. Pandey, 2012
82. Festinger, 1954
83. Schaefer, 2008, p. 69
84. Sinha, *et al.*, 2002
85. Oscar Lewis, 1959
86. Sinha, 2013
87. Pareek, 1970
88. D. Sinha, 1975
89. McLoyd, 1990
90. Friel et al., 2011
91. Zahn-Waxler, Duggal, & Gruber, 2002
92. Simons,et al., 1999
93. Conger & Donnellan, 2007
94. Holzmann, Sherburne-Benz, & Tesliuc, 2003
95. The Asian Development Bank (ADB), 2001, p. 1
96. Fearing that they might fall back into poverty without protection.
97. Baulch, Wood, & Weber, 2006
98. Edes, 2013
99. Handayani, 2014
100. Holzmann, Sherburne-Benz, & Tesliuc, 2003, p. i
101. http://www.gktoday.in/twenty-point-programme_22/
102. See Chapter 1.1. Appendix at the end of the chapter
103. The Socio Economic and Caste Census (SEC Census), 2015
104. For example, Deaton, 2005
105. The Planning Commission, 2009
106. The Planning Commission, available at the followinghttp://planningcommission.nic.in/plans/planrel/fiveyr/10th/volume2/v2_ch3_4.pdf. Retrieved on August 25, 2015
107. The Census. 2011
108. O'Keefe, 2007
109. O'Keefe, 2007
110. Bhalla, 2011 p. 23
111. The Finance Ministry study reported at http://www.iasscore.in/latest-news-11.html
112. Farrington, & Slater, 2009, p. 13
113. Sushmita, 2015
114. Bhalla, 2011, p. 24
115. The ideology is part of a universal belief reported in a multinational survey conducted over the period 1995-2000 that poor people were the product of an unfair society. The belief was held even in the USA (39 per cent), but more strongly in Chile, Argentina, Mexico and Brazil (60 to 78 per cent), and most strongly in Spain and Germany (81 to 87 per cent) (Joseph, Barrientos, & Hulme, 2010).
116. Designed by Nandan Nilekani, 2008
117. Aadhaar means 'basis'.

118. The Socio Economic and Caste Census (SEC Census), 2015
119. Lindert, et al., (2007)
120. Joseph, Barrientos, & Hulme, 2010
121. Harvey, 2007
122. https://www.givedirectly.org/give-now.php. Retrieved on August 29, 2015
123. Farrington, & Slater, 2009, p. 1, Italics added
124. Farrington, 2009; Farrington & Slater, 2009; Harvey, 2007; Slater & Farrington, 2009 among others
125. Tabor, 2002
126. Farrington, & Slater, 2009
127. Deaton and Grosh, 2000
128. Subramanian and Deaton, 1996
129. Deaton, 2005
130. Sen, 1999
131. Babdura, 1997
132. Holmes & Jackson, 2008
133. http://datab.us/i/GiveDirectly. Retrieved on August 29, 2015.
134. Diaz-Guerrero, 2000
135. Maathai, 2009
136. Moyo, 2009.

REFERENCES

Abramsky, J. and Drew, S. (2014). Changes to National Accounts: Inclusion of Illegal Drugs and Prostitution in the UK National Accounts. The Office of UK National Accounts, London.

Asian Development Bank (ADB) (2001). *Social Protection: Our Framework Policies and Strategies*. Manila, Philippines.

Bandura, A. (1997). *Self-efficacy: The exercise of control*. New York: Freeman.

Bandyopadhyay, S. (2013). *Why inequality in India is on the rise*. London School of Economics and Political Science, March 27.

Banerjee, R. (2015). *Who cheats and how? Scams, fraud and the dark side of the corporate world*. New Delhi: Sage.

Baulch, B., Wood, J. and Weber, A. (2006). Developing a social protection index for Asia. *Development Policy Review*, 24 (1): 5-29

Bhalla, S.S. (2003). Recounting the poor: Poverty in India, 1983-99. *Economic and Political Weekly*, 25-31 January: 338-349.

Bhalla, S.S. (2011). Inclusion and Growth in India: Some Facts, Some Conclusions. Asia Research Centre Working Paper 39. London School of Economics, London. Retrieved on June 14, 2015.

Conger, R.D. and Donnellan, M.B. (2007). An interactionist perspective on the socioeconomic context of human development. *Annual Review of Psychology*, 58, 175–199.

Damodaran, Harish (2008): *India's new capitalists—caste, business and industry in a modern* nation. New Delhi: Permanent Black.

Deaton, A. (1988). Quality, quantity and spatial variation in price. *American Economic Review* 78(3), 418-430.

Deaton, A. (2005). Measuring poverty in a growing world (or measuring growth in a poor world). *Review of Economics and Statistics,* 87(1), 1-19.

Deaton, A. (2010). Price indexes, inequality, and the measurement of world poverty. *American Economic Review* 100(1), 5-34.

Deaton, A. and M. Grosh (2000). Consumption. In M. Grosh, and P. Glewwe (Eds.), *Designing Household Survey Questionnaires for Developing Countries: Lessons from 15 Years of the Living Standards Measurement Study,* Oxford University Press, New York, NY, for the World Bank.

Diaz-Guerrero, R. (2000). Is abnegation a basic experiential trait in traditional societies? The case of Mexico. In. J.W. Berry, R.C. Mishra and R.C. Tripathi (Eds.), *Psychology in human and social development: A Festschift for Durganand Sinha* (pp. 68-85). Delhi: Sage.

Diener, E. (2013). The remarkable changes in the science of subjective well-being. *Perspectives on Psychological Science,* 8, 591-612.

Diener, E. and Diener, M. (1995). Cross-cultural correlates of life satisfaction and self-esteem. *Journal of Personality and Social Psychology,* 68, 653-663.

Diener, E., Kahneman, D., Tov, W. and Arora, R. (2010). Income's association with judgments of life versus feelings. In E. Diener, J. Helliwell, and D. Kahneman (Eds.), *International diferences in well-being.* New York: Oxford University Press.

Diener, E., Tay, L. and Oishi, S. (2013). Rising income and the subjective well-being of nations. *Journal of Personality and Social Psychology,* 104(2), 267-276.

Edes, B. (2013). **The Social Protection Index: Assessing Results for Asia and The Pacific.** Asian Development Bank. Manila, Philippines.

European System of Accounts (2010, June). European Commission. Office of the European Union Luxembourg.

Farrington, J. and Slater, R. (2009). Lump Sum Cash Transfers in Developmental and Post-Emergency contexts: How Well Have They Performed? London: Overseas Development Institute.

Festinger, L.A. (1954). A theory of social comparison process. *Human Relations,* 7, 117-140.

Friedman, M. (1970). The social responsibility of business is to increase its profits. *Times Magazine,* New York, Sept. 30.

Friel, S., Akerman, M., Hancock, T., Kumaresan, J., Marmot, M., Melin, T., *et al.* (2011). Addressing the social and environmental determinants of urban health equity: Evidence for action and a research agenda. *Journal of Urban Health, 88,* 860-874.

Fulmer, C.A., Gelfand, M.J., Kruglanski, A.W., Kim-Prieto, C., Diener, E., Pierro, A. and Higgins, E.T. (2010). On "Feeling Right" in cultural context: How person-culture match affects self-esteem and subjective well-being. *Psychological Science*, 21, 1563-1569.

Gajwani, K., Kanbur, R. and Zhang, X. (2006). Patterns of Spatial Convergence and Divergence in India and China. Paper prepared for the Annual Bank Conference on Development Economics (ABCDE), January 18-19 2006.

Gandhi, A. and Walton, M. (2012). Where India's billionaires get their wealth? *Economic and Political Weekly*, 47, No. 40, October 6. Retrieved on June 18, 2015 from http://www.michaelwalton.info/wp-content/uploads/2012/10/Where-Do-Indias-Billionaires-Get-Their-Wealth-Aditi-Walton.pdf

Gehring, K. and Kulkarni, K.G. (2006). Economic growth and income inequality in India. http://www.kulkarnibooks.com/assets/downloads/kishore_papers/Growth_and_Inequality_in India_with_keith.pdf. Retried on June 14, 2015.

Global Wealth (2015): Winning the Growth Game. Boston Consulting Group (BCG), Boston, USA, June 15.

Goldsmith, Oliver (1770/1907). *The deserted village*. London: Ginn & Company.

Grass, G. (2001). No gate can withstand the crush of the hungry: A conversation with S. Dasgupta. Outlook, Aug 20.

Handayani, Sri W. (2014). Poverty Dimension of the Social Protection Index: Assessing Results For Asia and The Pacific. Brief No. 22. Asia Development Bank, Manila, Philippines.

Harvey, P. (2007). Cash-Based Responses in Emergencies. Humanitarian Policy Group. Overseas Development Institute.

Helliwell, J. (2013). Humans are happier when they do the right thing; it also helps them overcome difficulties. *Springer's Journal of Happiness Studies*. Available at http://www.sciencedaily.com/releases/2013/06/130612133012.htm

Hofstede, G.H. (1980). *Culture's consequences: International differences in work related values*. Beverly Hill: Sage

Holmes, R. and Jackson, A. (2008). Cash transfers in Sierra Leone: Are they appropriate, affordable or feasible? Overseas Development Institute, London.

Holzmann, R., Sherburne-Benz, L. and Tesliuc, E. (2003). Social Risk Management: The World Bank's Approach to Social Protection in a Globalizing World. The Human Development Network, The World Bank, Washington DC.

International Monetary Fund (IMF) (2015). Asia: Stabilizing and Outperforming Other Regions. Economic Health Check: IMF Survey, Washington, D.C.

Joseph, H., Barrientos, and Hulme, D. (2010). *Just give money to the poor: The development revolution from the global South*. Sterling. Herndon, VA: Kumarian Press.

Kakar, S. (1978). *The inner world: A psychoanalytic study of childhood and society in India*. Delhi: Oxford University Press.

Kasser, T. (2002). *The high price of materialism*. Cambridge: The MIT Press.

Kim, U., Triandis, H.C., Kagitcibasi, C., Choi, S.C. and Yoon, G. (1994) (Eds.). *Individualism and collectivism: Theory, method, and application (pp. 31–55)*. Thousand Oaks: Sage.

Kinsey, M. (Ed.) (2008). *Creative capitalism: A conversation with Bill Gates, Warren Buffet, and other economic leaders*. New York: Simon and Schuster.

KPMG (2011). Corruption and Bribery Survey 2011: Impact on Economy and Business Environment, KPMG.

Kuznets, S. (1955). Economic growth and income inequality. *The American Economic Review*, 25 (1), 1-26.

Lewis, O. (1959). *Five families: Mexican case studies in the culture of poverty*. New York: Basic Book.

Lindert, K., Linder, A., Hobbs, J. and Bénédicte de la Brière (2007). Bolsa Família Programme: Implementing Conditional Cash Transfers in a Decentralized Context. SP Discussion Paper NO. 0709. Social Protection. The World Bank, Washington, DC.

List of Indian billionaires, 2015. Retrieved on July 14, 2015 from https://en.wikipedia.org/wiki/Category:Indian_billionaires

Maathai, W. (2009). *The challenge for Africa: A new vision*. London: Heinemann.

Mazumdar, S. (2008). Crony Capitalism and India: Before and After Liberalization. Working Paper No. 2008/04. Institute for Studies in Industrial Development. New Delhi.

McClelland, D.C. (1961). *The achieving society*. New York: Van Nostrand.

McClelland, D.C. (1965). Toward a theory of motive acquisition. *American Psychologist*, 20, 321-333.

McClelland, D.C. (1982). Leadership motive pattern and long-term success in management. *Journal of Applied Psychology*, 67 (6), 737-743.

McClelland, D.C. (1985). *Human motivation*. Glenview, IL. Scott, Foresman.

McClelland, D.C. and Winter, D.G. (1969). *Motivating economic achievement*. New York: Free Press.

McLoyd, V.C. (1990). The impact of economic hardship on Black families and children: Psychological distress, parenting, and socioemotional development. *Child Development*, 61(2, Special Issue on Minority Children), 311–346.

Mehta, V. (1967). *Portraits of India*. New York: Penguin Books.

Meyer, C. and Birdsall, N. (2012). New Estimates of India's Middle Class. Technical Note. Center for Global Development, Peterson Institute for International Economics, Washington D.C.

Misra, G. and Agarwal, R. (1985). The meaning of achievement: Implication for a cross-cultural theory of achievement motivation. In I.R. Lagunes and Y.H. Poortinga (Eds.), *From a different perspective: Studies of behaviour across cultures* (pp. 250-266). Lisse: Swets & Zetlinger.

Moyo, D. (2009) *Dead aid: Why aid is not working and how there is a better way for Africa.* London: Penguin.

Muller, J.Z. (2013). Capitalism and inequality: What the right and the left get wrong. *Political EconomyPolitics and Society,* March/April.

National Intelligence Council (NIC) (2012). Global Trends 2030 Alternative Worlds (Fifth Report). Washington D.C.

O'Keefe, P. (2007). People with Disabilities in India: From Commitments to Outcomes. The World Bank, Washington D.C., November.

Oishi, S., Diener, E., Lucas, R.E. and Suh, E. (1999). Cross-cultural variations in predictors of life satisfaction: Perspectives from needs and values. *Personality and Social Psychology Bulletin,* 25, 980-990.

Oxfam Briefing Paper (January, 2017). An Economy for the 99 Per cent. World Economic Forum. WWW. Oxfam.org

Pal, P. and Ghosh, J. (2007). Inequality in India: A survey of recent trends. DESA Working Paper No. 45. Department of Economic and Social Affairs, United Nations, New York.

Pandey, Madhu (2012). The middle class mentality: An ICSSR report. Patna: ASSERT Institute of Management Studies.

Pareek, U. (1968). A motivational paradigm for development. *Journal of Social Issues,* 24, 112-115.

Pareek, U. (1970). Poverty and motivation: Figure and ground. In V.L. Allen (Ed.), *Psychological factors in poverty* (pp. 300–317). New York: Academic Press.

Persson, T. and Tabellini, G. (1994). Is inequality harmful for growth? *The American Economic Review,* June.

Piketty, T. and Chanel, L. (2017). Indian income inequality, 1922-2014: From British Raj to Billionaire Raj? Paper Series, No. 11. In Alvaredo, F., Chancel, L., Piketty, T., Saez, E. and Zucman, G. (Eds.), *World Inequality Report, 2018*. Paris School of Economics, Paris.

Proto, E. and Rustichini, A. (2013). A Reassessment of the Relationship between GDP and Life Satisfaction. *PLoS ONE,* 8 (11).

Roland, A. (1988). *In search of self in India and Japan: Towards a cross-cultural psychology*. Princeton, NJ: Princeton University Press.

Schaefer, R.T. (2008). *Racial and ethnic groups* (11th ed.). Upper Saddle River, NJ: Prentice Hall.

Schumacher, E.F. (1973). *Small is beautiful: A study of economics as if people mattered*. London: Blond & Briggs.

Sen, A. (1999). *Development as freedom.* New York: Alfred A Knopf.

Simons, R., Lin, K., Gordon, L., Conger, R. and Lorenz, F. (1999). Explaining the higher incidence of adjustment problems among children of divorce compared with those in two-parent families. *Journal of Marriage and Family,* 61(4), 1020–1033.

Sinha, D. (1975). Studies of psychological dimensions of poverty: A challenge and necessity. Presidential address. Proceeding of the 13th Annual Conference of the Indian Academy of Applied Psychology. Dharwar: Karnataka University.

Sinha, J.B.P. (1968). The nAch/nCooperation under limited/unlimited resource conditions. *Journal of Experimental Social Psychology, 4,* 233-248.

Sinha, J.B.P. (1990). *Work culture in the Indian context.* New Delhi: Sage.

Sinha, J.B.P. (2013). Human development: Concept and strategy. In R.C. Tripathi and Y. Sinha (Eds.), *Psychology, development, and social policy* (pp. 59-80). New Delhi: Springer.

Sinha, J.B.P. (2014). *Psycho-social analysis of the Indian mindset.* New Delhi: Springer.

Sinha, J.B.P. and Pandey, J. (1970). Strategies of high aAch persons. *Psychologia,* 13, 210-216, Japan.

Sinha, J.B.P., Vohra, N., Singhal, S., Sinha, R.B.N. and Ushashree, S. (2002). Normative predictions of collectivist-individualist intentions and behaviour of Indians. *International Journal of Psychology, 37,* 309-319.

Slater, R. and Farrington, J. (2009). Cash Transfers: Targeting. Project Briefing No. 27. London: Overseas Development Institute.

Smith, Adam (1776). *An inquiry into the nature and causes of the wealth of nations.* London: Strahan & Cadell.

Subramanian, S. and Deaton, A. *(1996).* The demand for food and calories. *Journal of Political Economy,* 104 (1), 133-162.

Sushmita (2015). Mahatma Gandhi National Rural Employment Guarantee Act: A Review. *International Journal of Arts, Humanities, and Mangement,* 1 (7), 18-26).

Tabor, S. (2002). **Direct Cash Transfers**. Social Safety Net Primer Series. World Bank Institute.

The Census Of India (2011). **Data on Disability**. Office of the Registrar General and Census Commissioner, India, New Delhi, 27-12-2013.

The Human Development Report (2018). The United Nations Development Programme (UNDP). September 14, New Delhi.

The National Council for Applied Economic Research's (NCAER) Report (2015). Centre for Macro Consumer Research, New Delhi.

The Planning Commission, Feb 14, 2009, Retrieved from http://planningcommission.nic.in/reports/genrep/rep_hasim1701.pdf

The Socio-Economic Caste Census, 2011 (2015). Ministry of Finance, Government of India, New Delhi. *The Times of India,* Patna, February 2, 2018, p. 8.

The World Bank (2014). Purchasing Power Parities and Real Expenditures of World Economies: Summary of Results and Findings of the 2011 International Comparison Programme, World Bank, Washington, DC.

The World Bank (2015). A Measured Approach to Ending Poverty and Boosting Shared Prosperity. World Bank Group, Washington, D.C.

The World Economic Forum. (2012). Global Risk Report 2012. http://reports.weforum.org/global-risks-2012/?doing_wp_cron=1478086016.0533339977264404296875

The World Health Organization (WHO) (2014). Disability and health. Fact sheet No. 352 December 2014. Retrieved from http://www.who.int/mediacentre/factsheets/fs352/en/on August 15, 2015.

Tov, W. and Diener, E. (2007). Culture and subjective well-being. In S. Kitayama and D. Cohen (Eds.), *Handbook of cultural psychology*. (691-713). New York: Guilford.

Triandis, H.C. (1994). Theoretical and methodological approaches to the study of collectivism individualism. In U. Kim, H.C. Triandis, C. Kagitcibasi, S.C. Choi, and G. Yoon (Eds.), *Individualism and collectivism: Theory, method, and application* (pp. 41–51). Thousand Oaks: Sage.

Tripathi, R.C. (1988). Aligning development to values. In D. Sinha and H.S.R. Kao (Eds.), *Social values and development: Asian perspectives*. New Delhi: Sage Publications.

Tripathi, R.C. (2013). Education: Path to development and happiness in rural India? In R.C. Watkins, M. and Shulman, H. (2008). *Toward psychologies of liberation*. London: Macmillan-Palgrave.

Tripathi, R.C. and Y. Sinha (Eds.), (2013) *Psychology, development, and social policy in India* (pp. 81-102). New Delhi: Springer.

Weber, Max (1905/2002). *The Protestant ethic and the spirit of capitalism* (translated by Peter Baehr and Gordon C. Wells). New York: Penguin Books.

Zahn-Waxler, C., Duggal, S. and Gruber, R. (2002). Parental Psychopathology. In M.H. Bornstein (eds.), *Handbook of parenting* (Vol. 3, pp. 295–327). Mahwah, NJ: Lawrence Erlbaum Associates.

Appendix 1.1
List of Major Government Welfare Schemes

Aam Aadmi Bima Yojana (2007). Scheme extends the benefit of life insurance coverage as well as coverage of partial and permanent disability to the head of the family or an earning member of the family of rural landless households and educational assistance to their children studying from 9th to 12th standard as an extended benefit.

Atal Pension *Yojana* (May 9, 2015). Social sector scheme pertaining to pension.

Central Government Health Scheme (1954). Comprehensive medical care facilities to the central government employees and their family members.

Deendayal Disabled Rehabilitation Scheme (2003). Creation an enabling environment to ensure equal opportunities, equity, social justice and empowerment of persons with disabilities.

Deen Dayal Upadhyaya Gram Jyoti *Yojana* (2015) aims to provide 24x7 uninterrupted power supply to all homes in Rural India.

Digital India Programme (July 1, 2015) aims to ensure that government services are available to citizens electronically and people get benefit of the latest information and communication technology.

Gramin Bhandaran Yojana (March 31, 2007). Creation of scientific storage capacity with allied facilities in rural areas in order to meet the requirements of farmers for storing farm produce, processed farm produce, and agricultural inputs. To improve their marketability through promotion of grading, standardization and quality control of agricultural produce.

Indira *Awaas Yojana* (1985). To provide financial assistance to rural poor for constructing their houses themselves.

Indira Gandhi *Matritva Sahyog Yojana* (2010). A cash incentive of Rs. 4,000 to women (19 years and above) for the first two live births.

Integrated Child Development Services (October 2, 1975). To tackle malnutrition and health problems in children below 6 years of age and their mothers.

Integrated Rural Development Programme (1978). Self-employment programme to raise the income-generation capacity of target groups among the poor.

Janani Suraksha Yojana (2005). One-time cash incentive to pregnant women for institutional/home births through skilled assistance.

Jawaharlal Nehru National Urban Renewal Mission (December 3, 2005). To be replaced by Atal Mission for rejuvenation and urban transformation.

Kasturba Gandhi *Balika Vidyalaya* (July 2004). Educational facilities (residential schools) for girls belonging to SC, ST, OBC, minority communities and families below the poverty line in educationally backward Blocks.

Kishore Vaigyanik Protsahan Yojana (1999). Scholarship programme to encourage students to take up research careers in the areas of basic sciences, engineering and medicine.

Livestock Insurance Scheme. Insurance to cattle and attaining qualitative improvement in livestock and their products.

Mahatma Gandhi National Rural Employment Guarantee Act (February 6, 2006). Legal guarantee for 100 days of employment in every financial year to adult members of any rural household willing to do public work-related unskilled manual work at the statutory minimum wage of Rs. 120 per day (2009 prices).

Members of Parliament Local Area Development Scheme (December 23, 1993). Each MP has the choice to suggest to the District Collector for works to the tune of Rs. 5 Crores per annum to be taken up in his/her constituency. The Rajya Sabha Member of Parliament can recommend works in one or more districts in the State from where he/she has been elected.

Midday Meal Scheme (August 15, 1995). Free lunch to school-children on all working days.

***Namami* Gange Programme** (March 1995) For Clean and Protected Ganga.

National Literacy Mission Programme (May 5, 1988). To make millions adults in the age group of 15-35 literate.

National Pension Scheme (January 1, 2004). Contribution based pension system.

National Social Assistance Scheme (August 15, 1995). Public assistance to its citizens in case of unemployment, old age, sickness and disablement and in other cases of undeserved want.

Pradhan Mantri Adarsh Gram Yojana (July 23, 2010).

Integrated development of Scheduled Caste majority villages in four states.

Pradhan Mantri Suraksha Bima Yojana (May 9, 2015). Social Sector Scheme pertaining to Insurance Sector.

Pradhan Mantri Jeevan Jyoti Bima Yojana (May 9, 2015). Social Sector Scheme pertaining to Insurance Sector.

Pradhan Mantri Jan Dhan Yojana (August 28, 2014). National mission for financial inclusion to ensure access to financial services, namely banking savings and deposit accounts, remittance, credit, Insurance, pension in an affordable manner.

Pradhan Mantri Gram Sadak Yojana (December 25, 2000). Good all-weather road connectivity to unconnected villages.

Rajiv *Awaas Yojana* (2013). It envisages a "Slum Free India" with inclusive and equitable cities in which every citizen has access to basic civic infrastructure and social amenities and decent shelter.

Rajiv Gandhi Grameen Vidyutikaran Yojana (April 2005).Replaced by Deen Dayal Upadhyaya Gram Jyoti Yojana. Programme for creation of Rural Electricity Infrastructure and Household Electrification for providing access to electricity to rural households.

Rashtriya Krishi Vikas Yojana (August 1, 2007). Achieve 4 per cent annual growth in agriculture through development of agriculture and its allied sectors during the XI Plan period.

Rashtriya Swasthya Bima Yojana (April 1, 2008). Health insurance to poor (BPL), Domestic workers, MGNERGA workers, rikshawpullers, building and other construction workers, and many other categories as may be identified by the respective states.

Saksham **or Rajiv Gandhi Scheme for Empowerment of Adolescent Boys** (2014). Aims at all-round development of adolescent boys and make them self-reliant, gender-sensitive and aware citizens, when they grow up.

Sabla **or Rajiv Gandhi Scheme for Empowerment of Adolescent Girls** (2011). Empowering adolescent girls (Age) of 11–18 years with focus on out-of-school girls by improvement in their nutritional and health status and upgrading various skills like home skills, life skills and vocational skills. Merged Nutrition Programme for Adolescent Girls (NPAG) and Kishori Shakti Yojana (KSY).

Sampoorna Grameen Rozgar Yojana (September 25, 2001). Providing additional wage employment and food security, alongside creation of durable community assets in rural areas.

Skill India Programme (National Skill Development Mission) (July 15, 2015). To provide the institutional capacity to train a minimum 40 crore skilled people by 2022.

Swabhiman (February 15, 2011). To make banking facility available to all citizens and to get 5 crore accounts opened by Mar 2012.

Swarnajayanti Gram Swarozgar Yojana (April 1, 1999). Bring the assisted poor families above the poverty line by organising them into Self Help Groups (SHGs) through the process of social mobilization, their training and capacity building and provision of income generating assets through a mix of bank credit and government subsidy.

Swavalamban (September 26, 2010). Pension scheme to the workers in unorganised sector. Any citizen who is not part of any statutory pension scheme of the Government and contributes between Rs. 1000 and Rs. 12000/-per annum, could join the scheme. The Central Government shall contribute Rs. 1000 per annum to such subscribers.

National Rural Livelihood Mission (NRLM) (June 2011). To organize rural poor into self-help groups and make them capable for self-employment. The idea is to develop better livelihood options for the poor.

***HRIDAY* (Heritage City Development and Augmentation Yojana)** (2015). To preserve and rejuvenate the rich cultural heritage of the country.

Sukanya Samridhi Yojana (Jan 2015). The scheme primarily ensures equitable share to a girl child in resources and savings of a family in which she is generally discriminated as against a male child.

Smart Cities Mission (June 25, 2015). To enable better living and drive economic growth stressing on the need for people-centric urban planning and development.

Atal Mission for Rejuvenation and Urban Transformation (June 25, 2015). To enable better living and drive economic growth stressing on the need for people-centric urban planning and development.

Pradhan Mantri Awas Yojana (June 25, 2015). To enable better living and drive economic growth stressing on the need for people centric urban planning and development.

Source: https://en.wikipedia.org/wiki/List_of_government_ schemes_ in_India

2
Power Politics of Development

Samarath Ke Nahi Dosh Gusa.[1]

BASIC POWER PROCESS

From Micro to Macro Perspective

Development begins with human initiatives and culminates in human being's better state and sense of wellbeing. During this journey, it involves other individuals, groups, nations, and superpowers, which take upon themselves to define what development is and how it must be realized—often by imposing their own design and serving, advertently or inadvertently, their own vested interests that often constrain other's state and sense of wellbeing. They impose to the extent they have the power, skills, and motivation to do so. Let us see how it happens.

Genesis of Development and Wellbeing

At the most basic level, development is essentially an induced change process. Change is natural, pervasive, and inevitable. Everything around us changes and keeps changing. We keep changing too. Our body, our thinking, our skills, attitudes, experiences, and even mood keep changing. Similarly, the physical environment around us change, people change, their relationships change, and so on. Some changes are useful and hence desirable while others are harmful and hence undesirable. We all are hedonists in varying degrees. We avoid pain and seek out pleasure. So, we make efforts to make desirable changes and avoid undesirable ones. We tend to change the physical environment around us: Build houses, cities, dams, highways, and all those things of human creations that we see around us. We create social milieu too. We form family, groups, communities, organizations, nations, and international organizations to change the way we live, earn, work, and relate with each other. We tend to move out of inhospitable places, hostile people, and uncomfortable situations to the ones where we feel more secure, comfortable, and happy. We change ourselves too—our views, our habits, our ways of living, and so on to align with the demands of the places, the people around us, and the specific time (*desh, paatra,* and *kaal*). We feel empowered and enjoy this feeling of having the capabilities to impact the people and the environment around us. This is the genesis of development: *The efforts to escape the undesirable and to realize desirable changes that give us a sense of competence and self-worth, which are the defining properties of wellbeing.*

How do we know what is desirable and what is undesirable and how to seek out desirable and to avoid the undesirable?

The most natural way is to act upon places and people to see what happens and how we feel about that happening. If we do not know what to do, our acts are random. We make many trials and errors without knowing which one will work. We just try and watch. Then by chance, one of the moves hits the desired outcome. We try again, there are some errors, but now we succeed sooner. We repeat it again and again to be sure that it really works. Once confirmed, it is adopted as *the known effort to procure a positive outcome.* Not only human beings, but even rats do the same. When a hungry rat is put in a maze, it keeps jumping around the maze till it hits a lever that yields a pallet of food. Gradually, the rat learns to go and press the lever without any trial and error[2]. That's the way we form effort-outcome linkages that are the basis of knowing and reaching out to get to our desirables. This process of knowing the correct efforts and making them to get to desirables is is process of development.

Development in inter-personal context. However, we do not live in social vacuum. There are always other people with whom we keep acting and interacting. They too act to get to their desirables while interacting with us. We observe, cooperate, help, influence, compete, obstruct, or harm each other. We compare our constructions of desirables and undesirables with them. But suppose two persons are equally uncertain about what is desirable or undesirable and how to get it. They both will start exploring individually by trying out various ideas and options selecting some and dropping others, and will gradually come up with a set of their own. If they get together, they will naturally go for their own view. If the image of the desirable and the way to get it happen to be the same, there is no problem. They both will feel confident that they have the right vision of development and act in the same way to realize it. However, it rarely happens, particularly if the issue at hand is as complex or ambiguous as the desirable future about which individuals invariably have different views and personal interests. So, they try to influence each other partly for the sake of validating their own individual views. In the process, they might converge to find a solution half-way by compromising a bit.[3] It is a flexible, give and take process. It is ideal, but it too happens rarely because no two persons are either likely to be equally naïve about what is their desirable future, or have similar or compatible needs and perspectives. One of them is invariably more advantaged than the other in being more matured, experienced, intelligent, affluent, shrewd, articulate, imposing, manipulative, or exploitative. The advantaged one has an edge in power over the disadvantaged in influencing the latter. The advantaged may genuinely feel that he/she has a better view of desirable future and it is also in the interest of the disadvantaged to subscribe it. The advantaged may also have self-interest to see that his/her view prevails and serves his/her interest irrespective of how it affects the disadvantaged. The disadvantaged will yield only to the extent that he/she is unable to resist the advantaged.

It is a matter of relative power – power over each other. The more powerful has three major ways of influencing the less powerful person. The most ruthless way is to unilaterally impose upon and control the less powerful person by dictating what the latter must do. Another way is to promise a carrot – offer of an attractive reward, should the less powerful person fall in line. It is less coercive and more engaging process where the recipient's need (for a carrot) is evoked to make him/her yield. If the recipient does not care for a carrot, the power wielder has no influence. The third and most subtle way is to create a situation where the less powerful person feels that it is in his/her interest to think, feel, and behave as wished by the more powerful person. The more powerful does not have to exert power over the less powerful. The less powerful reaches out to him/her and seek out or guess what the more powerful wishes and act accordingly. Which of the three ways is evoked depends on the magnitude of relative power and the nature of relationship between the more and less powerful persons. Larger power differential tempts the more powerful to opt for unilateral imposition without any fear of retaliation from the less powerful. Smaller power differential requires manipulations or give and take. Quality of relationship in terms of close affinity and trust is conducive to a free flow of power and influence.[4] If we trust and respect a person, we let him or her decide for us. There is no negative feeling, hence, no resistance. We have parents, teachers, seniors, bosses, gurus, friends, and even the local musclemen who resort to one of these three measures (more often all three in various combinations, degrees, and sequences) to prevail upon us to accept their vision, their dreams, their commands, etc. and we do the same to define for those who are dependent on, close to, or helpless in face of our pressure. If our interactions continue for a while, they led to form a group where the less powerful yield to the more powerful, and together they create a majority that cultivates an image of a desirable future.

The majority in a group has tremendous power and influence on its individual members. It imposes on them the image of desirable future, irrespective of how individuals think and feel. Individuals may have different views or may even see that the majority is wrong, but still prefer to suppress their own ideas and go along with the majority. It may not be wise, they might think, to disagree with the majority; for there is a risk of getting rejected, ridiculed upon, or sanctioned on some excuses. So, there is a safety in following the flock. After all, group solidarity, they might think, is more important than individuals' idiosyncrasies. You may need, they think, their help in exigencies. Or, maybe, the majority is right. After all, the group has a shared wisdom that has been distilled from a variety of experiences over a time period. So, it is wise relying upon the majority. In other words, the individuals' mind turns and twists till they fall in line.[5] Only infrequently, a deviant stands out to follow his or her own ideas, serve own interests, or pursue what he or she views as desirables at the cost of being marginalized or sanctioned by the majority. More often, the majority's image of a desirable prevails.

When two groups interface, the more powerful dominates the less powerful, although the power dynamics are somewhat different from those in case of individuals facing a majority. The weak group also has its own core preferences, norms, dos and don'ts that it intends to retain in face of any pressure to change them. The dominant group still tends to coerce, impose, tempt with rewards, persuade, cajole, entice, and resort to various other devices to prevail upon the weaker one, but rarely succeeds to change fully the core beliefs and preferences of the weak group. Total assimilation of the worldview of the weak group into that of the powerful is rare. Uneven integration is more likely where the ideas from both clash and are negotiated to compose into a new whole. Of course, the dominant group still has a major say. In certain cases, the dominant group ignores or deprives the weak one of valuable resources, marginalizes, and leaves it high and dry. The opposite of it also happens at times. The weak group dissociates from the dominant one, remains defiant, and prefers to function in an alienated or independent way. The four modes of intergroup transactions—assimilation, integration, marginalization, and alienation—vary as a result of the groups' characteristics[6]; but relative power still remains the most critical factor in calibrating the four modes for designing of a group's desirable future.

Moving to large groups and to nations, we find that the same pattern—dominance of the stronger over the weaker-holds. History has witnessed, for example, the variety of ways in which the more powerful restructured the worldview of the less powerful people and shaped the latter's image of their desirable future. Just a few pointers are given here before we see the full play of the dynamics of dominance in India.

A large scale immigration of *Aryans* into the Indo-Gangetic plain led to assimilate the indigenous population. However, the *Aryans* integrated many religious practices, beliefs and rituals from them into their religion.[7] Among the *Aryans,* Brahmins, although in minority, established their superiority and hence legitimacy to impose on other castes their design of the human development, which was operationalized in terms of the progression in the life-forms. They envisioned the birth cycle of 8.4 million life-forms, in which all living beings ranging from plants through insects, birds, and animals to human being get born. Brahmins posited themselves at the top only next to divine while placing lower castes or indigenous people at the bottom of human beings, just above animals. Further, they prescribed to the lower caste people elaborate codes of conduct (*dharmashastras*) in order to get born progressively into higher castes (Vaishyas, Kshatriyas, and even Brahmins). The codes of conduct were steeply tilted in favour of Brahmins and Kshatriyas and quite unfair to lower castes.

As Europe developed, the powerful Europeans fanned over distant lands in order to dominate the indigenous people. Large number of them moved to North America and overpowered and ruled whom they called the Red Indians[8]. Red Indians ended in marginalization and alienation for the rest of their existence[9]. European design of development prevailed over the land since then. Same is the story of South America where we hardly see any significant continuation of the indigenous worldview which can compete with that of the European.

Europeans' domination of African and Asian countries is a blatant example of imposing an alien design of development. It was started in the fifteenth and sixteenth centuries, but got accelerated from the 19th centuries.[10] Europeans professed having the objective to "civilize the barbarian nations as "The White Man's Burden". That is, the efforts and costs they were supposedly incurring on a humanitarian ground to modernize and improve the conditions of undeveloped indigenous people[11]. In reality, however, it was European imperialism driven by their vested interests and the paternalistic belief in their racial superiority[12]. They were empowered by the industrial revolution, advancement of science and technology, new worldview emanating from Reformation and Renaissance, and their ability to control sea routes. On the contrary, African countries were fragmented and vulnerable to European domination. Merchants, missionaries, and rulers came on in increasing number to sell new products and grab land in return, spread Christianity, and rule over the native people by providing the Western vision of what a developed society and people should look like, think, feel, and behave.

On the other hand, the dominance by Hindus over the South-East Asia, which started about 1500 hundred years ago, was quite subtle and non-coercive. "Hindu kings were ruling over Indo-China and the numerous islands of the Indian Archipelago, from Sumatra to New Guinea. Indian religion, Indian culture, Indian laws and Indian government molded the lives of the primitive races all over this wide region, and they imbibed a more elevated moral spirit and a higher intellectual taste through the religion, art and literature of India" ...the indigenous people were "lifted to a higher plane of civilization.[13] Buddhism was also quite indirect in its influence. Buddhism was not designed to convert people directly[14]. It did convert people of many Asian countries in benign ways. Lord Buddha, for example, instructed his monks to help people overcome their unhappiness and suffering that they were creating for themselves by their ignorance and bad conduct. The idea was to help them learn how to get rid of suffering by cultivating right conducts. Those who did became Buddhists and most often their children became Buddhists too. On the contrary, Islamic dominance was coercive and violent.

DOMINANCE OVER THE NATIVES

Islamic Dominance

Sporadic Islamic invasions of India started in about the 8th century, but got more massive from the 12th century CE resulting into the establishment of the Delhi Sultanate (1206 CE), and finally the Mughal empire (1526-1707 CE) that lasted till the 17th century CE[15]. The invaders looted the enormous wealth concentrated in temples and monasteries. But that was not their primary motive. They tended to spread Islam by wiping out Hinduism and Buddhism through their superior martial prowess and fanatic ferocity. But, that was not the primary driver either. Hindu "monism was sufficiently flexible and accommodating to leave a wide area in which [Islamic] monotheism had freedom of movement...[so] the essence of the undoubted conflict must be looked for the *Muslim worldview* [Italic added] ...the the Muslim were expansionists with a tenacity of purpose in total contrast with the already shrinking, nostalgic, Indian worldview among Hindus of those days, this confidence invested even their ruthless and underhand exploits with an aura of exhilaration".[16]

Accounts of bloody assaults and ruthless exploitation "with an aura of exhilaration" differ widely and are strongly controverted. However, the evidence does confirm that most invaders and many Muslim rulers destroyed and looted temples and monasteries; demolished places of learning; enslaved Hindu men, women, and children and sold them to Muslim nobles from Delhi to Central Asia; coerced Hindus to get converted into Islam or else to pay *Jiziya;* impoverished people by taxing them very heavily; and so on. Wherever Muslim armies marched, people fled into jungles leaving behind their immovable belongings in order to save themselves and their women.[17] Ibn Battuta was quoted, "The Muslims dominate the infidels, but the latter fortify themselves in mountains rugged places, as well as in bamboo groves. Hence they cannot be subdued".[18]

The ruling class and those associated with them had a life of luxury based on dominance, exploitation, and corruption. The foreign born Muslim nobles looked down upon Indian born Muslim nobles as low born, who, in turn, detested Hindu nobles. The Delhi Sultans and Mughal emperors kept themselves above all by centralizing all power, treating their nobles as slaves, and playing with them like pawns. They lived the most luxurious life in despotic style that the nobles emulated to the extent that their power, position, manipulative skills, and exploitative behaviours permitted. They had an insatiable hunger for sensual pleasure, lust for luxuries, and ostentatious display of their status and wealth. Even the richest European courts, according to foreign visitors of the time, could not compare in richness and magnificence with the lustre of the Indian courts.[19] A famous historian, Jadunath Sarkar, was quoted observing that "All the surplus produce was swept into the coffers of the Mughal nobility and pampered them in a degree of luxury not dreamt of even by kings in Persia and Central Asia".[20]

Their palaces and mansions were fully carpeted and decorated with silver and gold, with orchards, gardens, fountains, and served by a large fleet, often running into hundreds and thousands, of servants and slaves. There were trainers, servants, and attendants for the horses and camels that they were supposed to maintain according to their status. While encamping, their tents were made equally magnificent. All the arcades and galleries were covered from top to bottom with brocade, and even the pavements had rich carpets. Their harems had many wives and concubines protected by eunuchs, but the nobles still visited the dancing girls and called them to their places for entertainment. They "were soaked in wine [and opium] and sunk in debauch".[21]

For all these lavish life style and ostentations, the nobles needed lots of money and power. Their salaries were not sufficient. So, they resorted to bribery, embezzlement, and exploitation. No one met his superior empty handed. They had to present a gift (*nazarana*); the more valuable the gift, the more favour it was likely to fetch. Nobles were looking for every opportunity of presenting gifts of extraordinary magnificence to the king either as ostentatious display, or to dissuade the king from instituting an inquiry into their excessive exactions, or to gain his favour such as an increase of salary, a larger military command, a more profitable political appointment, or a highly lucrative revenue assignment. Receiving and even demanding presents and money by men in powerful positions was the customary. For example, Nur Jahan's father, the prime minister under Jahangir, was open in demanding precious presents. A high officer, Jai Singh, for example, had to give Rs. 30,000 to the minister close to the emperor in order to allow him to retain the Deccan command.[22] In fact, everybody in the royal Court as well as outside had to pay in order to get or retain a petty or large favour. The royal court was an arena of conspiracy and intrigues where courtiers colluded and conspired to flatter and prostrate before more powerful and outwit, double cross, and eliminate their rivals. They posed to be loyal and subservient to their lord, but waited for an opportunity to rebel and over throw him.

Power and position were also used for the wide-spread embezzlement.[23] Some officers managed to receive double, even more than double, the salaries and the grants that they were entitled to. Some cheated from the salaries of the soldiers and the expenditure on their horses. Many who had the rank of maintaining 5,000 horses did not keep even 1,000. Others employed fewer men than shown in records to work on government jobs and reported inflated expenditures on them. Even the Master of Mint debased the new coins by putting in them less silver than approved, and still got way majestically by manipulating the evidence. The smart slaves rose into the ranks cf nobles and made fortunes. For example, a slave, Bashir, amassed 13 crore *tankahs* while the State's total revenue of the whole year was only 6.75 crore. Similarly, another slave had acquired wealth amounting to two years total revenue of the government. There were instances when the corruptible and greedy nobles were appointed as judges.[24]

Siphoning of government money, however, was not enough. There was pervasive exploitation.[25] Sir Thomas Roe was quoted observing, "the people of Hindustan lived as fishes do in the sea—the great ones eat up the little. For first the farmer robs the peasant, the gentleman robs the farmer, the greater robs the lesser, and the King robs all"[26]. The Ulama had referred to *Hidaya* for providing religious justification to confiscate the land and all moveable property of the conquered people or to levy capital tax to the extent that they were reduced to subsistence living. The land and the properties, thus confiscated, were distributed among officers, soldiers and Ulama in lieu of pay or reward. The Sultan had directed that only so much should be left to his subjects that they could live from hand to mouth without storing up anything in excess, lest they may likely to rebel or resist his oppressive regime. The artisans and craftsmen were equally exploited to produce luxury goods by working overtime, but were paid minimum for their products. Even the Hindu landlords were reduced to a deplorable position and were forced to seek sundry jobs from the nobles. The practice was continued by the Mughal administration which levied taxes on an ever-ascending scale. The farmers were so impoverished that some of them were compelled to sell their women and children to meet the revenue demand[27]. In sum,

> "The story of the exploitation of the poor, both rural and urban, was unending. And, the guiding principle of this pernicious practice was to leave the people with bare subsistence. ... It would appear that the lords and the upper classes ... derived a cynical pleasure in oppressing the poor."[28]

Socio-economic inequality was not new to India. The ancient Indians were not averse to making money and living luxuriously. Hindu kings, *samants* (Hindu lords), and merchants indeed lived lavishly.[29] However, their urge for luxury was probably contained to an extent by a strong tradition of asceticism that was rooted in the pre-vedic period. There was also a strong belief that the wellbeing of a king depended on the wellbeing of his subjects. The belief did not prevent the king from extracting wealth from the people, but certainly moderated the extent of inequality in the society. For example, during the Gupta period the country had indeed "a culture showing a wide variation in living". "The prosperous urban dwellers lived in comfort and ease with a variety of luxuries in the way of jewels and cloths...the degree of comfort in the urban centres at any rate was not restricted to the upper classes alone....The comfortably installed town-dweller had on the outskirts of his town the homes of the out-castes probably much the same as the modern shanty-town. Villages, however, showed less disparity in the standard of living".[30] In fact, "The condition of the peasantry in India, up to the 14th century, was not bad.... But thereafter, there is hardly any foreign visitor to India in the 16th and 17th century in particular, who was not struck by the extremely miserable existence of the lower class people".[31]

In sum, the nobles, both Muslim and Hindu but Muslims particularly, enjoyed a life of opulence, sensual pleasure and luxuries, and instant gratification and ostentations by coercing and exploiting those below them and being coerced and exploited by those above them including kings and overlords.[32] This was the model of a lavish life based on the misuse of power that was inherited by the colonial ruler and has lingered in the mindset of many Indians.

Colonial Dominance

The British further dominated and exploited Indians starting from the 18th century that later led to their rule over the country.[33] Despite the medieval exploitation at the time British started making inroads, the country was more developed than Europe in many ways. The farmers were productive and the craftsmen were skillful enough to generate wealth amounting to the second highest GDP in world, only next to China.[34] "Indian methods of production and of industrial and commercial organization could stand in comparison with that vogue in any other part of the world"[35]. And, "... there was almost nothing that England could export that the East [India] wanted to buy".[36] So, the British paid in gold and silver particularly for textiles. Hand-woven cotton had very fine quality. It had integrated agriculture with village-level industry leading to a viable decentralized economy.

Furthermore, vernacular education was quite widespread. For instance, William Adam[37] reported that in Bengal there was one school for about 73 children, which compared favourably with most countries in the world. The elementary education was sufficient to meet the demands of the time in trading and accounting. The schools did not depend on financial support of the State, they were maintained mostly by either public contributions or the landlords of the village. Thus, elementary education too was integrated with the village community. The situation was similar in Madras and Bombay presidencies[38] indicating the presence of a universally literate mass of Indians.

The British continued with the medieval exploitative policy, and executed it rather more efficiently having greater devastating impact on the economy and the people. "… in many of its structural features, as well as its substantive policies, the colonial state sustained what were essentially pre-colonial political forms until well into the nineteenth century".[39] They started with the aim of achieving a monopolistic trading position. Soon they got greedy realizing that India could be turned into a major market for British goods and a source of raw materials to feed British industries. They needed and acquired political power to control over the market and to reign over the country so that they could exploit the country freely and fully and to bleed it in order to enrich Britain. In the year 1600, Britain had only 1.80 per cent of the world's GDP while India had 22.54 per cent. By the year 1870, Britain increased is GDP by five-fold to 9.10 per cent while India lost almost half of it, getting reduced to 12.25 per cent.[40] India became the "jewel in the British crown" having the essential elements in the world power structure, in terms of geography, logistics, and military manpower.[41]

The British "de-industrialized" India by destroying its industries and crafts, tormented artisans and craftsmen mercilessly, forced farmers to produce indigo and opium for exports, imposed a new parasitic class of landlords who perpetuated the British raj, and siphoned off Indian wealth to Britain. They caused "appalling poverty"[42] of people, created a huge mass of landless labourers, and impoverished a large section of the traditional landed aristocracy, which led to the drying up of the main source of income of indigenous schools[43] and thereby rendered the masses illiterate. While the population of India increased from 170 million in the beginning of 1757 (the year of the first the British conquest) to 420 million by the India's Independence (1947), the country's income "probably did not increase at all".[44] The schemes of irrigations might have improved agricultural production and the railways improved its relatively more efficient transportation; but they still could not prevent the frequent occurrences of famines. There were famines in the pre-colonial centuries. However, the number and severity of famines in about the two centuries of the British rule were much higher than in the past centuries.[45] While there were only 14 famines occurred in 600 years (between the 11th and 17th centuries) before the colonial inroad, there were 12 famines and four "severe scarcities" only in about 100 years (between 1765 and 1858)[46] of the colonial rule. Famines were not caused so much by the poor production of food but due to the ways it was distributed among the people.[47] No wonder that Richard Becher of the East India Company wrote to his superiors in London on May 24, 1769, "It must give pain to an Englishman to have reason to think that since the accession of the Company to the *Diwani*, the condition of the people of this country has been worse than it was before.... This fine country, which flourished under the most despotic and arbitrary government, is verging towards ruin".[48]

Box 2.1: Mahatma Gandhi on British Rule

It [British rule] has impoverished the hapless millions by a system of progressive exploitation ... It has reduced us politically to serfdom, it has sapped the foundations of our culture ... it has degraded us spiritually.[49]

Having ruined the country, the British justified its "The White Man's Burden' to retrieve it from all the evils and modernize the people. Indians were portrayed "having no history" and Indian culture was said to be expressed in the "universal deification of all finite existence and the degradation of the Divine, a deprivation of man of personality and freedom", and "the morality which is involved in respect of human life was not found among the Hindus".[50] Indian village community was characterized by "the barbarian egotism'.[51] Every European held the conviction of their racial superiority over Indians. Seton Kerr, a Foreign Secretary of the Government, reported "the cherished conviction of every Englishman in India, from the highest to the lowest, by the planter's assistant in his lowly bungalow and by the editor in the full light of the Presidency town, from those to the Chief Commissioner in charge of an important province to the Viceroy on his throne, the conviction in every [English] man that he belongs to a race whom God has destined to govern and subdue [Indians]". ... Lord Kitchener, a most distinguished Commander-in-Chief of Ir lia, declared, "It is this consciousness of the inherent superiorit of the European which has won for us India. However well-ec ucated and clever a native may be, and however brave he may ave proved himself, I believe that no rank we can bestow on hir would cause him to be considered an equal of the British officer".[52] In order to prove their superiority, some of the British conducted ethnographic surveys to show that Indian society was fragmented in castes and communities[53] and Indians were afflicted by religious rituals, superstitions, and social evils. They were considered to be primitive with nothing to boast about,[54] "new-caught sullen people, half-devil and half-child".[55]

The medieval rulers and nobles were indeed corrupt and exploitative, but their exploits remained within the country and their lavish life style at least promoted the luxury industry that added to the country's GDP. On the contrary, the British, while being exploitative and corrupt, transferred their exploits to Britain and thus drained the economy permanently. The early British rulers were rapacious. Clive colluded with Mir Jafar to win the battle of Palasey in 1757. In return, he was taken through the treasury and was asked to take whatever he wished. He took £1,60,000, distributed another half a million among the army and navy of the East India Company, and gifted of £ 24,000 to each member of the company's committee. Mir Jafar further presented him a life time *jagir* worth £ 27,000 annually. When questioned by the British Parliament about his ill-gotten money, Clive defended himself by simply following the accepted company practice stating that "I stand astonished at my own moderation given opportunities for greater gain".[56] The first Governor General of India, Warren Hastings, was notably impeached on accounts of corruption.[57] Despite Victorian façade of having moral imperatives and restraints, the British officers and their wives were seduced by Indian opulence. They took bribes, extorted, and pocketed whatever they could misusing their official positions. Lady Willingdon, for example, had an unashamed habit of making it a point to visit the queens and the princes and make them gift their favourite jewels to her.

Corruption seemed to be deeply rooted in the historical formation in the West during the period of industrial revolution where complex economy and complicated rule of law led to the growth of corruption.[58] Later, when the Western financiers became the colonial rulers, their exploitative tendencies were instilled into the colonial officers.[59] The East India Company simply institutionalized it.[60] It kept the salaries of its officials low, but allowed them to augment their income by personal business that they conducted leveraging through their company's position. Later on, the British government raised the salaries of the officials abnormally high paying the Viceroy and the governors, for example, £25,000 and £10,000 annually (respectively). Even the starting salary of an engineer was £420. From 1757 to 1919, the country had to pay for the administrative expenses in London, first of the East India Company, and then of the India Office. The cost of British staff was raised by long home leave in the UK, early retirement, and lavish amenities in the form of subsidized housing, utilities, rest houses, etc. The cost kept rising till in 1856, as a result of which the East India Company transferred about £3.5 million annually to the UK. This was in addition to the private remittances of officers, and the other expenses such as purchases of military items, railway equipment, and a variety of civilian goods, which were almost exclusively procured from the UK.

The British demolished Mughal aristocracy, but left about one fourth of the population in the 565 princely States[62] and thousands of *zamindars* and *nawabs*, who perpetuated the Mughal tradition of living lavish life and ostentatious display of wealth through exploitative behaviour. The rulers in the princely States, Rajas and Maharajas, remained conspicuous in their extravagances with "large palaces, harems, hordes of retainers, miniature armies, ceremonial elephants, tiger hunts, and stables full of Rolls Royces"[63](*see* Box 2.2). Though on a smaller scale, the *zamindars* and *nawabs* in the British territory, like the rulers in the princely States, retained the lifestyle of Mughal aristocrats indulging in luxuries and exploiting the gullible and the vulnerable. Thus, the medieval mindset continued on.

The expatriates did not remain uncontaminated either. There were around 31,000 British expatriates (of which around 22,000 were in the army) in 1805. Later on, the number increased to about 1,64,000 to 1,68,000 (the majority still remained of army officers).

Box 2.2: Maharajas and Their Luxuries

The maharajas and nawabs mimicked the lifestyles of European aristocrats with an exuberance that soon brought architects and sculptors and sellers of outlandishly expensive knick—knacks hustling out to India. Parisian jewellers convinced many a ruler to melt down his ancient treasures of gold, and re-cut their gems to be in vogue with the latest fashions. The Maharaja of Bharatpur got great blocks of ice dumped into his swimming pool with a pretty servant girl sitting on one of the floating ice-cakes and passing out delicacies to royalty lolling in the pool. About 20 per cent of over 20,000 Rolls Royace (RR) built before the World War I got home in he princely states of India (According to Murad Ali Baig's 'Rolls Royce and the Indian Princes'). The Maharaja of Mysore always purchased RR in sevens. In the 1930s, Maharaja Bhupinder Singh of Patiala had the largest RR fleet: A total of 44. According to the daughter of the Maharaja of Patiala, whenever their Rolles were sent for servicing, armed guards would go along. The speedometers, the oil gauge, the dashboard, were all decorated with precious stones and jewels. And still, he famously used his RR to collect municipal waste to get even with the snobbish staff at the brand's London showroom who mocked him for his 'looks. Fitted with guns and cannons, searchlights, and safes, the 1925 Rolls-Royce New Phantom belonging to Umed Singh II, Maharaja of Kota, was especially designed for royal hunts. One of the kings of Jodhpur family ordered a special `purdah' car for his queen. It came accessorized with woodwork and ebony inlay, twin sunroofs, fly screens, darkened `purdah' glass, and blinds. The Maharaja of Jamnagar sent over his queen's pink slipper so that his Phantom II could be painted in that exact colour. The RR of the Maharani Sethu Parvati of Travancore had a small stool on the floor to seat a dwarf masseur who would massage her feet but remain invisible to other people.[61]

They lived in the luxuries of their clubs and bungalows in specially protected and privileged suburbs known as cantonments and civil lines and "maintained the Mughal tradition of official pomp, sumptuary residences, and retinues of servants" sprinkled with European flavours of elitism. They ruled ... "much the same way as the Roman consuls had ruled in Africa 2,000 years earlier, and were very conscious of the Roman paradigm". With classical education, they were quite happy establishing law and order by spending more than half of the government money on military, justice, police and jails, and living in their own brand of self-righteous arrogance" with contempt for the native Indians[64]. The native people were denigrated to introject a national sense of inferiority complex that continued to afflict Indians even after their Independence (and in many cases even today).

Conceding their racial inferiority, most of the Indian civil servants as well as the male members of the new urban class of industrial capitalists, lawyers, doctors, teachers, and journalists emulated the British and relished the English tastes for wearing European clothes and shoes, drinking imported beer, wines and spirits, and using European weapons.[65] They sported their Indianized English and proclaimed to hold the Western worldview while still smarting under the medieval mindset.

In sum, the medieval worldview wrapped in lavish lifestyle got deeply enshrined in the colonized Indian mindset, though manifesting differently in different sets of people. The Rajas and Maharajas in the princely States still indulged in the Mughal forms of pomp and show infused it with Western luxuries and lifestyles. The British, though drawn largely from the English middle class, were enamoured by Indian luxuries, and too indulged in them profusely, although sporting their racial superiority in having a modern outlook flaunting in their behaviour. The Indian civil servants and the male members of the new urban middle class Indians aspired to be a carbon copy of the British emulating them as much they could, but were largely driven by the medieval mindset.

Exceptions were the Western orientalists, who presented an exotic image of Indians and believed that India had earlier developed a high civilization.[66] However, they too were part of the colonial narrative reflecting "… a certain will or intention to understand, in some cases to control, manipulate, even to incorporate…".[67] Indians into the Western frame by evoking unequal political (imperial), intellectual (science and English), social (social reforms), cultural (taste, texts, values), and moral (behaviour) superiority of the Europeans.

Reactions to Colonial Dominance

Reactions to the British dominance were varied: Social, economic, as well as, political. Some of the Indian elites had a strong conviction of the spiritual superiority of the ancient civilization (thanks to the orientalists). However, they all had the realization of the decay in Indian society, impoverished conditions of the people, and the depression of Hindu religion. In contrast, they knew that Europeans were by far superior in science and technology, rationality, and statecraft.[68] Hence, "adaptation" and "resistance" were required simultaneously to cope with the new situation. Indians learnt English and acquired Western lifestyle, tried to gain political power in order to compete with the British, initiated economic activities, or drew on ancient thought from Vedas and Vedanta to match "the rival philosophies of the West" in order to counteract the onslaught of Christian missionary.[69]

English opened access to European liberal thoughts. They learnt lessons from the Industrial Revolution of England (1760-1830) and got inspired by the French Revolution (1789-1794). English language along with the uniform system of education provided Indians a common language for political thinking and action, and even more important, "a like-mindedness" in "community of thought, feeling and ideas" which created a fountainhead for Indian nationality.[70]

The first expression of this nationality was the three socio-religious reforms movements in the 19th century. They were the *Brahmo Samaj* of Raja Ram Mohan Roy[71], the Ram Krishna Mission of Swami Vivekananda[72], and the *Arya Samaj* of Swami Dayanand Saraswati.[73] They all drew on the Vedas and Vedanta to raise spiritually framed national consciousness that was expected to cleanse Indians of their superstitions, rituals, and social evils in order to revitalize the Indian society and enlighten Indians.[74]

The second response was primarily economic starting from the late 19th and early 20th century in the emergence of Indian industrial entrepreneurs from the ruins caused by the East India Company. Entrepreneurial activities, however, were initially limited to money-lending, procuring raw materials for the British trade and industry and selling British products in the local market, or joining the British in trading and limited mining activities. From such a circumscribed milieu, the Marwaris rose to dominate the jute industry in Calcutta (now Kolkata), primarily, because of their strong business disposition and well-knit community. They coped with the hostile attitude of English traders and jute mill owners, worked as well as competed with them, and gradually outwit them.[75] They made fortune between the two World Wars, and controlled about 70 per cent of the domestic market and 80 per cent of the deposits in organized banking[76]. Of them, the Birlas, Jalans, Goenkas, and a few others were the major ones.

The Kammas and Naidus in South India took advantage of the new system of irrigation, hybrid and Cambodian breed of cotton, and availability of textile machinery from Britain[77] to start textile industry in the South, particularly in Coimbatore.[78] The Parsis, another well-knit community with strong business orientation, took over from them starting cotton mills first in Bombay (now Mumbai) and then in Nagpur. The Parsis were in fact located in Surat and used to make lots of money in trade of opium with China and of cotton with London. The British encouraged them to move to Bombay and helped them start cotton mills. The Parsis were fast to recognize the value of learning English. They cultivated amicable relations with the British, many of them worked as translators between the British and the natives, remained loyal to the British, financed the British military apparatus, and made lots of money during the World Wars.

Of them, Jamsetji N. Tata was the most famous. He built technologically more sophisticated mills and pioneered many enterprises. Jamsetji was pragmatic to name one of his mills "Empress Mill" facilitating Queen Victoria as the Empress of India, but at the same time nursed strong nationalist impulses. Tata Steel, for example, was launched as a "*swadeshi* (indigenous) enterprise", for which London was unwilling to provide capital. Instead, "Within three weeks the entire capital for the construction purposes of £ 1.63 million was secured, contributed by 8,000 native Indians, and the working capital of £ 40,000 was subscribed by one Indian—the Maharaja Scindia of Gwalior".[79] The investors were as varied as princely States, Hindu and Muslim merchants, a Jewish merchant, and even a British banker. It has indeed a national identity.[80]

In contrast to Calcutta (now Kolkata) and Bombay (now Mumbai), which were built by the British and where Marwaris and Pais (respectively) were the migrants, Ahmedabad was built by the indigenous Indians who were Hindus and were already established in banking industry from which they moved on to textile. The British only played a supportive role to facilitate them in their business. An Indian civil servant, Ranchodlal Chhotalal, a traditional Nagar Brahmin, was first to establish a cotton textile factory in Ahmedabad. Others followed his successful example. Major ones among them were Sarabhai, Lalbhai, and Bhagubhai.[81] They are still the big names in textile.

There were other patches of emerging entrepreneurship in the country. The Patidars of Gujarat and the Marathas of Maharashtra controlled major part of the land. They established caste-based trust and had the bonding that was conducive to forming cooperatives for their entrepreneurial activities. Cooperatives were not so dependent on the British Raj and hence were more explicit in their nationalism and participated more openly in nation's freedom movement.[82] Besides, there were individuals such as Laxmanrao Kirloskar, Walchand Hirachand and P.C. Roy who made their mark in their respective areas and others—smaller ones—who were struggling at smaller places to establish themselves and to create wealth for the country.

Nationalism, it is reasonable to presume, was not the main driving force for most of the entrepreneurs. It did seep into them while they tried to create a gainful space for their business in the hostile landscape that was under British control and supremacy. They had to live with subtle and not-so subtle discriminations and humiliations. Marwaris were frequently referred to as "short sighted industrialists", "mugs with money", "pirates" and "up to do some dirty work".[83] G.D. Birla was accused of indulging in 'unfair competition". He was a member of the Board of Directors of various mills under the Yule Managing Agency, but was not allowed to use the elevator in the Yule office, and had to use the stairs.[84] Similarly, Jamsetji Tata, according to a legend, was not allowed entry in a European-owned hotel which displayed a sign forbidding entry to dogs and Indians. He got built the luxury hotel, Taj Mahal, where Indians could entertain and be entertained without being insulted.[85] Sir Dorabji Tata, son of Jamsetji Tata, once recalled that the chief commissioner for the Indian Railways, Sir Frederick Upcott did not believe that Tata Steel could produce quality steel. He mocked, "Do you mean to say that Tatas propose to make steel rails to British specifications? Why, I will undertake to eat every pound of steel rail they succeed in making".[86] There were numerous similar instances of sarcastic remarks and decimations that the industrial entrepreneurs had to live with. They did not afford to offend the British. They concentrated on creating wealth, building educational and other institutions for the nation, and supporting Indians in their struggle for the political power. G.D. Birla and Jamanalal Bajaj were the major financial support to the Congress. And yet, they were wary of going all the way out to support the Indian National Congress because of its increasingly confronting stance to the British, commitment to socialism, and support to trade unions. The balance of power was steeply in the favour of the British patronized by the State.

The third and the most important development in the late 19th and early 20th century was the emergence of political consciousness that manifested in diverse forms. There are different schools of thought about the source and expressions of this consciousness. The Cambridge School[87] gave credit to the colonial State for creating an opportunity by introducing English language, laws, and institutions, and later on limited political participation to those who were indoctrinated into the colonial perspective and were expected to contribute to better governance.[88] A retired British civil servant, Allan Octavian Hume invited, with the approval of the British Raj, a few privileged Indians to form the Indian National Congress in 1885. Indeed the early Congress leaders subscribed to the colonial ideology and were willing to work with the British government in its professed colonial policy of "civilizing" the natives. As a result, they turned into the mimic men"[89]—eulogizing the Raj, proving to be loyal, collaborating, but also competing with them for power and privilege.[90] An early Congress President (1897), C. Sankaran Nair, for example, credited the Raj to pave "the way to progress" and to introduce English education, which brought religious, social and political regeneration of the country. Without the British rule, Nair feared, the country was likely to drift into "anarchy, war, and rapine".[91] A little later, B.N. Dar, another Congress President (1911), lauded the British for providing "peace, order, and perfect security of life and property... [He added] I thank God that I am a British subject, and feel no hesitation in saying that the government of India by England...is still the greatest gift of providence to my race.[92]

The nationalist approach, in contrast to the Cambridge view, credited the native elites with greater agency arising out of growing spirit of nationalism in the country[93]. Even if the leaders were mimic men, their mimicry soon turned into a menace to the Raj[94]. They were of course enlightened by the liberal European thought and impressed by the modern institutions, but were soon started getting driven by the appalling conditions of the people caused by the exploitative colonial regime and their obligation to take people out of it. They claimed political power. They had factions and frictions among themselves; but their main adversary was the British. They, instead of collaborating and competing with them, assumed an increasingly confronting and conflicting stance to the British. They initiated a movement that got increasingly assertive demanding first a limited self-rule (*Swaraj*) and later on full independence in order to have an absolute power to develop the country and catch up with the West.

The subaltern studies[95] did not agree that the British ever had hegemony over Indian people. Over 100 rebellions between 1783 and 1900 were recorded to show that Indian peasants, workers, and tribal resented and resisted the British as well as their own overlords who were exploiting them. The elites had the rhetoric of democratic rights and justice, but were part of traditional system of social dominance, which aroused and angered the subalterns. Because their rebellions were spontaneous, sporadic, short-lived, and often violent, the critiques considered them as *primitive and pre-political*[96] in consciousness, sort of impulsive reactions in "stick and stones" having no "specific political content".[97] The subaltern studies maintained that they were neither pre-political nor mobilized by the elites. They were autonomous having their own dynamics that contributed directly and indirectly to the nationalist movement. They were indeed quite scattered before the *World War*, but converged to generate a mass movement that reinforced the national movement led by the Congress Party.

In sum, reactions to the colonial rule led to religious renaissance, industrial activities, and most importantly, an upsurge of nationalism. The nationalist movements and their achievements were not entirely due to the efforts of 'enlightened' elite leaders but were also contributed by the large scale popular struggles and revolts of the people.[98] Obviously, Indian nationalism was the composite of the interplay of many forces[99], which were often divisive and distractive, as well as converging and reinforcing. The Muslim League, for example, on one side, and the Hindu Mahasabha, on the other, weakened the thrust of the Congress, but diverse other groups and communities converged under the leadership of Mahatma Gandhi against the British. There was indeed a binding inner spirit of nationalism. It was indeed resurrected by the European liberal thought in reaction to the exploitative regime that has impoverished the people. A common language, new institutions, and the professed policy of colonial modernization created a conducive milieu. The aspiration was to gain political power in order to develop the country, reform the society, and to restore the dignity of Indians. Power, it was realized, was the only means to achieve the goal. People's rebellions, though sporadic, helped create a milieu of nationalism that was also reinforced by other revolutionary groups. The national movement remained elitist till Mahatma Gandhi appeared on the scene (1915) and turned it into a mass and encompassing movement led by the Congress Party. The power of non-violent *satyagrah* (civil disobedience) prevailed over the British and the country got independence (1947). Even before Independence, the Congress leadership was engaged in discourses on the nature and course of the country's socio-economic transformation. After Independence, the country found itself enmeshed in the new world system, which was reshaped after the World War II and was defining development as a part of the geopolitics.

IDEOLOGIES NESTED IN GEOPOLITICS AND CULTURE

Geopolitical Context

Development is defined by power-play and the name of the game is politics. Politics in the post-Independence India has been nested in geo-politics. The decade following the end of the Second World War (1945-1955) was highly turbulent in the geopolitics. Europe was devastated by the war. Many countries in Asia and Africa, including India[100], got or were about to get independence. They were badly impoverished by the colonial exploitation. America (the USA) had emerged as *the* supreme power, but still had a threat to its supremacy and the capitalist worldview from the Soviet Union, which controlled the Eastern Europe, the rise of Communist China, an increasing influence of communism in Greece and Turkey, and later on the Korean War (1950–1953). The World War had ended only to start a cold war between the USA and the Soviet Union.[101] Americans were afraid that "Communism goes where hunger is", and hunger was indeed stalking in the vast spread of the poor Asian and African countries. They were likely to be the soft targets, Americans feared, of the communism. America felt having moral obligations as well as vested interests to rebuild its allies in the Western Europe and to feed the hungry in Asia.[102] In order to do so, it had to develop its industry and agriculture at home and contain communism abroad by first rebuilding Europe and then assisting the Asians in their development. Billions of dollars were pumped into the Western Europe under the Marshall Plan (1948–1953)[103] for first providing food and fuel, then for reconstructing industrial and agricultural production facilities, renewing transport, and expanding free trade among European countries, and finally for rearming them under the NATO (North Atlantic Treaty Organization), which was meant to assume a confronting posture to the Soviet Union. The Soviet Union had its plan, COMECON, for rebuilding the Eastern Europe and the Warsaw Pact to counteract the NATO, although it was constrained by its weaknesses due to war time losses. Its triumph card, however, was the ideology of communism, which was attractive to the colonially exploited people in Asia, who were naturally cynical of the intention of the imperial West.

Marshall Plan was framed as a joint cooperative venture (*Organization for European Economic Co-operation*), but in reality, was mostly used for exporting American goods, technology, and expertise to Europe. Thousands of American economists, statisticians, engineers, and industrialists were sent to revamp European economy and train Europeans in American best practices of running industries, doing business, and managing farms. In fact in most cases, a prominent American businessman was posted in each of the participating European capitals to coordinate and oversee the reconstruction process. The Marshall Plan was a great success in improving infrastructure, rebuilding industries, and increasing agricultural production, but was also criticized as "the American plan for the enslavement of Europe."[104] It was part of the politics to prevent communism from infecting the next door—Western Europe.

America was equally earnest to intervene in the newly independent Asian countries, lest the communism cash on their impoverished conditions and hostility to the colonial West. In his inaugural address on January 20, 1949, President Harry Truman declared a 4-point approach, which besides supporting the United Nations and its related agencies and helping in world economic recovery, declared that "The old imperialism—exploitation for foreign profit—has no place in our plans. What we envisage is a programme of development based on the concepts of democratic fair dealings"..."a bold new programme for making the benefits of our [American] scientific advances and industrial progress available for the improvement and growth of underdeveloped areas."[105] This was the first time discourse on development.

However, the grants and credits to Asian countries by the end of 1953 were less than half of what the USA pumped into Europe. India was badly short of food and started getting wheat from the USA under the PL 40 (Public Law 480) from 1951. By 1959, the US provided $1.7 billion in grants and relief including $931 million in food.[106] India was neither able nor required under the PL 480 to pay in dollars. So, the money, paid in rupees, was used to sponsor the Fulbright exchange visitors fellowships to Indians and Americans. Indians were to visit the USA and learn science, technology, and American lifestyles and American consultants and scholars visited India in order to establish technical and management institutes, train Indians, and to advise the Indian government on how the country can develop and manage its farms and factories. The exchanges both ways were meant not only to assist India, but also to facilitate American inroads into the Indian socio-economic landscape.

However, the USA remained ambivalent to India. It was positive to India since 1930s in supporting its struggle for independence. President Roosevelt in fact strongly advocated for its independence after the Second World War.[107] It considered India's democracy as the frontline defense against the spread of Communism. If the large-sized and democratic India succumbed to communism, the Americans feared, the rest of Asia will go down readily. However, America had a binary mindset to see the world in black and white. It suspected and discriminated all those who did not join its military alliances or toe its line in international politics. Pakistan did by joining SEATO (South East Asian Treaty Organization) and CENTO (Central Treaty Organization) in 1954. India did't and received helpful aids as well as hostile bites from the USA.

India's attitude to America was also ambivalent. The largest democracy in Asia (India) had a natural affinity with the most powerful democracy of the world (USA). Long exposure of Indians to the Anglo-American culture, frequent exchanges between the people even before the Fulbright programme, the English language, and many shared strands in the lifestyles had created a bond of psychological proximity that tended Indians and Americans to naturally gravitate to each other.[108] However, the country under the leadership of Nehru had a different than the American design of development. Nehru had the conviction that the country needed evolutionary, democratic, but independent ways of development by cultivating science, technology, and modern forms of organizations.[109] He was impressed by the Russian model of planned development of the economy[110]. He believed that "economic achievements were also to serve the grander schemes of attaining economic independence, preserving political freedom, gaining military security, and enhancing national power".[111] He has a natural aversion for capitalism, which, according to him, was inappropriate for alleviating poverty in India[112]. Above all, he was a staunch nationalist driven by "...his deep-rooted and earnest concern for the removal of poverty, his passion for economic progress, his commitment to egalitarian goals and social justice, ...".[113] He was a world leader who was determined not only to keep India but all newly independent Asian and African countries clear out of the cold war and let them develop in their own ways by balancing their relations with both the USA and the Soviet Union. In order to do so, he helped organized the Bandung Conference (1955) that led to form the Non-Aligned Movement (NAM) in 1961 involving Nasser (Egypt), Nkrumah (Ghana), Sukarno (Indonesia), and Tito (Yugoslavia)[114]. Nehru was also instrumental in formulating the *Panchsheel* (five principles) for the world order: Respect for each other's territorial integrity and sovereignty, non-aggression, non-interference in each other's domestic affairs, equality and mutual benefit, and peaceful co-existence of the nations.

In this spirit of independence, Nehru did not listen to American advice for resolving the Kashmir issue (1948), defied American pressure and recognized the communist regime in China (1949) for which he had great admiration[115] till the Chinese aggression in 1962, but supported the American resolution in the United Nations condemning North Korea's aggression (1950). He did not hesitate to ask and receive wheat and technical assistances from the USA for developing agriculture, mining, minerals, but leaned on the Soviet Union and its allies for establishing basic industries in steel, coal, machines, and tools manufacturing, and others. The Soviet Union was not in a position to give India as much financial assistance as the USA, but it did align with the Indian vision of development by offering financial and technical assistance for establishing basic industries at much lower interest rate (2.50%) while similar assistance from the West was available at higher (about 6%) rates of interest. Most valuable were the consistent Soviet political support to India on the Kashmir issue and supply of arms (including the MIG fighter planes despite Chinese protest).

Thus, the Soviet Union proved to be an enduring friend and a role model for India's Five Years Plans for development while the USA remained a generous, though unreliable, benefactor and a custodian of democratic values that India cherished. India's development efforts in 1950s and 1960s reflected the influences of both under the leadership of Nehru.

MODELS OF DEVELOPMENT

Nehru's Socialist Plan for Development

India's vision for development started taking shape as early as the 1930s during the freedom movement—much before President Truman's declaration (1949). There were three sets of influences: Russian communism, Fabian socialism, and Gandhian philosophy. The Indian National Congress Party was the umbrella organization for the freedom movement, Mahatma Gandhi was the guide, and Jawaharlal Nehru was the most powerful influence for steering the movement as well as for creating a vision for the country's future. Nehru had deep respect for Mahatma Gandhi, but did not share Gandhi's vision of development.

As back as 1928, Nehru visited Russia and was immensely impressed by it. On return, he wrote, "... if the future is full of hope [for india], it is largely because of Soviet Russia and what it has done....".[116] He wrote again, "Both [India and Russia] are vast agricultural countries with only the beginnings of industrialization and both have to face poverty and illiteracy. If Russia finds a satisfactory solution for these, our work in India is made easier[117]. He did not, however, subscribed to the idea of class conflicts and violent revolution. Mahatma Gandhi had already got the Congress committed to non-violent civil disobedience (*satyagrah*). Mahatma Gandhi too was agreeable to communism: "I believe in non-violent... communism.... if communism came without any violence, it would be welcome. For then, no property would be held by anybody except on behalf of the people and for the people".[118] Russian impact, however, was quite deep in (a) in adopting Five Years Plans of development, (b) prioritizing heavy industries for creating industrial base for the development of other industries and sectors, and (c) resorting to detailed industrial licensing and regulation through the Industrial Regulation Act (1961) for differentially stimulating industries and preventing concentration of wealth and power within a small number of business houses.[119]

"Turning on its head, the traditional Western economic notions that heavy industry should come in the later, rather than the earlier"[120], Nehru set country's priority on heavy industries: "It is clear that in India today the development of cottage industries on a vast scale is essential for the well-being of the masses. It is equally clear the rapid development of large scale machine industry is an urgent need of the country. Without industrialization no country can have political or economic freedom and even cottage industries cannot develop to any large extent if economic freedom is absent"[121]. The National Planning Committee (1938), of which Nehru was the Chairman, asserted that "There can be no planning if such planning does not include big industries".[122]

While adopting planning and prioritizing heavy industries, Nehru drew his ideas of development from the Fabian socialism. Fabian socialism favoured parliamentary democracy, which, through socialist legislations, was believed to help rectify the injustices of capitalism and improve the conditions of poor, deprived, and the exploited people. Its methods were evolutionary, peaceful, and persuasive in realizing incremental changes and development.[123] Nehru wrote in the early 1930s, "Capitalism, having had its day, had reached the stage when it was time for it to retire in favour of socialism".[124] He further noted, "Socialism is more than an economic doctrine, it is a philosophy of life...I see no way of ending poverty, the vast unemployment, the degradation and the subjection of the Indian people except through socialism. That involves vast and revolutionary changes in our political and social structure, the ending of vested interests in land and industry as well as the feudal and autocratic Indian States system".[125] Socialism signified that "... the means of production should be socially owned and controlled for the benefit of society as a whole".[126] However, it did not require hasty nationalization of the entire private sector industries. There could be enough room for the private sector to function and prosper so long as they remained within the broad framework of socialism.[127] The economy, however, was to be kept under government control.[128] Twenty major industries were to be brought under the control of the central government, while other basic industries of national importance were to be nationalized only if adequate private capital for their development was not forthcoming.

Further, socialism did not necessarily mean workers' control over or extensive participation in management like in the Yugoslav system. Rather, the scientific knowledge of professionals and the wisdom and acumen of eminent individuals were considered to be essential, because they were the ones who could see the complexity of problems that the people faced, foresee their attainable future prospects, and help plan how to get there. Thus, the intellectual core of socialism suited the elite orientation of Nehru. Economy was to be built first at the top by the individuals at the top of the politics, administration, and business.

Nehru was exceedingly open to suggestions and advices, particularly from those who were close to him or if the suggestions and advices were based on surveys and empirical reports. He tended to remain as inclusive as possible. Back in 1938, his *National Planning Committee* included "well-known industrialists, financiers, economists, professors and scientists as well as representatives of the trade unions.... hard-headed big business was there, as well as people who are called idealists and doctrinaire, socialists as well as near-communists".[129] Similarly, the *Second Report on Reconstruction Planning* (1945) aimed at balancing regional development by allocating industries in different provinces and in rural backward areas, building up infrastructure for irrigation and improving agricultural productivity, and promoting popular participation through cooperative societies and *panchayats*.[130] Twenty nine sub-committees were formed to collect information and prepare the First Five Year Plan covering agricultural, industrial, social, economic, financial, and other sectors of development.[131] This consensus building often led to many compromises. Despite having strong commitment to the socialist form development, Nehru did not even mention 'socialism' in his speech on the First *Five Year Plan* in the Parliament (1951). The Plan was presented as "a realistic survey of what it is possible to do with the resources likely to be available within the limitations of our Constitution and without a marked break from our existing social and economic framework".[132] It was only in the *Second Five Years Plan* (1956-1961), which was drafted by his close adviser, P.C. Mahalanobis, that the "socialist pattern of society" was unequivocally accepted as "the national objective". Since then, the subsequent governments increasingly moved towards the socialist measures till the socialist regime lost its spirit, the economy ran into serious problems, and the geo-political events and forces forced India to embrace the market economy by following the Western design of development.

Western Design for Development

Modernization of the traditional societies had been a long concern since the colonial days. The independence of Asian and African countries, end of the World War II, and the cold war between the USA and the Soviet Union turned it into a discourse on development by the 1950s. There was an underlying assumption that the world was divided into under-developed and developed countries. Developed countries had an economy that was *capitalist* in being market-driven and efficient, a political system that was *democratic* and egalitarian, and a society that was *individualist* in its social relationships. The first world—Europe and the USA—was developed while the third—Asian and African countries—was under developed (Eastern Europe dominated by the Soviet Union was the second world). The under developed countries had to be helped to develop following the Western design. "The White Man's Burden" in the colonial era had a new version in the "moral obligation" of the USA to help develop the under developed, as President Truman declared, in "democratic ways" by employing American "scientific advancement and industrial progress". The road map for this progression was derived from the Western experience of rising through industrial revolutions to the mass consumption society. Development had turned into a global faith.[133] It is the partnership of the developed and under developed countries, in which under developed, with the assistance of the developed, rise above their poverty and social evils and catch up with the developed in economic affluence and lifestyles.

Following the Western model, development was assumed to be driven primarily by economic growth, which impacts social structure and functions that in turn shape individuals' thoughts and behaviour. The composite of the three—economic, social, and psychological—changes occur in five sequential stages that the under-developed countries must pass through in order to be like the West. They were identified as traditional, pre-condition for a take-off, take-off, maturity, and mass consumption.[134] The most under-developed countries are those that have a **traditional society,** which is characterized by subsistence agriculture, primitive technology, lack of economic and social mobility, static social relations, and dislike for change. However, changes can be induced by increasing demands for agricultural and industrial products, not only for self-consumption, but also for selling to others. As a result, a **precondition for the take-off of the economy** is created where investments are made for more production, employment of better technology, trade, and commerce. Such new activities impact social structure, disturb social equilibrium, and begins social mobility. People start thinking and behaving differently, particularly for improving their conditions of living. The **Take-off stage** witnesses the acceleration of these processes through a shift from agriculture to industrialization with the accompanying growth in urbanization. The scenario is best depicted by the Great Britain's classic industrial revolution. Such a revolution **drives the economy to maturity** by diversification of the industrial base, expansion of multiple industries, shifts from manufacturing of capital goods towards consumer durables for domestic consumption, rapid development of transportation, infrastructure, large-scale investment in social sector consisting of schools, universities, hospitals, and so on. Finally, the society achieves the state of **mass consumption** with the "promises of abundance" of increasing variety of goods and services to meet ever expanding needs and choices, rapidly innovating technology, large disposable income, and open society with highly mobile people having flexible social norms, idiosyncratic values, and individualistic lifestyles.

The five stages were compressed into three where an undeveloped—*traditional*-society was reported to pass through a *transitional phase* in order to become a developed—*modern*-society. The factors that were responsible for this progression were the degrees of urbanization, literacy, media participation, and political participation.[135] Concomitant to this social and political progression were the changes that were identified in people's which are primarily material and economic. Their individual achievements accumulate into the national wealth. Training programmes were conducted in underdeveloped countries, including India,[140] to inculcate high *nAchv* in people in order to help facilitate the economic growth of the countries.[141]

Underlying these psychological characteristics was the assumption of Adam Smith's[142] self-interested rational individuals who strive to maximize their gains by competing in the market.[143] The primary driver is the expanding needs. People have to keep creating new needs that become new demands for more and more as well as better and better variety of goods and services. The producers and suppliers of goods and services too have to invent new needs in order to expand their market. An essential part of this dynamics is the sanctity of the private property that individuals acquire and to which they have unlimited and legitimate access. It is this process of acquiring and protecting private property that the seeds of capitalist mode of development lay. In order to compete for private property, individuals have to fight and, if possible, elbow out the rivals, exploit the nature, and innovate technology. They have to have power and hence to be politically alert and active. Naturally, capitalism and democracy co-evolved driven by individualist values in symbiotically facilitating each other.

In sum, it was this package of capitalism, democracy, and individualism backed by the scientific advancement, material affluence, and political power that the West presented to India with an underhand pressure to join them against communism. India embraced it partly because of the failure of socialist model of development and partly as a pressure from the geo-political events and forces. But it did not join the West against communism.

Mahatma Gandhi for *Sarvodaya*[144]

There was another—Gandhian—stream of thought that remained ignored during this whole period of socialist to free market regimes of development. Mahatma Gandhi's ideas of development were basically different from those of Nehru's and were diametrically opposed to the Western model of development. Gandhi denounced the Western view that source of development lies in the self-interests of rational individuals who keep accumulating material the other hand, were found to have the people who were functionally specific, universalistic, and achievement-oriented.[136] In other words, traditional people allocate status, rewards, and recognition on the birth-based indicators such as race, caste, age, gender, family wealth, and so on. They favour people who are close such as family and friends, and distance and discriminate those whom they believe to be outsiders and unfamiliar. They do not distinguish work, family, and social roles; the boss, for example, is like the father. The modern ones, on the other hand, allocate status, reward, and recognize others on the basis of their individual achievements, do not differentiate between personally related and unrelated others, and make decisions and act on them following largely objective norms and standards. A survey in six countries, including India, revealed that the persons who were educated, urbanized, and had industrial work experiences were holding modern attitudes, values, norms, and practices. They aspired to advance economically, valued education, had a sense of personal efficacy, assumed personal responsibility, planned their life including family size, did not submit to parental authority, assumed autonomy as well as granted autonomy to lesser people around them, kept themselves informed of world affairs, and participated actively as citizen.[137]

Economic growth indeed supposed to affect social structure, functions, and people's behaviour, but reverse was also argued to be true. For example, the factors that were reported to have the potential to facilitate economic growth were the "planning, concern for time and for future, willingness to defer gratification, accuracy of keeping appointments, assembling many elements of production into coordinated systems, interpersonal trust, willingness to cooperate with others on the basis of role rather than familiarity, small power distance, moderate risk taking, self-control, and hard work."[138] Another line of research documented massive evidence from a large number of countries to show that high need for achievement (*nAchv*) of people leads to greater economic growth of their country.[139] High *nAchv* people strive for excellence, explore new opportunities, create new resources, take reasonable risks, and have perseverance to achieve their goals, possessions for satisfying their endless needs. Gandhi called it "animal appetite" that can never be satiated, nor does it make people happy. Unlimited lust for material possessions instigates people to usurp other's possessions and in the process causes conflicts and violence. Such a view is devoid both of humanity and morality.

Private property is sacrosanct in the Western model, but displacing other's from their property is justified as part of the struggle for existence and the survival of the fittest. On the contrary, Gandhi posited that cultivating the value of *aprigraha* (non-possession) while searching for *satya* (truth) through *ahimsa* (non-violence) is essential for human wellbeing.[145] Drawing probably from his favourite guide, *Bhagawad Gita,* he believed that people should contain their needs. He wrote:

> "... the mind is a restless bird; the more it gets the more it wants, and still remains unsatisfied. The more we indulge our passions the more unbridled they become. Our ancestors, therefore, set a limit to our indulgences. They saw that happiness was largely a mental condition. A man is not necessarily happy because he is rich, or unhappy because he is poor".[146]

According to Gandhi, one should own just enough for meeting the basic needs. If he earns more, the earnings belong to the people at large, and he is, not an owner, but just a "trustee" of it to see that such a wealth is used for common good, particularly for the most poor and deprived people.[147] Gandhi wrote: "I want the concentration of wealth, not in the hands of a few, but in the hands of all".[148] Some of the industrialists such as G.D. Birla, Ambalal Sarabhai, Jamnalal Bajaj and J.R.D. Tata, accepted at least partly Gandhi's ideas of trusteeship in managing labour relations with good results.[149] In the Gandhian scheme, individuals must not compete with each other for their material advancement. Rather, they should cooperate and cultivate socio-economic harmony for justice and spiritual development.

Similarly, the Western prescription of enlarging market (from local through national to international) for enabling competing individuals to actualize their full potentials for profit making was unacceptable to Gandhi. It is *the plain living people in self-sufficient villages* are what Gandhi envisaged as the building blocks of economic wellbeing. In such a scenario, small scale and locally-oriented production, using local resources and meeting local needs, thereby creating employment opportunities for many was considered to promote the well-being of all.[150] His *ashrams* were the model of community where the inhabitants produced their own food, clothing and means of living, while promoting a lifestyle of self-sufficiency, mutual help, personal and spiritual development as well as working for wider social harmony.[151] The ideal society, according to Gandhi, was the one where the highest attention was paid to the prime needs of the weakest sections of the population, where the untouchables, whom he called *harijans* (god's children), were fully accepted as equals, and Hindus and Muslims live in harmony.

Gandhi rejected the plea that India should modernize by following the British pattern. He wrote in *Young India* (1921): "I feel that if India will discard 'modern civilization', she can only gain by doing so".[152] Further, "If India copies England, it is my firm conviction that she will be ruined".[153] It will not be called Hindustan; but Englistan[154]. "This [English] civilization takes note neither of morality nor of religion... It is eating into the vitals of the English nation. It must be shunned"[155]. Civilization, according to Gandhi, was "that mode of conduct which points out to man the path of duty. Performance of duty and observance of morality are convertible terms. To observe morality is to attain mastery over our mind and our passions. So doing, we know ourselves".[156] He had harsh words for the British Parliament:

> "That which you consider to be the Mother of Parliaments is like a sterile woman and a prostitute. Both these are harsh terms, but exactly fit the case. That Parliament has not yet, of its own accord, done a single good thing. Hence I have compared it to a sterile woman. The natural condition of that Parliament is such that, without outside pressure, it can do nothing. It is like a prostitute because it is under the control of ministers who change from time to time. ... If the money and the time wasted by Parliament were entrusted to a few good men, the English nation would be occupying today a much higher platform. Parliament is simply a costly toy of the nation".[157]

Not that he wanted India to remain immune to outside influences. True to the core values of openness and receptivity of the Indian culture, he accepted C.F. Andrews' Christian influences and sourced his ideas of *satyagrah*, ethics and religion in politics, and so on from some of the Western thinkers (their work in Italic) such as the following:

- John Ruskin (1880). *Unto the last.*
- William Salter (1889). *Ethical religion.*
- Henry David Thoreau (1849). *On the duty of civil disobedience.*
- Leo Tolstoy (1894). *The kingdom of god within you.*
- Leo Tolstoy (1908). *A letter to Hindu.*[158]

However, he indigenized them by reformulating them in Indian cultural images, symbols, and ethos, and concretized them in actionable mass movement in order to mobilize Indians in an unprecedented scale.

Box 2.3: Gandhi's Endogenous India

I do not want my house to be walled in on all sides and my windows to be stuffed. I want the cultures of all the lands to be blown about my house as freely as possible. But I refuse to be blown off my feet by any. I refuse to live in other people's houses as an interloper, a beggar or a slave.[159]

Therefore, he did subscribe to democracy; but not the Western democracy which, according to him, was a "diluted fascism' where a small group of people, sitting at the top in the government, make most of the decisions that affect the rest of the people. Democracy for Gandhi was not only a political but also a moral system which was meant to decentralize power, assist the development of every social class especially the lowest, create principles and practices to settle disputes in non-violent manner, recognize individuality of all human beings, promote freedom of their thought, and helped communities to maintain self-discipline and live and function in harmony.[160]

Similarly, *Swaraj* (self-rule) was not only political independence of the country to run its affairs without any dominance and interference from other nations. It also means a self-rule of the various groups and communities in having freedom from poverty and social evils that afflict them and to live in harmony with other groups and communities without being dominated and exploited by them. *Swaraj* (self-rule) is incomplete without being practiced at individual level.[161] The true self-rule means that every person rules his or herself and that the State does not imposes laws upon the people without their consent. Contrary to the pyramid of power in the existing political system, Gandhi envisaged that that society should be the exact opposite, where nothing is done without the consent of people, down to the individual.[162] However, individuals and groups were to be governed by self-control, mutual responsibilities, and sense of duties towards each other rather than their rights.[163]

Gandhi's emphasis on *simplicity, economic morality and religiosity, self-sufficiency of villages, decentralization of power, and self-ruling individuals*[164] was radically different from the grandiose, elitist, secular, scientific, and socialist style of Nehru who planned development on the foundation of heavy industries. When Nehru met Gandhi for the first time in 1916, he was unable to relate to Gandhi's style and rhetoric of politics characterized by "a blend of grass-root activism, asceticism, religion and philosophy".[165] Though they developed unalienable attachment to each other, but never agreed on the ways to development. Gandhi considered centralized planning as a "waste of effort and labour".[166] He was against large machineries: "Machinery is like a snake-hole which may contain from one to a hundred snakes. Where there is machinery there are large cities; and where there are large cities, there are tram-cars and railways; and there only does one see electric light".[167] He was not really against all machineries, but the attitudes underlying mechanization: "What I object to is the craze for machinery, not machinery as such.... I want to save time and labour, not for a fraction of mankind but for all. ... "The saving of the labour of the individual should be the object, and not human greed the motive." ..."I am socialist enough to say that such factories should be nationalized, State-controlled...."[168]. He was against large dams and irrigation projects, advocating that small projects were more efficacious, organic manure was better and less dangerous than man-made chemicals, and forests should be managed with the goal of water conservation rather than revenue maximization.[169] He was thus concerned of how the Nature was being degraded in the process of development.

His aim was the development of each and every human being.

"In modern terms, it is beneath human dignity to lose one's individuality and become a mere cog in the machine. I want every individual to become a full-blooded, full-developed member of the society".[170] Development indeed has to be *sarvodaya*—the rise of all.

The means to realize *sarvodaya* was *satyagrah*[171]: "the Force which is born of Truth and Love or non-violence".[172] It is person-centric and reflects the ancient Indian dictum that if you want to change others, first change yourself; for the changes in you will radiate and strike right cords in others and they would naturally respond by changing themselves. According to the ancient Indian thought, changes—real changes—in self require efforts. *Tap*—to burn or suffer—is the right word to reflect the process of initiating such self-changes. *Tapasya,* the process of engaging in *tap,* involves self-suffering that enables the person to rise on the scale of moral and spiritual merit. So self-suffering is the source of gaining courage to stand for truth and call upon others, without indulging in violence, to rally around.[173] Others are in fact believed to be attracted to the self-realized person and seek inspirations for similar changes. The underlying assumption is that individuals share the same entity, *atman,* or in the largely collectivist Indian culture, the same identity[174], and hence self-suffering resonates in other's self and create a nucleus for reciprocal changes.

However, others may not be in communication with their self and may not be aware of their resonating self. So, the *satyagrahi* (the person who is engaged in *satyagrah*) should resort to communication, reasoning, and persuasion to let them realize the good sense and resist from harmful or dysfunction habits and practices. If others still do not see the truth or the right course of conduct, the *satyagrahi* can resort to non-cooperation, disengagement, and dissociation (that is, civil disobedience). The crucial consideration is not to dislike, hate, or hurt the person or persons, but to target the conduct that needs to be changed, the conflicts that have to be resolved, and the harmony that has to be restored.[175]

Gandhi perfected *satyagrah* during the freedom movement. He went on 17 fasts often for days (one of 21 days) for arousing the conscience of Hindus and Muslims to desist from communal riots and to stop discriminating untouchables. It is worth noting that none of his fasts was meant for arousing good sense in the

British government. He rather negotiated with the British and when a talk failed, resorted to civil disobedience by breaking English laws and boycotting British clothes.

There is ample proof that Indians often resort to this three-stage method of conflict resolution within the family. It is not unusual for a family member to refuse taking meals to either express a grievance or to seek a redress, to argue and argue till a particular view prevails on other family members, or to carry a sullen face and refuse talking and cooperating in the daily household chores till the person's cause is taken care of. The whole idea is that the members are and have to remain enfolded emotionally within the family.

In sum, the Gandhian ideas of development had roots in the indigenous Indian thought, though they also drew on Western thinkers. They were meant for bonding the Indians of diverse background, religious, castes and communities. Some were indeed highly idealistic, but others had high potential to facilitate inner growth and inculcate morality in politics. No serious efforts were made either in the Nehruvian era or thereafter to delineate those that could have given a fundamentally different direction to our development efforts.

COMPARATIVE VIEW OF THE MODELS

Gandhian Thought: A Mixed Bag

Gandhi admitted losing his influence on Nehru and the Congress at the time of the partition of the country and its Independence (on August 15, 1947)[176] allowing Nehru a free hand to build the nation according to his socialist convictions. Nehru was a charismatic leader having an overwhelming power on the Congress Party and the State apparatus. Despite his immense respect for Gandhi, he was at best willing to accommodate some of the Gandhi's ideas (e.g., cottage and small scale industries) subordinated to his grand plans for development. Gandhi's disciples did not have Gandhi's stature and influence to create a mass movement pressurizing the government to take Gandhian model seriously. Gandhians did try on their own with rather limited success, others kept paying lip service to Gandhian thought, and Gandhism got almost lost from the Indian development discourse. Hindus and Muslims reverted to occasional riots; scheduled castes and tribes continued to be discriminated and deprived despite their quota in government jobs and educational institutions; and the country kept moving first towards socialist pattern, and later on changing the track to head for a market-driven economy.

Not that it was only the power politics that marginalized Gandhism in the national scenario. There were some unresolved issues in Gandhian thought too. For example, the assumption of person-centric self-suffering as the driver for positive change in others, though part of the ancient Indian wisdom, was not quite a convincing means to change others. India does have a long and continued tradition of having a few saints, yogis, and gurus who by their moral, spiritual, or charismatic power inspire many to get self-transformed and achieve extraordinary altruistic feats. Even common people are occasionally enthused to display outstanding courage and sacrifice for common causes. Gandhi galvanized the whole people during the freedom movement. However, once that inspiring figure leaves the scene (as Gandhi did), some of the followers still carry on, but the spirit seems to evaporate, and the common people revert to the same old habits and existential mode of coping with the daily exigencies. As if, the surrounding milieu smothers the inspiration and the conscience by its sedative effects.

Positive changes, in order to be sustained and accelerated, have to be supported by systemic forces and reinforcing experiences. A few people are sure to be idealistically fired, but the rest have to, at least initially, goaded by systems and live experiences to take to and stay on the right track. Probably, people have to be approached from both sides: to be inspired by a moral, spiritual, and charismatic leader and supported and sustained by conducive systems and experiences. An emergence of such a leader is the good fortune of a society, but putting in place an appropriate system and procedures to reward the initiative is a function of wisdom and planning. In other words, the State has to play a critical role in planning and piloting development for the country.

Unless such a systemic milieu is created, people are likely to misconstrue their inner impulses and attribute motives to others for all their real or imagined sufferings. Instead of being firmly anchored in the Gandhian *satyagrah,* they are likely to resort to protest, and worse, burst into aggressive violence taking it for a fight for their just cause. The frequency, intensity, and variety of individual, group, and sectoral conflicts and violence in the country only confirm the view that Gandhi is being remembered on his birthdays (October 2) and death anniversaries (January 30) and remains forgotten for the rest of the year. Only a limited number of scholars (referred above) are still struggling to retrieve some of Gandhian ideas to see their relevance in the present scenario.

Another constraint in the Gandhian thought was the centrality of self-sufficient villages as the building blocks of the nation. It was against the irreversible trend of growing globalization that was initiated in the colonial period and was accelerating particularly after the World War II. Development does not remain a local or entirely a national issue now. Countries are caught in geopolitics; international trade is growing; and companies, capital, technology, and people are moving seamlessly across the national boundaries. Ideas fly even faster. In fact, there is powerful rhetoric of "partnership for development", which is being sponsored by a number of international agencies. In such a globalizing world, the idea of self-sufficient villages, which are closed to the outside world, do not seem to be realistic. Instead, what seems to be realistic and desirable is to search for the essence in the Gandhian emphasis on self-sufficiency of villages in terms of greater degree of decentralization of economy and political decision-making for development. Self-sufficient closed villages locked in primitive technology are ruled out. But locally vibrant economy that is empowered by Internet, mobile, and other innovative technology and having access to international market—the glocalized (local and yet global)—that can get us closest to Gandhian ideas that can be tried out.

A highly promising was the Gandhi's advocacy of simplicity and primacy of the weaker sections in development decisions. The value of simplicity stands in stark contrast to the consumerism of the market economy and the medieval values of lavish life style. Consumerism invariably cost the Nature unnecessarily. Simplicity draws on the Indian cultural ethos of containing rather than compulsively chasing galloping needs and desires. Simplicity allows minimum damage to the environment and more resources available for distribution to more people. It is a paradigm shift in our approach to development that Gandhi advocated.

The most important was Gandhi's emphasis on social harmony and inclusive development where the weakest and the most discriminated are given the highest priority in resource allocation and attention. Emphatic understanding of other's suffering (*peer parayi jane re*) is the best impulse to personal and social bonding. This is the only way to attain a wholesome wellbeing of all Indians.

Rise and Fall of the Socialist Regime

Nehru's socialist form of development had its run. It got more focused in the Second Five Year Plan (1961-1965), gained momentum in the subsequent four Plans, but got mired in its own structural deficiency, beauropathy,[177] corruption, and political expediency compelling the country to turn around and head towards a capitalist mode of development, which was assuming almost universal endorsement.

Despite laudable objectives, the socialist form of development neither served "the capitalist objective of efficiency nor and the socialist objective of equity".[178] During this period (1950-1980) the GDP grew at an average rate of around 3.5 per cent per annum[179], while per capita income of Indians increased on an average of 1.30 per cent only inviting a sarcastic remark of being the "Hindu rate of growth".[180] The public undertakings indeed laid a solid foundation for industrial growth, where earlier there was almost none. However, the mixed economy and the policy of extensive licensing for production and import of scarce goods allowed a large group of unscrupulous businessmen and industrialists who manipulated and misused licensing to make huge profit. "The licensing mechanism, at best, produces redistribution essentially outside of the poverty sector from the rich to the not-so-rich-and generates considerable economic inefficiency which, in reducing the productivity of investment, compromises the strategy of rapid growth to provide increasing jobs to the poor".[181] Further, it did not only fail to prevent the concentration of wealth in a few business houses, but also led to increased corruption because procuring licensing required the collusion with government officers with whom the booty had to be shared.

At the end of the Second Five Year Plan, it was officially observed that "while it is to be recognized that they [public sector undertakings] have made considerable contribution to the economy of the country, it is equally evident that their performance has not been up to the mark. The size of cumulative and annual losses that a number of them have incurred causes concern. The quality and price of goods manufactured have not in many cases given full satisfaction".[182] The losses were invariably written off by the government and the poor quality of goods and services were no problem, because they were invariably short of supply.

There were not enough managers available in the country. So, the government spared a large number of its functionaries as well as hired retired officers to manage public undertakings. According to a count, over 80 per cent of top executives of the public undertakings in the mid-sixties were either government officers on deputation or the retired ones.[183] They had acquired a bureaucratic mindset that was dysfunctional to a pathological extent. A foreign consultant of the Government of India had vividly described this bureaupathic (pathological bureaucracy) system of government administration:

> Granted prior agreement in principle on the kind and dimension of programme to be undertaken and the amount of money to be made available for the purpose, specific decisions incident to the effectiveness of purpose in India, are reviewed by too many organs of the Government in too detailed, too repetitive, and too negative terms. Perhaps nowhere else have so many systemic barriers been erected to prevent the accomplishment of that, which it has been determined, should be done.[184]

One of the reasons for such a bureaupathic orientation was the government norms regarding accountability. It did not matter if one made 10 good decisions, but was held responsible for one bad decision that checkered his confidential report and hence career. There was no scope for experimentation or any entrepreneurial venture for the good of the undertaking. The wise thing was to follow the due procedure and not to step on anybody's toes. The trade union leaders often had close connections with the powerful politicians who were more than willing to pull strings for them. On numerous occasions the managers lamented that they work at a place where "action, not inaction has to be defended".[185]

Furthermore, public undertakings were proclaimed as a model employer, as a result of which the employees construed them as predominantly welfare oriented organizations where profit and viability were subjugated to employees' welfare. As a result employees' gains were independent of the organization's profit, and dependent on how much pressure they could mount on the management. So, employees formed trade unions that attracted membership by competing in making aggressive demands. The *mantra* in the political parlour was not to aggravate labour relations, but to "buy peace" to run the organization; instead of confronting the trade unions.[186]

Consequently, "socialist pattern" turned to be "socialist patter". Socialist measures failed to yield the desired results, but socialism still remained an effective political instrument to attract the common people and those who systemized with them. Thus, what Nehru launched as a pragmatic programme out of economic necessity, turned into political expediency[187] employing measures that were only manifestly in the socialist form. "Such a [socialist] tradition surely ran the risk, both of degenerating, over time, into socialist patter, without a concrete programme being executed by an ideologically-inspired cadre of socialists, and, indeed, of being captured and turned into an instrument of bourgeois classes pursuing their own interests behind a socialist screen".[188]

By 1980s, the economy got into a mess and India's foreign exchange reserve fell to a low of $240 million, just enough to support only two weeks of imports. The International Monetary Fund (IMF) and the World Bank offered help on the condition of economic reforms towards opening of the Indian economy. The government ran out of options and finally, had to give up the socialist pattern for a market-oriented capitalist mode of development in the early 1990s.

Cracks and Caveats in the Western Model

A landmark in the shift from the socialist mode to the Western design of development was the *New Economic Policy* in 1991. Since then, liberalization of economy is getting faster and the pressure for more market reforms is still mounting. The GDP has been growing at a faster rate, per capita income has been increasing, and the country has made remarkable achievements in almost all domains. However, the country is accumulating wealth without the wellbeing of the most people.[189]

A number of scholars even in the West have challenged the viability of the capitalist mode of development calling for demolishing it: "the idea of development stands like a ruin in the intellectual landscape" and "it is time to dismantle this mental structure".[190] This development model, they argued, is the legacy of the Western imperialistic mindset, cannot be de-linked from insatiable profit making, and is intrinsically destructive to the environment, social relations, non-Western cultures causing far more misery than it alleviates.[191] It is "a system that is neither viable, nor sustainable, nor fit to live in. The (substantial) benefits that it still confers on a tiny minority are not enough to justify its continuing acceptance, in view of the lethal dangers that it entails".[192] There is a book, *"The White Man's Burden: Why the West's Efforts to Aid the Rest Have Done So Much Ill and So Little Good"*[193] documenting the failure of the model. Furthermore, the Western development model alleged to be congenitally afflicted by a bad faith (although there were some exceptions), because it meant to contain communism by enticing material and technical assistance.[194] The top down technocratic solutions indeed started "the tyranny of experts"[195] ignoring the basic needs of the vast majority.

Social modernization has happened too, but not in the way envisaged in the Western model. There is a shift from collectivism to individualism, particularly among the young, urban, and professionals. But collectivist orientations are not eliminated completely. Rather the two, collectivism and individualism, have interpenetrated, as a result of which Indians serve their individual interests by collectivist and the collectivist purposes by individual initiatives.[196] Indians indeed are adopting Western lifestyles ranging from food to fashion, from music to movies, and so on. There is hardly a domain where the Western footprints are not clear and deep. However, deeper down into the Indian psyche, high power distance and the medieval lust for a lavish lifestyle seem to rob cherished ancient values of seeking peace of mind and living in contentment with what they have. Money is the main judging scale for everything including relationships and self-worth. It has pushed back the values of modesty, austerity, contentment, and other cherished traditional values. And yet, some of the deeply enshrined dispositions have managed to resist the Western onslaught. For example, Indians, unlike their Western counterparts, still prioritize personalized over contractual relationships, yield to large power distance rather than respecting egalitarianism, prostrate before more powerful persons, and impose upon the lesser ones. They make money by adopting the capitalist mode, but spend it lavishly like the medieval lords. Their vulgar display of wrongly accumulated wealth defies their modernized façade. What we have are not the modernized Indians in the Western mould, but the ones who are wearing Western modernity over their medieval mindset.

Western concept of modernization was rooted in their historical experience where economic, social, and political development co-evolved reinforcing and pushing each other forward in specific stages and combinations. However, India, like many other developing countries, experienced a "temporal compression".[197] They took advantage of the Western experience, but opted for different forms and features of modernization. Tradition and modernity were thus seen as supplementing rather than supplanting each other. They were not defined as stark opposites or as "mutually exclusive".[198] The modern even revived and integrated with some of the traditional features[199] resulting into ideas and institutions that were modern and traditional at the same time.

Caste and religion are typical examples. Caste, the most resilient Indian institution, has been transformed to carry on the "ancient regime" and yet lead to "democratic political revolution".[200] In other words, the caste associations are both "natural" formations for serving traditional purposes as well as voluntary organizations for vertical, horizontal and differential political mobilization. Caste system in India indeed has turned into "more flexible networks of caste associations, organized around modern economic, professional, and political activities".[201] It has become a power plow to claim economic gains, positions of power and influence, and control vote banks.

Indians are highly religious, but the country opted for secularism—a modern worldview. However, Indian secularism is not the negation of religious faith (as in the West); rather is accommodative of multi-religiosities. Politicians exploited it to fan communalism while still posing to be secular. *Caste and religion were modernized but mainly to serve narrow political rather than national interests.* Naturally, they have turned into the most formidable systemic deterrents to development.

Political modernization manifested in the West in democratic processes in governance. Parliamentary democracy in the West evolved out of the Industrial revolution. Political participation grew slowly in Europe mostly in the upper class. On the contrary, India was declared a republic in 1950 granting universal suffrage while major industrial activities were started later in the sixties. It was not claimed by the people but was given to them like a gift. It was "puzzling" to Western scholars because the societal conditions such as "rigid caste system, oriental despotism, parasitic landlordism, and stunted agricultural development" were hardly conducive to democratic ethos and practices.[202] As the people were divided along caste, class, religion, language, and many other lines, there happened "politicization of a fragmented social structure through a penetration of political forms, values and ideologies ..operating against the background of an essentially apolitical [and elitist] condition of society.[203] The elites occupied powerful positions and rationalized their acts of "refusing to overhaul on any massive scale a social structure that maintains their privileges"[204]. In other words, the political democracy in India did not result into a clash between traditional social structures and modern political system but rather the modern survived only by becoming part of the hierarchically structured Indian society, that is, by "traditionalizing" itself.[205] It was indeed "a simultaneous rather than sequential model of [political] development".[206]

Tradition rather claimed modernity causing serious consequences. For example, national political parties were fragmented along traditional divides. Many regional parties emerged, but that too got fragmented along caste and other lines. Each of them was recognized solely by its leader who, like the traditional chieftains, centralized power and expanded his support base by mobilizing people on the basis of caste, religion, or whatever other parochial and local incentives he could offer. The leaders continuously negotiated with each other to gain access into the positions of power by forming coalitions and alliances. The coalitions were based not on ideology, but expediency that required continuous "political accommodations, bargains and compromises"[207] failing which the parties parted ways and clobbered another set of coalitions in order to keep the game going on and on. The parties lacked democracy in their internal structure. They were generally controlled by a single person with his or her coterie of confidents. The chief remained at the top through perfunctory election process, till one of his confidents rebelled and formed another party. The driving force for joining and parting ways was the ego or lust for power and position or greed for money and material benefits rather than any principle, ideology, or national interests.

Such an opportunistic politics gave wrong signal to the people who were sensitized more to the politics than any other factors. Mobilizing them for electoral purposes increased their political participation even in remote places,[208] but not necessarily cultivating democratic values and norms in them. They could now seek any favour, press for any demand, or cause any nuisance as part of their democratic rights without thinking of their responsibilities. Political parties seeking their support could hardly desist or resist.[209] It raised a crucial issue: "How can one inculcate into organized groups the belief in some sort of public interest which would moderate the kinds of demands made and the techniques used to influence government, so that government can function with a minimum of recourse to coercive methods to maintain law and order?"[210] or can remained focused on its development agenda? The reality is that the parties have largely failed to maintain a balance between people's demands and good governance: "The evidence for eroding political order is everywhere. Personal rule has replaced party rule at all levels....Below the rulers, the entrenched civil and police services have been politicized. Various social groups have pressed new and ever more diverse political demands in demonstrations that often have led to violence"[211]. They block traffic, destroy public property, encroach on public lands, turn violent, and bully whoever cross their way. They enjoy freedom to ignore all law and order without any sense of responsibility for public goods and national interests. All they need is to collect supporters who join them in the xpectation of sharing the spoils of their aggressive activities. Caste nd religion are often the easiest available sources to form such ands of self-seeking groups.

INTEGRATIVE THOUGHTS

Development is a vision of desirable state and sense of living that the more powerful define for themselves and then impose on the less powerful ones. Islamic rulers relished living a lavish life by exploiting those below them. The colonial rulers perpetuated it while professing to civilize the natives as a part of "the white men's burden". This charm of lavish living even at the cost of others is the dream that most Indians have inherited and cherished at the heart of their heart. The elites today realize it to varying extent and the rest only fantasize about it. Gandhi wanted to salvage Indians from such a mindset by positing the moral superiority of simplicity and decentralized decision-making, which have far reaching implications for shifting development focus from elites to the common people, particularly poor and the weaker sections.

Box 2.4: Paradigm Shift in Approach to Development

A shift from elitist, lavish, and exploitative to modest and sharing life style is essential for a wholesome and inclusive human development as well as the preservation of the Nature.

Gandhi's ideas of development were not given a chance because Nehru was committed to socialism and elitism. He had overwhelming influence on the Congress as well as on the State apparatus. Nehru's socialism laid down a sound foundation for industrial growth, but failed in its expectations because of the collusion of corrupt politicians, bureaucrats, and businessmen. It neither created sufficient wealth for alleviating poverty nor prevented concentration of wealth in a fewer hands. Its failure paved the way of the country to embrace the Western design of development consisting of market-driven economy and individualism in social relationships. Its third component, democratic politics, was already introduced in the country. All three have been filtered through the ground reality. Market- driven economy has created wealth that is usurped by a few for living by the medieval values of opulence and causing alarming inequality and widespread deprivation in the masses. Individualism has gained ground turning into selfishness and causing exclusive development. Democratic politics, devoid of democratic spirit, was confined to electoral politics that is a game devoid of ideology or idealism. Politicians need more and more money for winning elections and live lavishly. So, it breeds crimes and corruption that are seeping into the whole society. Electoral politics has turned into caste and communal politics fragmenting political parties and groups into self-seeking entities. The result is an anomic society where castes and communalism are the most readily available source of rallying political power. A culture of *baljori* (by force of power) has emerged from the top to the bottom distorting the process of development in one's own interest.

Notes

1. Powerful cann't be faulted, Tulasidas, *Ramcharit Manas*.
2. Skinner, 1983.
3. Based on evidence from Levinea, Higginsb, & Choic, 2000.
4. See details in Sinha, 2014, pp. 63-72.
5. Constructed on the bases of the studies by Asch, 1956; Levinea, Higginsb, & Choic, 2000.
6. Berry, 1997.
7. Thapar 1972, p. 132.
8. It started in the 15th century and got accelerated to the extent that in the 19th century, 5 million Europeans migrated to North America. See https://en.wikipedia.org/wiki/European_colonization_of_the_Americas.
9. Peroff, 2002; Vividly depicted in the epic film: *How the West was Won*, 1962 https://en.wikipedia.org/wiki/How_the_West_Was_Won_(film)
10. *Gale Encyclopedia of U.S. History*. War (2008); Panikkar, 1953.
11. This was a poem composed by Rudyard Kipling (1889) referring to the American colonization of the Philippines. Later on, it was taken for as a noble enterprise: developing the colonized for their own benefit. French justified its colonial rule by way of *the mission civilisatrice* (civilizing mission), Easterly, 2014.
12. Carter & Harlow, 2003.
13. Majumdar *et al.* 1960, pp. 222–223.
14. Berzin, 1996.
15. Elliot & Dowson, 1952.
16. Lannoy, 1971/2008, p. 228.
17. Chatterjee & Eaton, 2006, p. 11; Wink, 1991 pp. 14-16, 172-174.
18. Lal, 1992b, p. 1.
19. Manucci & Pelsaert cited by Lal, 1992a, p. 5.
20. Lal, 1992a, p. 1.

21. Lal, 1992a, p. 7.
22. Lal, 1992a, p. 19.
23. See details in Lal, 1992a.
24. Lal, 1992b.
25. See details in Lal, 1992b.
26. cited by Moreland, 1992, p. 269.
27. Moreland, 1992, pp. 253-55.
28. Lal, 1992b, p. 45.
29. The lavish life of a *samant* (Hindu noble) during the Gupta period has been vividly described in a famous Hindi novel *Chitralekha* by Bhagawati Charan Verma, 2000.
30. Thapar, 1972, p. 151.
31. Lal, 1992b, p. 2.
32. Mayo 1927/1969, pp. 276–277.
33. Panikkar, 1953.
34. Robins 2006.
35. Anstey 1929, quoted by Nehru 1946/2001, p. 284.
36. Robins 2006, p. 7.
37. Adam, William, 1941.
38. Willian Adam's Report on Bengal 1835-1838, cited by Panikkar, 2013.
39. Frykenberg, 1977, pp. 141-42.
40. Maddison 2001.
41. Maddison, 2013, p. 1.
42. Nehru 1946/2001, p. 299.
43. Panikkar, 2013.
44. Maddison, 2013, p. 23.
45. Davis, 2001.
46. The Famine Commission (1901) cited by Desai, Raychaudhuri, & Kumar, 1983.
47. Sen, 1982.
48. Cited by Panikkar, 1953, 85.
49. Mahatma Gandhi's letter to the Viceroy Irwin, dated March 2, 1930.
50. Hegel, 1956, cited by Islam, & Rasel, 2012, p. 2.
51. Karl Marx, 1969, cited by Islam, & Rasel, 2012, p. 3.
52. Panikkar, 1953, p. 123.
53. see details in Dirks, 2001.
54. Mill, 1817/1958.
55. Kipling 1889, p. 371.
56. https://en.wikipedia.org/wiki/Robert_Clive.
57. Marshall, 1987; Pavarala, 2004.
58. Robb, 1992.
59. Abraham, 2009, p. 67.
60. Marshall, 1987; Pavarala, 2004.
61. Shobita Dhar, April 5, 2015.

http://timesofindia.indiatimes.com/india/Royal-Royce-tales/articleshow/46810553.cms.
62. https://en.wikipedia.org/wiki/Princely_state.
63. Maddison, 2013, p. 7.
64. All cites and most observations are from Maddison, 2013, p. 6.
65. Maddison, 2013, p. 13.
66. see Sen 2006, pp. 151–153.
67. Said, 1977, p. 13.
68. Chatterjee, 1993, p. 6.
69. Panikkar, 1953, p. 245.
70. Panikkar, 1953, 255.
71. Kopf, 1979.
72. Chaturvedi, 2006.
73. Chaturvedi, 2006; Rai, 1915.
74. Details are given in Chapter 4.
75. Oonk, 2004.
76. Varma, 2004, p. 71.
77. Export of textile machinery was permitted only after 1843.
78. Damodaran, 2008.
79. Frasser, 1919, p. 51.
80. Bahl, 1995, p. 73.
81. Oonk, 2004.
82. Damodaran, 2008.
83. Oonk, 2004, p. 3.
84. Oonk, 2004, p. 6.
85. http://parsikhabar.net/bombay/the-story-of-the-taj-mahal-hotel/2620/
86. Verrier Elwin 1958. Both Hotel Taj Mahal and Tata Steel were completed after Jamsetji's death.
87. See Seal, 1971; Gallagher, John, & Robinson, 1953; Ganachari, 2010; Gordon Johnson, 2005; Spodek, 1979, among others.
88. As designed by Macaulay (Shani, 2005).
89. Bhabha, 1994.
90. Seal 1968.
91. Parekh 1989, p. 50.
92. Parekh 1989, p. 51.
93. Chandra, 1969.
94. Bhabha 1994:85-93.
95. Chakrabarty, 2000; Ranjit Guha, 1982 to 1989; 1997; Gyanendra Pandey, 1991; among others.
96. Hobsbawm, 1978, p. 2.
97. Anil Seal, 1968, p. 1.
98. Gyanendra Pandey, 2002.
99. Desai, 1948; Spodek, 1979.
100. India got Independence on August 15, 1947.

101. McMahon, 2003.
102. Cullather, 2010.
103. Hogan, 1987.
104. Wettig, 2008, p. 142.
105. Available at http://www.bartleby.com/124/pres53.html
106. Stebbins, 1959, p. 297.
107. https://en.wikipedia.org/wiki/India%E2%80%93United_States_relations.
108. Furber, 1965.
109. Shaw, 1889.
110. Nehru, 1928, p. 5.
111. Mitra, 2009, p. 256.
112. Nehru, 1982.
113. Mitra, 2009, p. 256.
114. *History and Evolution of Non-Aligned Movement*, 2012.
115. China was referred to as India's "great sister in the East", Nehru, 1982, p. 270.
116. Bright, 1946, p. 94.
117. Nehru, 1928, p. 5.
118. *Harijan*, 13 February 1937, p. 45.
119. Desai & Bhagwati, 1975.
120. Desai & Bhagwati, 1975, p. 216.
121. *National Herald*, 1939.
122. Report of the *National Planning Committee*, 1938, pp. 28 & 36–37.
123. Shaw, 1889.
124. Nehru, 1982, pp. 946 –947.
125. Nehru cited by Zaidi et al., 1980, p.95.
126. Nehru, 1956, p. 17.
127. Nehru, 1956.
128. Industrial Policy Statement, 1945.
129. Nehru, 1985, p.372.
130. Hanson,1966, p. 37.
131. Ganguli, 1964.
132. Zaidi, 1980, p. 36.
133. Rist, 1997.
134. Rostow, 1962.
135. Lerner, 1964.
136. Apter, 1965.
137. Inkeles & Smith, 1974.
138. Triandis, 1984, p. 94.
139. McClelland; 1961.
140. McClelland & Winter, 1969.
141. See details in Chapter 1.
142. Smith, Adam, 1776.
143. See details in Chapter 1.

144. *Sarvodaya* means 'Rise of All". The term was coined by Mahatma Gandhi.
145. Gandhi, 2001.
146. Gandhi, 1938, pp. 56-57.
147. Mathur, 1971, p. 65.
148. Gandhi, 1938, p. 6.
149. Diwan & Lutz, 1987, p. 25.
150. Nadkarni, 2014, pp. 45–54; Nadkarni, 2015, pp. 90-103.
151. Ghosh, 2007, p. 17.
152. Gandhi, 1938, p. 13.
153. Gandhi, 1938, p. 29.
154. Gillen, & Ghosh, 2007, p. 30.
155. Gandhi, 1938, pp. 33-34.
156. Gandhi, 1938, p. 56.
157. Gandhi, 1938, pp. 27-28.
158. Srinivasa, Ed., 1987.
159. Avilable at http://www.quotationspage.com/quote/3849.html, retrieved on March 2016.
160. Tewari, 1971.

161Parel, 2000.

162. Srinivasa Murthy, 1987.
163. Easwaran, 2011.
164. Agarwal, 1944.
165. Mitra, 2009, p. 101.
166. Gandhi, 1939, pp. 378-379.
167. Gandhi, 1938, p. 90.
168. Gandhi, 1938, p. 6.
169. Guha, R. 2004, Kumarappa, 1951.
170. *Harijan*, 28 January 1939, p. 438.1.
171. Gandhi coined this term, Uma Majmudar, 2005.
172. Gandhi, 1928, p. 109; Chakrabarty, 2006.
173. Rudolph, 1963.
174. Sinha, 2014.
175. D. Sinha, 1987.
176. Chakrabarty, 2006.
177. Bureaucracy that turns pathological.
178. Desai & Bhagwati, 1975, p. 216.
179. Bhalla, 2011, p. 4.
180. http://archive.financialexpress.com/news/redefining-the-hindu-rate-of-growth/104268.
181. Desai & Bhagwati, 1975, p. 217.
182. Administrative Reform Commission, 1967, p. 1.
183. Nigam, 1967.
184. Appleby, 1956, p. 17.
185. Sinha, 1973.

186. Sinha, 1973.
187. Desai & Bhagwati, 1975, p. 217.
188. Dessai & Bhagwati, 1975, p. 218.
189. See Chapter 1.
190. Sachs, Wolfgang, 1992, p.1.
191. Rist, 1997, Rist, 2007, p. 488.
192. Rist, 2007, p. 489.
193. Easterly, 2006.
194. Rist, 2007, p.486.
195. Sachs, J., 2005.
196. Sinha et al., 2001.
197. D. Sinha, 1984, p. 19.
198. Bendix, 1967, p. 326.
199. Heesterman, 1985, p. 9.
200. Rudolph & Rudolph, 1967.
201. Eisenstadt, 1965, p. 669.
202. Paradoxical and puzzling expressions were used by Moore, 1993, p. 315.
203. Kothari, 1970, p. 11.
204. Moore, 1993, p.431.
205. Kothari, 1970, p. 93.
206. Kothari, 1970, p. 422.
207. Manor, 1990, p. 22.
208. Khilnani, 1999; Singh & Mishra, 2004.
209. For example, the affluent castes' agitation for job reservations.
210. Weiner, 1959, pp. 103-119.
211. Kohli, 1990, p. 3.

REFERENCES

Abraham, S. (2009). The making of colonial law, discipline, and corruption in British India. *Manupatra, 2*, 64-82.

Adam, W. (1941). *Reports on the State of Education in Bengal, 1835 and 1838.* Calcutta: Calcutta University Press.

Administrative Reform Commission (1967). *Report on the public sector undertakings.* New Delhi: Government of India Press.

Agarwal, S.N. (1944). *The Gandhian plan of economic development for India.* Bombay: Padma Publications.

Anstey, V. (1929). *The economic development of India.* London: Longman, Green & Company.

Appleby, P.H. (1956). Reexamination of India's administrative system with special reference to administration of government's industrial and commercial enterprises. Government of India, New Delhi.

Apter, D.E. (1965).*The politics of modernisation*. Chicago: University of Chicago Press.

Asch, S.E. (1956). Studies of independence and conformity: A majority of one against a unanimous majority. *Psychological Monographs, 70,* (Whole Number 416).

Bahl, V. (1995). *The making of Indian working class: The case of the Tata Iron and Steel Company, 1880-1946*. New Delhi: Sage.

Bendix, R. (1967). Tradition and modernity reconsidered. *Comparative Studies in Society and History*, 9(3), 292-346.

Berry, J.W. (1997). Immigration, acculturation, and adaptation. *Applied Psychology*, 46(1), 5-34.

Berzin, A. (1996). *Buddhism and its impact on Asia*. Asian Monographs, 8. Cairo: Center for Asian Studies, Cairo University.

Bhabha, H. (1994). *The location of culture*. London: Routledge.

Bhalla, S.S. (2011). Inclusion and Growth in India: Some Facts, Some Conclusions. Asia Research Centre Working Paper 39. London School of Economics, London. Retrieved on June 14, 2015.

Bright, J.S. (1946) (Ed.). *Collection of most significant speeches delivered by Jawaharlal Nehru from 1922 to 1946*. Lahore: Dewans Publications.

Carter, M. and Harlow, B. (Eds.) (2003). *Archives of empire (Vol. 1)*. Durham: Duke University Press.

Chakrabarty, B. (2006). *Social and political thought of Mahatma Gandhi*. Oxford: Routledge.

Chakrabarty, D. (2000). *Subaltern studies and postcolonial historiography*. Position Paper. Duke University Press.

Chandra, Bipan (1969). *The rise and growth of economic nationalism in India: Economic policies of Indian national leadership, 1880–1905*. Delhi: People's Publishing House.

Chatterjee, I. and Eaton, R.M. (2006) (Ed.). *Slavery and South Asian history*. Bloomington:: Indiana University Press.

Chatterjee, Partha (1993). *The nation and its fragments*. Princeton: Princeton University Press.

Chaturvedi, B. (2006). *Swami Vivekananda, the Living Vedanta*. New Delhi: Penguin Books.

Cullather, N. (2010). *The hungry world: America's cold war battle against poverty in Asia*. Cambridge, Mass: Harvard University Press.

Damodaran, H. (2008). *India's new capitalists: Caste, business and industry in a modern nation*. New Delhi: Palgrave Macmillan.

Davis, M. (2001). *Late Victorian holocausts: El Nino famine and the making of the Third World*, London; New York: Verso Books.

Desai, A.R. (1948). *Social background of Indian nationalism*. Bombay: Popular Prakashan.

Desai, M., Raychaudhuri, T. and Kumar, *D. (1983). The Cambridge economic history of India (*Volume 2*).* Cambridge: Cambridge University Press.

Desai, P. and Bhagwati, J. (1975). Socialism and Indian economic policy. *World Development*, 3(4), 213-221.

Dirks, N.B. (2001). *Castes of Mind: Colonialism and the making of modern India*. Princeton: Princeton University Press.

Diwan, R.K. and Lutz, M.A. (1987) (Eds.), *Essays in Gandhian economics*. New Delhi: Gandhi Peace Foundation.

Easterly, William (2006). *The white man's burden: Why the West's efforts to aid the rest have done so much ill and so little good*. New York: Penguin Group, USA.

Easterly, William (2014). *The tyranny of experts: Economists, dictators, and the forgotten rights of the poor*. New York: Basic Books.

Easwaran, E. (2011). *Gandhi: the man*. Tomales, CA: Nilgiri Press.

Eisenstadt, S.N. (1965). Transformation of social, political and cultural orders in modernization. *American Sociological Review*, 30(5).

Elliot, H.M. and Dowson, J. (1952). *The history of India as told by its own historians*. Calcutta: S. Gupta.

Fraser, I. (1919). *Iron and steel in India: A chapter from the life of Jamsetji Tata*. Bombay: The Times Press.

Frykenberg, R.E. (1977). Company Circari in the Carnatic, 1799-1859: The inner logic of political systems in India. In R.G. Fox (Ed.), *Realm and region in traditional India*. NOIDA, UP: Vikas Publishing House.

Furber, H. (1965). Historical and cultural aspects of Indo-American relations. *Journal of the University of Bombay, 34* (67/68), 95-116.

Gale Encyclopedia of U.S. History. War (2008). Farmington Hills, MI, USA

Gallagher, John, and Ronald Robinson (1953). The imperialism of free trade. *Economic History Review*, 6 (1), 1–15.

Ganachari, A. (2010). Studies in Indian Historiography: The Cambridge School. *Indica*, 47(1), 70–93.

Gandhi, M.K. (1928). *Satyagraha in South Africa*. Ahmedabad: Navajivan Publishing House.

Gandhi, M.K. (1938). *Hind swaraj or Indian home rule* (2nd Edition, Prefaced by Mahadev Desai). Ahmedabad: Nav ajivan Publishing House.

Gandhi, M.K. (1939). *Gandhi to Nehru, on August 11*: in *A Bunch of Old Letters*. Bombay: Asia Publishing House, 1958.

Gandhi, M.K. (2001). *Non-violent resistance (Satyagraha)*. Mineola, N.Y: Dover.

Ganguli, B.N. (1964). Nehru and socialism. *The Economic and Political Weekly: Special Issue*. July, 1213-1218.

Ghosh, B.N. (2007). *Gandhian political economy: principles, practice, and policy*. Aldershot, England; Burlington, VT: Ashgate.

Gillen, P. and Ghosh, D. (2007). *Colonialism and modernity: Histories and themesÿÿ:*. Sydney, Australia: *UNSW Press*.

Gordon, Johnson (2005). Provincial Politics and Indian Nationalism: Bombay and the Indian National Congress, 1880-1915.

Guha, Ramchandra (2004). *Anthropologist among the Marxists: And other essays*. Kolkata: Orient Blackswan.

Guha, Ranjit (Ed.) (1982 to 1989). *Subaltern studies: Writings on South Asian history and society* (8 Volumes). New Delhi: Oxford University Press.

Hanson, A.H. (1966). *The process of planning: A Study of India's Five Year Plans. 1950-64*. London: Oxford University Press.

Heesterman, J.C. (1985). *The inner conflict of tradition: Essays in Indian ritual, kingship and society*. Chicago: University of Chicago Press.

Hegel, Friedrich G.W. (1956). *Philosophy of history* (translated by J. Sibree). New York: Dover Publications.

History and Evolution of Non-Aligned Movement (2012). Ministry of External Affairs, Government of India, New Delhi, August 22. Available at http://mea.gov.in/in-focus-article.htm?20349/History+and+Evolution+of+NonAligned+Movement.Retrieved on December 15, 2015.

Hobsbawm, E.J. (1978). *Primitive rebels: Studies in archaic forms of social movement in the nineteenth and twentieth centuries*. Manchester: Manchester University Press.

Hogan, M.J. (1987). *The Marshall Plan: America, Britain, and the reconstruction of Western Europe, 1947–1952*. Cambridge: Cambridge University Press.

Industrial Policy Statement (1945). Government of India, New Delhi.

Inkeles, A. and Smith, D.H. (1974). *Becoming modern*. Cambridge, MA: Harvard Press.

Islam, M.M.A. and Rasel, R. (2012). Discourse on colonialism, colonial state and nationalism in India: A critical study of historiography. Available athttp://azizulrasel.wordpress.com/2012/04/16/discourse-on

Khilnani, S. (1999). *The idea of India*. New York: Farrar, Straus and Giroux.

Kipling, R. (1899). *The white man's burden*. In R. Kipling (Ed.), Verse (pp. 371–372). New York: Doubleday

Kohli, A. (1990). *Democracy and discontent: India's growing crisis of govern ability*. Cambridge: Cambridge University Press.

Kopf, D. (1979). *Brahmo Samaj and the making of modern India*. Princeton: Princeton University Press.

Kothari, R. (1970). *Politics in India*. Boston: Little, Brown & Co.

Kumarappa, J.C. (1951). *Gandhian economic thought. Bombay:* Library of Indian Economics.

Lal, K.S. (1992a). Chapter 5, Upper Classes and Luxurious Life. In K.S. Lal, *The Legacy of Muslim Rule in India*. New Delhi: Aditya Prakashan. Available at http://www.voiceofdharma.org/books/tlmr/ch5.htm. Retrieved on December 12, 2016.

Lal, K.S. (1992b). Chapter 7, Lower Classes and Unmitigated Exploitation. In K.S. Lal, *The Legacy of Muslim Rule in India*. New Delhi: Aditya

Prakashan. Aailable at http://www.voiceofdharma.org/books/tlmr/ch7.htm. Retrieved on December 12, 2016.

Lannoy, R. (1971/2008). *The speaking tree: A study of Indian culture and society*. New Delhi: Oxford University Press.

Lerner, D. (1964). *The passing of traditional society.* New York, The Free Press, Levinea, J.M., Higginsb, E.T. and Choic, Hoon-Seok (2000). Development of strategic norms in groups. *Organizational Behaviour and Human Decision Processes*, 82 (1), 88–101.

Maddison, A. (2001). *The world economy*. Paris: Organization for Economic Cooperation and Development.

Maddison, A. (2013). *Class structure and economic growth: India and Pakistan Since the Moghuls.* Oxford, New York: Taylor & Francis. Available at http://www.ggdc.net/maddison/articles/moghul_3.pdf. Retrieved on January, 17, 2017.

Majumdar, R.C., Raychaudhuri, H.C. and Datta, K.K. (1960). *An advanced history of India.* London: Macmillan.

Majmudar, Uma (2005). *Gandhi's pilgrimage of faith: From darkness to light.* New York: SUNY Press.

Marshall, P.J. (ed.) (1987). *The speeches and writings of Edmund Burke, First report of the select committee: Observations.* Oxford: Clarendon Press, pp. 183-184.

Marx, Karl (1969). *On colonialism and modernization* (edited by Shlomo Avineri). New York: Doubleday & Company.

Mathur, J.S. (1971). *Industrial civilization and Gandhian economics.* Allahabad, Pustakayan.

Mayo, K. (1927/1969). *Mother India.* New York: Greenwood Press.

McClelland, D.C. (1961). *The achieving society.* New York: Van Nostrand.

McClelland, D.C. and Winter, D.G. (1969). *Motivating economic achievement.* New York: Free Press.

McMahon, R.J. (2003). *The cold war. Very short introductions.* Oxford: Oxford University Press

Mill, J. (1817/1958). *The history of British India.* London, Chicago: Chicago University Press.

Mitra, S.K. (2009). Strategy and vision in politics: Jawaharlal Nehru's policy choices and the designing of political institutions. FakultätfürWirtschafts-und Sozialwissenschaften der Ruprecht-Karls-Universität Heidelberg, Germany.

Moore, B. (1993). *Social origins of dictatorship and democracy.* Boston: Beacon Press.

Moreland, W.H. (1992). *From Akbar to Aurangzeb: A study in Indian economic history.* New Delhi: Orient Book Reprint Corporation.

Moyo, D. (2009). *Dead aid: Why aid is not working and how there is a better way for Africa.* London: Penguin.

Nadkarni, M.V. (2014). *Ethics for our times: Essays in Gandhian perspective*. New Delhi: Oxford University Press, 2014. *pp. 45–54.*

Nadkarni, M.V. (2015). Gandhi's civilizational alternative and dealing with climate change. *Journal of Social and Economic Development*, June, 90-103.

National Herald, (June 21, 1939.) In S. Gopal (Ed.), *Selected works of Jawaharlal Nehru* (Volume 9), pp. 386-387. New Delhi: Orient Longman.

Nehru, J. (1928). *Soviet Russia: Some random sketches and impressions*. Allahabad: Law Journal Press.

Nehru, J. (1946/2001). *The discovery of India* (Paperback). New Delhi: Oxford University Press.

Nehru, J. (1956). *Planning and development: Speeches of Jawaharlal Nehru, 1952-56*, Delhi, Publications Division, Government of India.

Nehru, J. (1982). *Glimpses of world history*. New Delhi: Oxford University Press.

Nehru, J. (1985). *The discovery of India*. (4th Edition). New Delhi, Oxford University Press.

Nigam, R.K. (1967). Pattern of directorship in public undertakings. *Lokudyog*, 4, (1).

Oonk, G. (2004). Industrialization in India, 1850-1947: Three variations in the emergence of Indigenous industrialists. Rotterdam, The Netherlands: Erasmus School of History, Culture and Communication (ESHCC).

Pandey, Gyanendra (1991). *The construction of communalism in colonial North India*. Delhi: Oxford University Press.

Pandey, Gyanendra (2002). *The Ascendency of the Congress in Uttar Pradesh: Class, community and nation in Northern India, 1920-1940*. London: Anthem Press.

Panikkar, K.M. (1953). *Asia and western dominance*. London: George Allen & Unwin.

Panikkar, K.N. (2013). Religion and politics in colonial India. *The Hindu*, October, 23.

Parekh, B. (1989). *Colonialism, tradition and reform: An Analysis of Gandhi's political discourse*. London: Sage.

Parel, A. (Ed.) (2000). *Gandhi, freedom, and self-rule*. New York and Oxford: Lexington Books.

Pavarala, V. (2004). Cultures of corruption and corruption of culture: The East India Company and Hastings Impeachment. In E. Kreike and W.C. Jordan (Eds.), *Corrupt histories* Rochester, NY: University of Rochester Press, pp. 291-292.

Peroff, N.C. (2002). Who is an American Indian? *Social Science Journal*, 39 (3), 349.

Rai, L.L. (1915). *The Arya Samaj: An account of its aims, doctrine and activities, with a biographical sketch of the founder*. London: Longman.

Rist, Gilbert (1997). *The history of development: From western origins to global faith*. London & New York: Zed Books.

Report of the National Planning Committee (1938). Indian National Congress. Indian Institute of Applied Political Research, New Delhi.

Rist, Gilbert (2007). Development as a buzzword. Routedge, *Development in Practice*, 17 (4–5), 485-491.

Robb, G (1992). *White-collar crime in modern England*. Cambridge: Cambridge University Press.

Robins, N. (2006). *The corporation that changed the world: How the East India Company shaped the modern multinational*. Hyderabad: Orient Longman.

Rostow, W.W. (1962). *The stages of economic growth*. London: Cambridge University Press.

Rudolph, L. and Rudolph, S. (1967). *The modernity of tradition: Political development in India*. London: University of Chicago Press.

Rudolph, S.H. (1963). The New Courage: An Essay on Gandhi's psychology. *World Politics **16** (1), 98–117.*

Sachs, Jeffrey (2005). *The end of poverty: Economic possibilities of our time*. New York: Penguin Books.

Sachs, Wolfgang (Ed.) (1992). *The development reader. A guide to kowledge and power.* London: Zed Books.

Said, E. (1977). *Orientalism*. London: Penguin

Seal, Anil (1968, 1971). *The emergence of Indian nationalism: Competition and collaboration in the latter nineteenth century*. Cambridge: Cambridge University Press.

Sen, Amartya (1982*). Poverty and famines: An essay on entitlements and deprivation*. Oxford, Clarendon Press.

Sen, Amartya (2006). *The argumentative Indian: Writings on Indian history, culture and identity*. New York: F Picador, Farrar, Straus, and Giroux.

Shani, G. (2005). Indigenous Modernities: Nationalism and Communalism in Colonial India. *Ritsumeikan Annual Review of International Studies*, 4, 87-112. Available at http://www.ritsumei.ac.jp/acd/cg/ir/college/bulletin/e-vol4/shani.pdf. Retrieved on March 14.

Shaw, G.B. (1889). *Fabian essays in socialism*. London: Scott.

Singh, M.P. and Mishra, A. (2004). *Coalition politics in India: Problems and prospects*. New Delhi: Manohar Books.

Sinha, D. (1984). Psychology in the context of Third World development. *International Journal of Psychology*, 19, 17-30.

Sinha, D. (1987). *Ahimsa* as conflict resolution technique and instrument of peace: A psychological appraisal. Paper presented during a seminar on Peace and Conflict Resolution in the World Community. New Delhi.

Sinha, J.B.P. (1973). *Some problems of public sector organizations*. New Delhi: National.

Sinha, J.B.P. (2014). *The psycho-social analysis of the Indian mindset*. New Delhi: Springer.

Sinha, J.B.P., Sinha, T.N., Verma, J. and Sinha, R.B.N. (2001). Collectivism coexisting with individualism: An Indian scenario. *Asian Journal of Social Psychology, 4*, 133-145.

Skinner, B.F. (1983). *A matter of consequences*. New York: Alfred A Knopf.

Smith, Adam (1776). *An inquiry into the nature and causes of the wealth of nations*. London: Strahan & Cadell.

Spodek, H. (1979). Pluralist politics in British India: The Cambridge cluster of historians of modern India. *American Historical Review*, 84 (3), 688-707.

Srinivasa Murthy, B. (1987) (Ed.), *Mahatma Gandhi and Leo Tolstoy letters*. Long Beach, CA: Long Beach Publications.

Stebbins, R.P. (1959). *The United States in world affairs*. New York: Harper.

Tewari, S.M. (1971). The concept of democracy in the political thought of Mahatma Gandhi. *Indian Political Science Review, 6 (2), 225–251.*

Thapar, R. (1972). *A history of India* (Vol. 1). London: Penguin Books.

Triandis, H.C. (1984). Toward a psychological theory of economic growth. *International Journal of Psychology*, 19, 79–96.

Varma, P. (2004). *Being Indian: The truth about why the 21st century will be Indians*. New Delhi: Viking, Penguin.

Verrier, Elwin (1958). *The story of Tata Steel*. Bombay: Tata Steel.

Weiner, M. (1959). India's political future. *World Politics*, 12 (1), 103-119.

Wettig, G. (2008). *Stalin and the cold war in Europe: The emergence and development of East-West conflict, 1939–1953* (The Harvard Cold War Studies Book Series.). Lanham, MD.: Rowman & Littlefield.

Wink, A. (1991). *Al-Hind: the making of the Indo-Islamic world* (Volume 1). Boston, MASS.: Brill Academic Press.

Zaidi, A.M., et al. (Eds.) (1980). *The encyclopaedia of the Indian National Congress*. New Delhi: S. Chand.

3

Legacy that Started Decaying

Religion, Castes, and Politics

AN OVERVIEW

Endogenous development is ideal: "When a country develops endogenously, its way of life should be based on respect for its traditional values, for the authenticity of its culture, and for creative aptitudes of its people".[1] However, it never happens entirely. Development is invariably a joint function of the factors that are partly external to the country and partly internal. The preceding chapter showed how the Western design of development prevailed upon the socialist model of the Soviet origin negating the Indian ethos permeating in the Gandhi's thought. The *mantra* from the West was to "Grow economically with us by being like us". India indeed grew economically, but could not become a Western replica. Western design was filtered through internal factors causing unanticipated consequences. Among the major internal factors, castes and religions persisting from the ancient time and the mindset from the medieval period diluted, distorted, and diminished the western influences. The Western design itself had many faults. The outcomes naturally have been disappointing. It means neither all external nor all internal factors are likely to cause a desirable development. Development depends on how they are selectively employed. It is here that the State politics plays a pivotal role.

State Politics mediates the interplay of external and internal factors and determines the course of development of a country. Politics is the game of power for allocating resources as well as distributing benefits, which may or may not be directed to development. The State and its leaders set the norms for politics wielding enormous power over the rest of the society. However, politics is not entirely vested only in the State and the activities of the politicians in power. It also props up, though less explicitly, whenever two or more individuals or groups are competing to gain an edge over each other in accessing to and controlling some important resources. The State politics as well as the politics in a society have some common mechanisms. They both draw on the cultural construction of how power should or could be exerted to serve a purpose or realize a goal that one aspires for. "Politics is a competitive enterprise, its purpose is the acquisition of power for the realisation of certain goals, and its process is one of identifying and manipulating existing and emerging allegiances in order to mobilise and consolidate positions".[2] Politics in itself is amoral and devoid of ethics, neutral to goals, and values-free in adopting means for realizing the goals. Left to itself, it is more likely to drift into immoral and short-cut course that seems most promising for serving selfish ends by adopting even corrupt methods and colluding with wrong people disregarding common interests and larger goals. Religion and caste are the soft targets of it.

Religion, being central to the life of people, naturally attracts politics. Mahatma Gandhi contended that religion and politics are blended like blood and body and that politics without religion is a "dirty game".[3] However, people do play amoral politics with religion or use religion for serving political purposes. Politics can use religion to enthuse people to upscale their social behaviour and also make sacrifices for nation building. It can also evoke religious identity to arouse passion in order to exclude, discriminate, and coerce people of other religions. History tells us that political leaders had in the past done both, and now are misusing more than using religion for the benefit of people. There are also godheads who are more politicians than religious leaders. They hobnob with politicians, play power game, amass wealth, demand loyalty from their subordinates, weed out deviants and dissenters, and run their religious outfit like a political party.

Caste is another pervasive and enduring social formation. It "is so tacitly and so completely accepted by all, including most vocal elements in condemning it, that it is everywhere the unit of social action".[4] Hence, politics uses castes to reach out and expand its power base, while casteism moderates the way politics is played. Castes originated as a system of occupational differentiations for specialization of skills, but got locked into the 4-tiers of *Varnashram* (framework of *varna*) specifying dos and don'ts for castes at the different levels of the hierarchy. Caste system, over the centuries, got so endemic that even the non-Hindus (Muslims, Sikhs, Buddhists, Jains, and Christians) maintained the caste hierarchy.[5]

Castes and religion indeed have been playing politics within as well as with each other. The State has been playing politics with both of them. They all competed for societal resources, political space, and relative superiority. In the process they impacted each other and also got themselves changed. The relationships among them evolved over time affecting the nature and course of development. As long as the State politics was benign and positive-facilitating castes in their intended purpose of skills specialization and patronizing religion equitably, they led to enormous development in science, technology, and philosophies. Together, they led to the "golden" period of India's development, which was marked by people's sense of cultural superiority, vitality, vigour, creative imagination, and the spirit of adventure to explore distant lands as well as to meditate into the inner layers of mind[6]. However, as the politics degenerated into feuds and infightings regressing into a self-serving mode, it misused castes and religion for its own advantage. As a result, religions were ritualized cultivating superstitions and dysfunctional practices, caste hierarchy was petrified and got discriminating, and the State politics was disabled to face the invasions and alien rules. Development was thwarted and people fell deeper and deeper into poverty and poor quality of life, of which they have yet to come out. Let us take a historical view of this down-sliding dynamics.

DYNAMICS OF CASTE, RELIGION, AND POLITICS

Genesis of Castes

The Aryans who settled down in the Indo-Gangetic plain were agriculturists. In fact the word, 'Arya' comes from a root word meaning 'to till'. Some of them took up the roles of warriors and priests. The warriors were recognized as Kshatriyas and the priests were Brahmins, and the rest were called Vaishyas meaning 'the members of the tribe'. There was neither any rigid division of roles[7] nor any privileged order among them.[8] Those whom the Aryans captured or overpowered were called *daasas* (servants). Later on (during *Atharva-Veda*), *daas* were renamed Shudras. *Daasas* were darker skinned than Aryans. Thus, came the label of *varna* that means colour. There were Aryan-*varna* and *daas-varna*—former being superior to the latter. Thus, Kshatriyas, Brahmins, Vaishyas, and Shudras constituted four *varnas*. The *Vedic* texts did not mention the concept or practice of untouchability.[9] Later on, those who were engaged in menial activities such as scavenging, skinning dead cattle, etc. were denigrated as untouchables.

The chief among Kshatriyas was the king. The king had temporal power over all. But Brahmins claimed superiority to even Kshatriyas because the former had spiritual merit and religious role. The scholars and teachers among Brahmins developed a highly comprehensive worldview where the society and the kingship were conceptualized hinging on *dharma* (religion), which was believed to be divine in origin providing all-time valid laws for conducting one's life. Scriptures revealed that "the people during the *Vedic* and later periods firmly believed that the state had been set up by god Himself ...God created the state for administering a benevolent yet strict rule over the people".[10] Hence, the king promoted the wellbeing of his subjects, who in turn, were expected to see king's divine form. The most self-realized among Brahmins were said to be blessed enough to receive the divine laws, compile and communicate them to people for their benefits and wellbeing. Therefore, Brahmins had the duties and the responsibilities to guide and sanction people to live a life of *dharma*. It was only they who anointed the king with the divine right to rule over his subjects and helped him in performing religious rites and ceremonies[11]. They constituted the council of ministers that advised the king in discharging even his temporal duties. One of them was revered as the *raj-guru* who guided and blessed the king on all policies and practices. The king was supposed to protect *dharma* by enforcing the laws of *dharma* without being its custodian. Not only the king but the rest of the people too were required to solicit Brahmin's help in performing religious rites and ceremonies and to seek their guidance in day-to-day matters.

Thus, Brahmins succeeded in establishing a caste hierarchy among the *varnas* and substantiated it by inserting a new hymn, *Purusha Sukta,* in the later part of the *Rigveda* about a mythic origin of four *varnas*: Brahmins from the mouth of *Brahman* (the Supreme Being), Kshatriyas from the arms, Vaishyas from the belly, and Shudras from the legs. Once the hierarchy among the *varnas* was established, there was an effort to substantiate it by adding behavioural features. During the epics, for example, Brahmins were believed to be dedicated to truth, austerity and pure conduct; the Kshatriyas were inclined to anger and pleasures; the Vaishyas were involved in cattle rearing and living off the plough; while Shudras were prone to violence, covetousness, and impurity.[12]

Not only Brahmins had the privilege to deliver the divine laws (*dharma*) to the people, but they were in fact via-media between the gods and the people. That is, they were also responsible for approaching and praying gods on behalf of people for blessings them. The *Rigveda consisted* of over thousand poems and hymns that were prayers to 33 nature gods such as Indra (rain), Agni (fire), Rudra (storm), Vayu (air), Soma (drink for immortality), and so on for blessing the king and the people with wealth and prosperity.

Diversions from the Vedas

The *Rigveda* also contained two profound philosophical ideas that shaped the Indian mindset for the centuries to come. It propounded the idea of henotheism that one *Brahman* (the Supreme Being) takes many different forms signifying that there are many paths to the reach Him. If there are many valid paths to reach Him, there are also many new ways to explore the truth or to comprehend the reality. Therefore, the *Rigveda* also proclaimed that "Let noble thoughts come to us from all directions" (I.89.9). It was this pluralistic integrative approach that allowed the Vedic religion to incorporate, for example, 'fire-altars', '*linga-yoni* of the Indus valley civilisation into its own rituals and ceremonies.[13] "The religion that the Aryans brought with them mingled with the religion of the native people, and the culture that developed between them became classical Hinduism".[14]

Philosophical ideas and religious rites and rituals were intertwined in the *Vedas*. These two strands were later on disentangled following the Vedas. The first one, *jnana-kanda or marg* (the path of knowing) manifested in the Upanishads. Through episodes, commentaries, stories, and dialogues, the Upanishads explored the mysteries of life, death, and immortality. The second strand, *karma-kanda*, meticulously elaborated religious rites and rituals in in the *Brahmanas*. The *Aranyakas* bridged the two by elaborating the intricacies of rites and rituals and providing deeper meanings to them by drawing on the Upanishads. Together they covered the whole life space of people from the innermost layers of concerns and curiosities about the fundamental issues of life to the external routines of religious rites and rituals. According to the *Satpath Brahmana*, the religious rites and ceremonies as well as social and political norms that people were required to follow were settled by around 500 BCE.[15] Performing *yajna* was one of the most important duties for both the king and the commoners. Elaborate calculations were necessary to establish an appropriate configuration of the various objects on a *bedi* (sacrificial arena) for *hom* (offering to fire) during *yajna* (elaborate and collective worship) and animal sacrifices, the timing of *yajna*, the sequence of acts, and so on. Following the *Vedic* tradition of painstaking emphasis on proper pronunciation of prayers, recitation of hymns and on the exact sounds of *mantras*, the *Bramanas* contained elaborate manuals of sacrificial rites and religious rituals and provided detailed guidelines to people for daily routine. While these reflected Brahmins' creative imagination, extraordinary capacity of abstract thinking, and vested interests in working out complicated details for imposing upon others their superiority, they proved to be over-bearing and discriminating to those who were lower in the *varna* order.

Emergence of Buddhism and Jainism

In protest, Buddhism and Jainism arose as reformist movements. Buddhism drew on the ancient Indian tradition of asceticism that antedated the *Vedas*, which had also incorporated it.[16] Jainism claimed to have even an earlier origin. The 24th Tirthankar Mahavir was roughly a contemporary of Lord Buddha—both preached sometime between 6th and 4th century BCE.[17] Buddhism agreed on the Vedic faith in the fundamentals of metaphysics and ethics, but "refused to acquiescence the Vedic ceremonialism".[18] They denied the existence of gods, denounced violence in sacrificial rites, rejected the caste hierarchy, and challenged Brahmin's superiority. In fact, in certain instances they also defied the temporal authority[19] of kings. They were indeed focused on the ways of reducing and coping with human sorrows and sufferings, but were not agreed to subscribe to metaphysical speculations about them.[20]

Brahmins used Sanskrit in performing *yajna* (religious ceremonies) and other religious rituals. Instead, Buddhists prescribed to follow the Noble Eightfold Path (road map)[21], and preached in common people's language, *Prakrit*. Further, in contrast to the inexplicable actions and objects involved in *yajna* and other rituals, the Noble Path consisted of straightforward acts of learning through direct experience or from right persons, renouncing sensuous pleasure, having compassion for others, speaking truth kindly and wisely without offending others, earning one's living by fair means, and so on. These required cultivating positive thoughts, attempting full mindfulness, driving out negative ideas, concentrating, contemplating, and meditating.

Similarly, Jainism focused on compassion believing that everything in the universe, such as plants, trees, birds, insects and animals, like human beings, live and breathe, and hence have to be treated with equality and equanimity. Human beings can be free from all sorrows and sufferings by following the path of right faith, knowledge, and conduct, which consisted of nonviolence, truthfulness, honesty, *Brahmacharya* (celibacy) and *aparigraha* (renunciation of material things), and detachment from people and places.[22]

State in a Proactive Mode to Competing Religions

For about 1,000 years (500 BCE to 500 CE) or more, Buddhism and Jainism, particularly Buddhism, competed with Brahminism[23] in order to gain royal patronage and people's acceptance. Initially, they had strong appeal to the people who were wary of the rituals of the *Brahmanas* (the orthodox treatise of *karma-kand*). Brahminism, as a result, was subdued till Kautilya, a Brahmin, was able to establish Chandra Gupta Maurya on the throne of Magadh (322 BCE), Brahminism got an opportunity to reclaim its lost ground. His book, *Arthashastra,* explicates how the State came to be controlled once again by the priestly class. But the next Emperor, Ashok (268 to 232 BCE), saw to it that Buddhism spread almost all over India as well as many countries outside India. Buddhism was at its peak in India during this period. Similarly many Hindu kings, like Ashok, became either Buddhist or Jain and promoted their religion. For example, Kanishk (127–163 CE) and Harsha (606 – 647 CE) got thousands *stupas,* monasteries, and *sarais* (resting places) constructed as well as sent monks to spread Buddhism from India through Central Asia to China. The Chinese traveller Hiuen Tsang found Buddhist monasteries all over Central Asia.[24] Indeed, there were Buddhist monasteries in Persia, Iraq, Mesopotamia, Khorasan, and right up to the frontiers of Syria.[25] Later on, the Pal kings developed Nalanda, Vikramashila, and many other places as seats of Buddhist learning. They got so many monasteries constructed that the area was known as Vihar (the present State of Bihar).

While the kings promoted the religion they belonged to or were converted into, they donated lavishly to both temples and monasteries. They also organized religious congregations for the scholars of different faiths to dialogue and debate (*shastrartha*). There had been a long tradition going back to the mythic King Janak to organize such *shastrarthas*. Emperor Ashok followed it.

Box 3.1: Emperor Ashoka Defined *Dhamma* (religion)

Dhamma was aimed at building up an attitude of mind in which social responsibility, the behaviour of one person towards another, was considered of great relevance. It was a plea for the recognition of the dignity of man, and for a humanistic spirit in the activities of society.[26]

This tradition of philosophical and religious encounters continued till the Emperor Harsha. Harsha was initially a Shaiva but later on was converted into Buddhism. He still used to attend the *Kumbha* at Prayag at every five years where he provided food to 1,00,000 needy persons every day. On this occasion, he used to distribute all the surplus of his treasury including gold, jewellery, silk, etc. He even gave away his crown and rich clothing and took from his sister, Rajashri, a used common garment to wear. Once converted into a Buddhist, he prohibited the use of animal food and killing of any living being. In honour of the Chinese pilgrim

Hiuen Tsang, he organized an assembly, which was attended by 20 kings, 1,000 scholars from the Nalanda University, 3,000 Buddhists of both Hinayan and Mahayan schools, 3,000 Brahmins and Jains. The Assembly went on continuously for 23 days.[27] Similarly, the Gupta-kings (320 CE to 540 CE) were the devotees of Vishnu, but one of them Kumar Gupta, was the one who established Nalanda University, which the Pal kings later on developed as a great centre of Mahayan Buddhist learning. Jainism had fewer chances of gaining royal patronage, and hence had less visible presence among the common mass. Further, Buddhism seemed to over-shadow it by prescribing 'middle path' and adopting a more assertive stance than Jainism, which was rather extreme in its views. "Jainism maintained itself as a 'parish' religion with more determination than Buddhism, and hence the number of its adherents has remained fairly constant".[28]

In sum, the supportive policies and practices of the State regarding the religions were directed to create a tolerant society and an intellectually invigorating environment for the growth of various philosophies.

Development through Empire Building

There were other areas of fast development steered by the State power during this classic period (500 BCE-500 CE, according to some from 700 BCE to 700 CE). Monarchies and republics started emerging in North India that "replaced traditional tribal patterns of governance with a system based on rules and regulations".[29] This initiated a chain of developments.[30] Land size in agriculture increased by clearing forests and claiming wastelands. The captives from a conquered State were deported en masse to work on the conqueror's land.[31] New settlements increased land revenue that enabled the king to raise larger armies, conquer more States, and extend his kingdom. Clearing of forests provided timber for building townships and also made available larger number of elephants for the armies. By that time, iron was available for better implements and weapons. The Maurya Empire (322 BCE-183 BCE) was able to set up centralized and stable administration and formalized taxation leading to faster urbanization and increasing industrial activities. Officers of the State were appointed on merit and were paid salaries. There were elaborate system of monitoring their performance, and so was a spies system to watch on the enemies of the State. Better roads were built for facilitating easy travel and trade. New dams and ponds improved irrigation and agricultural yields. The rivers provided access to sea ports for trades with distant lands. India had in the third century BCE extensive trading relationships with Persia, Mesopotamia, Egypt and in particular with Sumeria where there was a colony of Indian merchants.[32] The Maurya Empire created enormous wealth and achieved a high level of urbanization.

Guilds Driving Development

As back as the 4th century BCE, artisans and craftsmen started organizing themselves into guilds[33] for producing high-quality products both for sophisticated urban consumption as well as exports. Guilds grew as highly powerful organization by the Gupta period (320 CE to 540 CE).[34] There were guilds from highly specific work such as oil crushing, dyeing, and silk-weaving to the cooperatives of architects, engineers, stone-cutters, brick layers, carpenters, iron-smiths, and others who pooled their specialized knowledge for as complex enterprises as designing and building ships, temples, and even cities. Then, there were guilds of bankers, traders, and transport merchants. In fact, artisans and craftsmen of every specific set of skills were organized into guilds. Guilds had their own system of governance. Guilds of same craft elected representatives to a corporate like body that formulated laws for the functioning of the guilds. The State accepted the laws and in many instances provided financial support to the guilds. The guild leaders had not only economic power and resources, but also factual control over urban institutions. Besides creating enormous wealth, the guilds also helped advance science and technology. While Brahmin and Buddhist scholars created theoretical knowledge, guilds advanced applied knowledge and imparted training in engineering, mining, metallurgy, architecture, ocean-navigation, and so on.

As specialization of guilds increased, diverse occupations were distinctly recognizable requiring life-long cultivation of specific knowledge and skills. Children joined the guilds of their parents in order to acquire, carry on, and improve further the expertise from generation to generation. The members of a particular occupation were recognized by their birth. Thus, *jati*, which means 'birth', comes into being. It is *jati* that is considered to be equivalent to 'caste'.[35] There were as many *jatis* as occupations.[36] They were functionally specific and hence more useful than *varnas* for social transactions. Naturally, social norms consisting of dos and don't, food taboos, and endogamy got associated with *jati*.[37] Further, *jatis* were differentiated in terms of purity and pollution.[38] As the nomenclature of the *jati* was specific to a place, the peoples of similar occupation elsewhere were recognized by a different *jati* name. Thus *jatis* kept multiplying and proliferating. There was another source of proliferation. Expanding trade and commerce brought people of different origin in contact with each other. Then, there were immigrants and invaders who settled down in the country. Although they were distinctly different, they have to be accommodated in the community. Hence, they were recognized as sub-castes. Expansion of trades and commerce also provided scope for some of the *Shudras* (lowest in *varna* hierarchy) to take up the occupations of artisans, and thereby gain some upward mobilization.[39]

They all were still parts of the *varna* system. *Jatis* thus manifested differentiation in social stratification, while *varnas* provided a broad hierarchical integrative frame within which *jatis* compared, contrasted, and strived for upward mobilization in the social hierarchy. As more and more Vaishyas took up non-agricultural occupations, Shudras started cultivating land, and thereby improved their position in the caste hierarchy.

Vaishyas, despite their prosperity through guilds, were still lower with respect to Kshatriyas and Brahmins in the *varna* hierarchy. Many of them decided to bypass the superiority of Kshatriyas and Brahmins by embracing Buddhism; because "Buddhism and Jainism began as anti-ritualistic, intellectually oriented movements of self-inquiry which appealed precisely to those urban classes who were affluent, educated, and emancipated from magico-religious superstition".[40] They donated generously and helped Buddhists establish affluent monasteries. Their contributions were instrumental in reshaping caves and furnishing them with paintings such as Ajanta and Ellora, and enriching the centres of learning such as the Nalanda and Vikramshila universities. There was a nexus between them. Buddhist and Jain monasteries constituted nodal points on a far-flung trade system linking coastal cities to those in the interior.[41] They offered shelter to the merchants, who in return made generous donations.[42] Monasteries too at times served as bankers to the guilds and invested in their ventures. "In almost the entire expression of this age, whether architecture or sculpture, was centred on Buddhism and most of it was made possible through the patronage of wealthy merchants, guilds, and royal donations".[43]

Height of Development

From the Maurya to the Gupta period (322 BCE-540 CE) was, broadly speaking, the most developed period of the ancient India, particularly its second half, which is often called the classical or the golden period. "... it was a period of a vigorous national life, bubbling over with energy and spreading out in all directions. Culture developed into a rich civilization flowering out in philosophy, literature, drama, art, science, and mathematics. India's economy expanded, the Indian horizon widened, and other countries came within its scope.[44]

Guilds produced fine goods, particularly the various kinds of textiles such as silk, muslin, calico, linen, and wool for both domestic and international markets. International trade and commerce created immense wealth. "Indian ships were now regularly traversing the Arabian Sea, the Indian Ocean, and the China Sea, and were seen at every port in these areas".[45] Indian traders, Buddhist preachers, and colonizers went over to whole of the South East Asia, which was often referred as Greater India. Probably, "trade and commerce must be a supreme passion in India" and the spirit of "adventure and an urge for expansion" must be propelling Indians to seeking opportunities in distant lands.[46] Back home, "The prosperous urban dwellers lived in comfort and ease with a variety of luxuries in way of jewels and clothes"....there were disparities between urban, town, and village dwellers, but even the latter "were reasonably prosperous".[47]

There were a number of great centres of learning. Of them, Nalanda was the most famous attracting scholars from China, Japan, Tibet, Korea, Mongolia, Bokhara, and other places. It had a very comprehensive curriculum. Besides, Buddhist philosophy, it taught Vedic texts, architecture, medicines, agriculture, art, and so on. Other famous centres of Buddhist learning were Vikramashila and Taxila, while Kashi (now Varanasi) was the seat of Brahminical learning. Kashmir was a centre for both Buddhist and Brahminical learning. Bhallabhi in Kathiawar and Amaravati in the South were, among others, famous seats of learning.[48] There were masterpieces of arts and architecture, cave paintings, and well-established traditions of music and drama.

There existed highly stimulating intellectual milieu. Prolonged *shastrartha* between Brahmin and Buddhist scholars had led to the development of six orthodox and three heterodox schools of Indian philosophy.[49] Guilds fostered pioneering developments in science and technology. Mathematics interested both—scholars and guildsmen[50] leading to the concepts of zero, decimal system, position and values of numerals, and letters in algebra for unknown values and numerical order, etc. These proved to be the foundations of modern arithmetic and algebra.[51] Aryabhata made discoveries in astronomy that were ahead the time by centuries. For example, he measured the length of the solar year, posited that earth rotates on its axis, and showed, contrary to the religious superstition, that the shadow of the earth falling on the moon causes eclipse. Later Varahamihira distinguished astronomy and mathematics from astrology and horoscopy. Charak is called the father of medicine and his *Samhita* was a classic compilation of medical encyclopaedias and pharmacopoeias. On the other hand, Sushruta was the father of surgery and he compiled his findings in the book *Sushruta-Samhita*.

There were other classics. For example, Panini was a Sanskrit grammarian who gave a comprehensive and scientific theory of phonetics, phonology, and morphology. His major work was *Astadhyayi*. Patanjali's *Yog Sutra* laid the foundation of yoga that is still followed all over the world (of course with modifications). Vatsyayan's *Kaamsutra* is still the most extensive treatise on love making. Bharat's *Natyashastra* initiated a tradition in drama. In literature, *Shakuntala* and *Meghaduta* of Kalidas are still considered to be superb. Manu's *Dharmashastra*, a comprehensive work on social codes of conduct was composed during this period, besides numerous other commentaries on the ancient texts and scriptures as well as popular writings like *Panchatantra*.

In sum, "Age of India and the writings of that period ... revealed a serenity, a quiet confidence of the people in themselves, and a glow of pride of being privileged to be alive in that high moon of civilization, and with it the urge to use their great intellectual and artistic powers to the utmost".[52] This was made possible by the proactive royal patronage to both religion and guilds, which competed with each other for excellence.

SEEDS OF THE DECAYING PROCESS

The process of decay started while the country was at its height of development: "... an inner weakness seemed to have seized India, which affected not only her political status but her creative activities.... all these [achievements] appeared to be the afternoon of a civilization; the glow of the morning had long faded away, the high noon was past....The sense of curiosity and the spirit of mental adventure gave way to a hard and formal logic and sterile dialectic...." There was "...drying up and losing her [India's] creative genius and creativity.[53]

Radhakrishnan attributed this decay to the loss of political freedom. But the political freedom was lost to the Islamic invasions much later, while, as Nehru suspected, the process of decay started much earlier. There was no sudden, sharp, or dramatic collapse. The process was slow and invisible for the first five hundred years of this glorious period. The powerful Gupta kings were able to keep the development edifice raising high and shining in almost all spheres of national life, and lastly Harsha was able to cover up the decaying process by maintaining the superstructure in an apparently good state, and the South carried it on for another 500 years. But all such efforts eventually succumbed and the edifice of high Indian civilization started collapsing primarily because of inner corrosion even before the onslaught of Islamic invasions starting from the 8rth century CE.

What were the dynamics that were corroding the foundations of this edifice and forced the final collapse?

Radhakrishnan was partly right; the cause was primarily political, though not exactly the loss of political freedom. It was the self-centred existential politics of the fragmenting States beginning from the post-Maurya period that set in the decay process—even while the country was manifestly riding high on the trajectory of development. The signs and symptoms were not noticeable till the end of the Gupta period, but got conspicuous by the end of Harsha's regime.

As the highly efficient and centralized Maurya Empire

collapsed, smaller kingdoms became independent. There were local chieftains, who were now free from the empirical control, nursed an ambition to become a sovereign power. Similarly, the chiefs of foreign invaders and immigrants who settled down in India sought a royal status. All three—the small kings, chieftains, and invading and immigrating rulers—wanted to be sanctified as kings having the divine right to rule. They bargained with Brahmins, and Brahmins returned the favour. They sensed this as an opportunity to reclaim the ground they had lost to the Buddhists during the reign of Emperor Ashoka.

Brahmins had the opportunity and privilege to oblige the king-aspirants. Brahmins claimed to be the inheritors of the Aryan tradition, had the monopoly of the religio-spiritual knowledge[54] and were the custodians of Sanskrit. They had the cultural competence and the habit to accept local traditions and cults in order to adapt with the demands of the time. They had already assimilated, as stated earlier, the some of the religious ideas and symbols of the Indus valley civilization. They were already claiming that Buddhism did not have anything new—all their ideas were drawn from the Vedas and the Upanishads. They were now able to accommodate image worshiping, Krishna-cult, and tantric elements with their orthodox beliefs. In short, "Brahmins orthodoxy had the capacity to adjust itself to this formidable range of religious expression in order to maintain its position. This it did most successfully... when a cult or sect became popular; it was gradually made respectable by being included at some level in the orthodox hierarchy".[55]

Because of this assimilating mindset, Brahmins already had accepted the Greek and other invading and immigrating tribes into the *varna* system. Now they started assimilating the Sakas, Kushans, later on Huns, and the other tribes which came along with Huns, by assigning them, depending on their skills and specialities, to sub-castes under the *varna* system. The presence of so many different castes and sub-castes necessitated to define codes of conduct to regulate their social transactions and inter-caste relationships. The *Manusmriti*—a *dharmashastra* (a compendium of moral laws and principles) was composed in the first or second century CE. It prescribed detailed norms for different castes and the nature of sanctions for their transgressions, which were highly favourable to Brahmins and Kshatriyas and horribly biased against others, although some believed that the *Manusmriti* provided "models rather than descriptions";[56] that is, the ideals rather than what actually were practiced. Others have suspected that the highly discriminatory and contradictory verses were interpolated later into the *Manusmriti* when the Brahmincal order prevailed over the society.

The most critical, however, was the privilege of the Brahmins to anoint a person as a king that placed them in a more advantaged position than the Buddhists. Buddhists did not believe in the divine origin or right of kings. A king, according to Buddhism, had a contractual role to his subjects[57] and the ceremonies by which he attained a royal status were elaborate donative in nature entailing gifts to Buddhist monks and the installation of a symbolic Buddha in a stupa.[58] It was only a Brahmin priest who had from the ancient time the authority to anoint a person as a king before his subjects accepted him in a god image. Brahmins now refurnished this tradition employing very elaborate rituals for consecration that culminated in *ashwamedha* (horse sacrifices) *yagna* sanctifying the king of his suzerainty over his kingdom. Further, in order to inflate the royal status of the newly anointed kings, they gave them the titles that were apparently exaggerations. Even those ruling over a small territory were given the titles of *Maharaja* (Great King), *Maharajadhiraj* (Great Emperor), *Prithwipati* (King of the whole earth), or *Chakravarti* (World-conquering). The Saka, Kushan, and later on Hun rulers, among similar other invader-chiefs or their sons, were given Sanskrit names and were "crowned according to the traditional rites meant for Kshatriyas".[59] They were titled as *Devaputra* (Son of God) and *Dharmika* (Spiritualist). Brahmins had in their belief system the epic characters of Rama and Krishna as the human kings incarnation of God Vishnu. The same god images of Shiva and Vishnu were evoked and attributed directly or indirectly to the new kings. They were addressed as gods in human form and were conferred the titles of *Maheshvara* (Great God) and *Survaloka Ishwara* (Universal God)—even superior to the gods. And, in other instances, were made to appear that they inherited the essential qualities of divine origin.

In bargain against this over-driven royalization, Brahmins received the royal patronage and the grants of land to own. When the king was a Brahmin or an invader turned into Shaiva, royal patronage to Brahmins was assured. For example, a Brahmin,

Pushyamitra, who ended the Maurya Empire by usurping the throne of Magadh, was bent upon to undo what Ashoka had done for Buddhism. He strictly re-established Brahminical order, and probably massacred a large number of Buddhists in his attempt to drive Buddhism out of his kingdom. The son of the Hun invader, Toraman, Mihirkula turned into a Shaiva, and violently promoted Brahminical order by demolishing Buddhist monasteries and killing people and devastating towns and cities. Later on in the South, the Pallava King, Mahendra-Varman (630 CE), and other kings, who were either Jain or Buddhist, renounced their faith, became Shaiva, and even prosecuted Buddhists and Jains by way of promoting Brahminism. On the other hand, Harsha, who was a Shaiva and got converted into Mahayan Buddhism, did not oppress Brahmins. Lord Shiva had evolved from the Vedic god Rudra[60] who symbolized thunder, that is, power and potency. Therefore, Lord Shiva attracted the aggressive kings more than Lord Vishnu, whose human forms, Rama and Krishna, were potent, but not unnecessarily violent or oppressive.

The intolerant kings, however, were not the only factor for accelerating the decaying process in the Indian society and civilization. It was the land grants in the context of fragmenting States that was the chief culprit. There was indeed a long established tradition to grant land to Brahmins. The *Anusasana Parva* of the *Mahabharata* devoted a whole chapter to the praise of making gifts of land. *Manusmriti* and *Purans* also prescribed it. The ancient Nalanda University was financed by the revenues collected from about 100 to 200 gifted villages.[61] "The temple of Somnath was endowed with more than 10,000 villages".[62] However, in all such grants, lands were granted as charity and royal generosity for promoting religious and scholarly activities. Grants were limited to revenue collection for generating resources to promote collective good. Now grants were part of an exchange of favours between the newly anointed kings and the anointing Brahmins. This was a shift not only from religious to secular nature of grants, but also from a religious call to reciprocating favours. It had profound implications for the centuries to come. The grantees had not only power to collect taxes, but also to control, punish, and reward the people living on the land. The grantees turned from priests to landlords—a miniature of small kings having autonomy to rule over the land.

Not only lands were granted to Brahmins, but they were also granted to the military officers in lieu of their salaries or to those who had provided special services to the king. They were called *samants*. During the Gupta period, the institution of *samants* came into prominence, although the making of *samants* started during the Maurya period.[63] *Samants* too had the autonomy to rule over the people on their land. Then, there were the small kings who were subjugated by a more powerful king or emperor, but were reinstated to rule over their territory on the condition that they would pay tributes. There were also others who yielded to the suzerainty of the king by paying tributes. They too were called *samantas*. The more powerful among them ruling over larger territory were called *Maha-Samants* and the largest among them were designated as *Maha-Samant-Raja* (king)[64]. A cluster of *samants* of varying sizes was called the *Samants-Chakra* (Circle of *Samantas*). Harsha brought them into the control of his empire by allocating them hierarchical positions in his court.

From the Gupta period to the early medieval period of Harsha and increasingly thereafter, a large part of the country was ruled by a variety of landlords, *Samants,* and small kings restricting the direct control of the emperor over the territory and constraining his writ over the people. They subordinated to the emperor (if any one of them emerged as such), but not quite full-heartedly. The kings and particularly *samants* probably remembered that earlier, according to the *Arthshastra,* the *samants* were independent kings neighbouring the Maurya Empire. They were free to replicate the pattern of governance of an emperor by having the autonomy, a court and courtiers, land grantees, but most important, an ambition to conquer over neighbouring territories in order to emerge as an overlord of larger territory. They indeed rallied behind the Guptas and Harsha to fight against the Huns, but more often they fought among themselves for either survival or supremacy or both. "The possession of kingdoms was a precarious business and the competition for territory a perpetual activity".[65] So, when later on, the Rajputs came into prominence in the western India, they fought each other unceasingly till they were subdued by the Islamic rulers.

The Guptas, for example, were probably "wealthy landowners who gradually gained political power..." to form the empire and assume the title of *Maharajadhiraja* (the great king of kings), although the two successive Guptas directly controlled only the Ganges valley while the *samantas* and kings from the neighbouring territories paid only tributes.[66] Only after the successive emperors pushed backed the Huns, defeated other kings, married in the family of a powerful king of Deccan that the empire could be extended to the whole of northern India.

The Gupta kings were probably a model to emulate by other kings, *samantas*, and landlords, not only in expanding their regime, but also in running the State in the Brahminical order. The Guptas fully followed the injunctions of the *Manusmriti,* had Brahmin ministers and advisers, and performed religious rites and rituals including *ashwamedha* (horse sacrifice) *yajna.* They were ardent devotees of Lord Vishnu and were also attracted to the devotional tradition (*bhakti marg*). Combining the two they entertained an "ideology of kingship" which was drawn from the epics; *Ramayan* and *Mahabharata.*[67] However, they did not think that they were, like Rama and Krishna, incarnations of Lord Vishnu; they only drew their divine rights to rule from them. But, the *Vishnu Purana* and the *Markandeya Purana* entitled them as *Paramesvara* (Supreme God)—a sure instance of how Brahmins ingratiated the kings.

Unsettling Polity and Expansive Brahminism

The post-*Gupta* political milieu got increasingly turbulent and inimical to development. Economy was already weakened by the frequent wars with the Huns. Once the Huns occupied Western India, the trade with Africa and Europe was blocked shifting the prosperity to the South, which still maintained trades and commerce with the South East Asia for another 500 years or so. Thereafter, they too collapsed like the North. Small kingdoms kept on fighting endlessly with each other. National perspective was lost to parochial outlooks and existential compulsions. Harsha did restore a seemingly well-knit empire by his military campaigns to whole of North India, personal charisma, vigilance and surveillance through extensive travelling, and wide ranging welfare measures. However, the empire was actually sitting over badly fragmented States—apparently subdued but intentionally hostile to each other. Soon after Harsha, the animosities burst open into fights for survival and superiority that ushered the North into an unsettled polity till the end of the early medieval period (around 1200 CE).

The unsettled political milieu caused uncertainties and insecurity where the dominant anxiety was self-preservation. It was not confined to the top players such as kings, *samants,* and landlords, but percolated down to the common people. With a change in suzerainty, the rest of the set-up and the society were shaken up too. Earlier the common people were required to pay one tax to the State, irrespective of who held the throne. But "with the increase in the number of intermediaries, the variety of taxes, in addition to land tax, were imposed"[68] and the money thus collected were not invested in either farms or crafts or public causes, but were used for conspicuous consumption. The people were getting impoverished, oppressed, insecure, anxious, and helpless, because of the fighting among kings, *Samants,* and lords. All – kings-to-commoners were looking for a source for solace and assurance.

Brahmins offered to be the saviours to all of them. The strong royal patronage by the Gupta emperors had already put them in a dominant position compared to Buddhists. Because of their command on cosmogony and cosmology, astrology and horoscope, religion and philosophy, Upanishads and Brahmanas, epics, and so on, they claimed to be able to know people's past, interpret their present, and not only predict their future, but also to reconstruct it. They prescribed rites and rituals, *vrat* (fasting accompanied by ascetic practices), celebrations, and *yajna* for all major life events ranging from birth through marriage to death in order to ensure material prosperity, happy life, and a sure berth in heaven. There were norms prescribed for daily routines and social transactions contingent on the stages in one's life and the castes within the *varna* hierarchy. As a result, castes cleavages were petrified. Transgressions by people of different kinds and seriousness were said to cause distressful events in life, their regression in re-birth as animals or insects, or a fall in the hell. Brahmins claimed to know what take people either to a hell or heaven. After putting people in such a predicament, Brahmins were ready with remedial measures that people could undertake with the assistance of Brahmins or Brahmins performed them on their behalf. All misfortunes as well as fortunes were interpreted not only in terms of previous conducts, but were traced to the past lives as well as the impact of the specific constellations of stars and planets. The people would not know, but must trust Brahmins to find out and rectify the misfortune and help them attain prosperity and well-being. There were auspicious time, place, and procedure for all major and minor decisions and actions and inauspicious ones to avoid, even if an invasion was looming on the boarder or an urgent matter needed immediate attention. Brahmins were to be consulted on all occasions and followed strictly. Of course, a few were likely to default, digress, and indulge in things that were considered to be sins. But then the must solicit Brahmin's assistance for penances and elaborate redemptive rituals and *pooja* with the help of Brahmins.

In sum, every bit of people's life was said to be determined by the forces on which the people had no control, but can be regulated if the people undertook redemptive measures either assisted or performed by Brahmins on their behalf. Kings as well as commoners were dependent on their destiny that only Brahmins, in communion with gods, were said to be able to improve or reshape.

These favours, however, were not free. There was a fee (*daan* & *dakshina*) in cash and kind for every bit of assistance, prescription, and proxy performance by Brahmins. The fees varied and were given directly or in a variety of ways depending on, how serious was the plight of a person, how pliable he was, and what was his capacity to pay, which was often stretched to the maximum.

Such a total hold over the life-events of kings-to-commoners was based on an impeccable credibility of Brahmins and unquestioned faith of the people in the Vedic religion, its texts, and scriptures that the Brahmins evoked in dealing with people. The texts and scriptures were composed orally over centuries. There was a strong tradition of annotations, commentaries on them, and commentaries on commentaries involving an intricate web of argumentations, disputations, logical sophistications, and interpolations.[69] This classical tradition continued. However, Brahmins needed an encompassing religious literature that could narrate the classical literature in such ways that people could accept them readily The *Purans* were composed for such a purpose. The *Purans* were in the making from the ancient time[70], but from the 4rth century CE onward they were composed and re-composed several times by different scholars addressing to anything and everything in the universe, "weaving and integrating the diverse beliefs from ritualistic rites of passage to *Vedantic* philosophy, from fictional legends to factual history, from individual introspective yoga to social celebratory festivals, from temples to pilgrimage, from one god to another, from goddesses to *tantra*, from the old to the new".[71] They included diverse topics such as the origin and description of the universe, genealogies of gods, goddesses, kings, heroes, sages, and demigods, folk tales, pilgrimages, temples, medicine, astronomy, grammar, mineralogy, humour, eroticism, love stories, as well as theology and philosophy. They were not free of evils either.[72]

Pauranic Brahminism invariably traced the sources of all *Purans* to the Vedas, Upanishads, Brahmanas, and so on in order to assert their divine origin. However, they incorporated local deities, took local priests in their fold, accommodated totems and taboos of people, sanctified cultish traditions, accommodated tribes and groups of people into *varna*-system, and adopted a down-to-earth populist stance for preaching a mass religion. In the process, they created millions of gods and goddesses, of whom the trinity—Brahma, Vishnu, and Mahesh—was recognized as the primary ones. Lord Vishnu was believed to pervade all connoting that Vishnu is "one who is everything and inside everything",[73] and hence could take any form—as varied as a fish, tortoise, boar, half lion, and human beings in forms of a dwarf, a sage, and kings. King Rama and King Krishna were the incarnations of Lord Vishnu. The Krishna cult led the growth of devotional approach (*bhakti marg*) that popularized *Vaishanism* among kings as well as commoners, particularly from the lower castes. Shiva evolved from the Vedic god Rudra and the Tamil god, Murugan.[74] Lord Buddha was claimed to the 9th incarnation of the god Vishnu[75] who preached a variant of the ideas of Upanishads and aimed to cleanse the religion of its unacceptable practices (for example, animal sacrifices). In the process, Brahmins created vast and varied mythology that provided models of behaviours to be emulated and avoided, ideals to aspire and mundane to live with, dilemmas to resolve, and so on—all dependent on the Brahminic worldview that hinged on following Brahminic dictates and paying Brahmins in return for the prosperity and well-being.

It was this expansive and inclusive Brahminism that moved to the South India from the 4th century CE and grew more and more dominant after the 6th century onwards.[76] It replaced Buddhism and Jainism, which were the earliest religions, particularly in the Tamil part of the South. Brahminism absorbed local traditions and religious practices into their own. Local deities were incorporated into the galaxy of Brahminic gods and goddesses by fabricating stories and parables. They were believed to "to represent the multiple facets of the same god or else were supposed to denote different forms and appellations by which the god came to be known and worshipped. Thus, while Vishnu came to subsume the cults Narayana, Jagannatha, Venkateswara, and many others, Shiva became identified with countless local cults by the sheer suffixing of Isa or Isvara to the name of the local deity, e.g., Bhutesvara, Hatakesvara, Chandesvara"[77]. On the other hand, new gods such as Ganesha (elephant-headed god) and Hanuman (monkey god) were incorporated into the *Pauranic* gods, the former as a son of god Shiva and the latter as a god dedicated to serve Lord Rama.[78]

Interestingly, the temple complex that evolved in the South grew out of the images and structure of the kingship, and in turn reinforced king's divine and temporal authority over his subjects.[79] There were three tiers of deities. Shiva and Vishnu were the pan-Indian supreme gods. They were viewed, like kings, as the ruling gods. Then, there were family gods of the *Samants* and powerful chiefs. Finally, there were village gods. The word, temple, in Tamil also means palace. So, the temple was the palace of Shiva and Vishnu where the god was believed to hold a court surrounded by the deities of the second tier. The gods of the powerful families were superiors to the village gods. They all had to rally around the supreme god during festivals, just as the village chiefs were also required occasionally to attend the royal court.

Priests were the administrators who were acting on behalf of the god. They blessed and honoured kings and commoners, rich and poor, men and women who worshiped at the temple and donated whatever they could: Land, produces, money, and jewels. Some, generally poor, dedicated their girl child to the god through a marriage like ceremony. She was called a *devadaasi* (servant of god), who sang and danced in the temple. The more valuable and frequent were the donations, the more privileges were granted to the donors during the worships and greater was their recognition and respect in the community. Kings lavished wealth on the temple.

The big donors such as *Samants* and rich landlords shared the god's sovereignty in the same way as did those who presented valuable gifts to a king. Donors to a temple competed with each other, as courtiers did, in making donations and thereby gaining power and privileges in the society.

Thus, there was a close correspondence between the religious and royal practices, values, and ideologies. Quite often the kings' temples were also palaces where royal business was conducted and royal rituals were enacted. As a result, royal capitals were also temple cities. They were not only sacred places for the royal deity, but also the place where the kings lived. For example, the Chola and Pandya kings developed Chidambaram and Madurai (respectively) as the capital cities. The close proximity, both physical and symbolic, enhanced the divine and temporal authority of the king as well as the power and status of the Brahmin priests. The less powerful kings upgraded their guardian deities into the *avatars* of either Vishnu or Shiva in order to upgrade their own power and position. Similarly, Brahmins kept on elaborating the temple rituals of worship and accumulating more and more wealth in order to make the temples more impressive. Pooja was to be performed three to six times a day, besides there were elaborate ones for special occasions, and for the expiration of sins, alleviation of natural calamities or crisis, or blessing of powerful persons. These rites and rituals got increasingly more elaborate and expensive enhancing Brahmin's grip on the life of people.

Brahminism in both—the North and the South—assumed an overwhelming influence on the life events of all, kings-to-commoners, by claiming to have the capabilities to help them out of all exigencies and ensure them prosperity and wellbeing. They started regulating more and more aspects of public life, administered caste-based codes of conduct, controlled all local economic production and much of its distribution, and transfer of property.[80] All these were for a fee that they called *daan and dakshina* (donations) in cash and kind. The payment was sanctified by relating it to an ancient institution of *Daan* (giving away valuable resources) emanating from the Vedic civilization.

In the exchange-oriented worldview of the West, giving away valuable resources to someone is supposed to oblige the recipient who must reciprocate at the earliest and in equal value lest he remains indebted[81] losing his status in comparison to the donor.

But not in the ancient Indian tradition, where *daan* was believed to give an opportunity to the donor to discharge his *dharma* (duties) in addition to the tangible and intangible gains that he is likely to get. It is the recipient, Brahmin, who obliges the donor. The Taittiriya Upanishad, for example, proclaimed that "The offering (*daan*) should be with honour ... should be plenty ... with modesty ... with awe ... with sympathy".[82]

Brahmins evoked this tradition in glorifying the acts of giving *daan*. Indian mythology, particularly the *Purans*, was full of the episodes of giving, justifying, and celebrating *daans* on all important occasions. For example, the sage Dadhichi gave his bones to Lord Indra so that Indra could make *vajra* (thunder) to kill the demon Vritrasura. King Shivi cut off his limbs piece by piece and offered them to a falcon in exchange for life to a pigeon who sought his protection from the falcon. Brahmins, however, stretched the compulsion to give *daan* to the extreme. The *Garuda Purana*, for example, showed the greedy priests exploiting the grief of a mourning family by fabricating stories about how the family's *daan* to them would be transferred to the deceased in heaven, while failing to do so would land the deceased into the hell. Further, the family of a diseased must donate a cow so that the diseased can hold the tail of the cow and cross over the river Vaitarani into the heaven lest the diseased get stuck in the hell.

Concern for *daan and dakshina* probably tilted the balance of favour more towards men over women, higher castes over the lower castes, and the privileged over the commoner. These discriminations were there from the early period, but seemed like accentuated lately. The *Manusmriti* (probably partly due to interpolations) and the *Purans* manifested highly discriminatory and contradictory prescriptions. Punishments for the transgressions of lower castes were unreasonably harsher than that of Brahmins and Kshatriyas. The pronouncements that "women must be honoured and adorned", and "where women are revered, there the gods rejoice; but where they are not, no sacred rite bears any fruit" now had to coexist with the prescriptions that "a woman must never seek to live independently" and that she must obey father as a child, husband as a wife, and mother as a widow.[83] Further, a wife should listen, obey and worship her husband, irrespective of howsoever unworthy and unfaithful he might be.[84] A girl should be married between the age of four to ten, before she reach puberty, or a man should marry a girl one third of his age.[85] And, when her husband died, she should jump into his pyre become a Sati—a goddess!

Goddess Sati did jump into fire and self-immolated, but not because her husband, Shiva, was dead, but because he was humiliated by her father Daksha. However, Brahmins were able to twist the mythic story to make it like a pious duty of a wife to die with her husband.[86] There was no mention of the *sati-pratha* (practice) in any of the ancient texts such as Vedas, Upanishads, Brahmanas, *Aranyakas,* or *Manusmriti*[87]. It appeared first time after the 4rth century CE[88]. The *Purans* prescribed it repeatedly. For example,

> When a woman's husband has died, she should either practice ascetic celibacy or ascend (the funeral pyre) after him.[89]
> A wife who dies in the company of her husband shall remain in heaven as many years as there are hairs on her person.[90]

There were other numerous instances where contradictory prescriptions were made or deviations from a norm were accepted expediently. For example, Lord Shiva was an ascetic god, but the *Shiva Purana* contained vivid descriptions of his erotic conducts.[91] Further, let us compare the following two views in the *Manusmriti*:

> Those who permit slaying of animals; those who bring animals for slaughter; those who slaughter; those who sell meat; those who purchase meat; those who prepare dish out of it; those who serve that meat and those who eat are all murderers[92], and
> There is no fault in eating meat, in drinking liquor, or in having sex; that is the natural activity of creatures. Abstaining from such activity, however, brings great rewards.[93]

Lord Krishna in the *Bhagavad Gita* highlighted the importance of *jnana marg* (through knowing), then considered *karm marg* (doing one's duties dispassionately) superior, and finally favoured the *bhakti marg* (devotional approach) asking, "Fill thy mind with Me, be My devotee, sacrifice unto Me, bow down to Me; thus having made thy heart steadfast in Me, taking Me as the Supreme Goal, thou shalt come to Me".[94] The three ways to realize the Supreme, despite their differential salience, were to coexist.[95] But, later on, the *Bhagavata Purana* tilted the balance to the *bhakti marg*. "The practice of yoga, *jñàna*, living in *dharma*, prayer or ascetic renunciation—none of them—is as successful in obtaining me as is the daily increase in loving devotion".[96] These are just a few examples. Indian mythology is replete with contradictions.

INTEGRATIVE THOUGHTS

The religious texts during the early medieval period were full of diverse, discrepant and contradictory beliefs, norms, and practices. Coexistence of such contradictory ideas, however, was not new in the history of Indian thought. The origin was rooted into the *Rig Veda* that held a pluralistic worldview soliciting different ways to approach the Supreme Being (Ultimate Reality). Combined with the oral tradition for transmitting the texts and scriptures over generations, the worldview caused numerous interpolations that only now are being distinguished from the original. Although interpolations were a regular feature from the ancient time, the intentions behind the interpolations were likely to vary across different time periods. It is difficult to distinguish the intentions behind the interpolations made earlier from those that were made later during the *Puranic* period. However, we may assume that the changing worldview as a result of unsettling socio-economic-political milieu affected the mindset of the scholars to see and interpret the religious texts differently, which then led to the kind of interpolations that they made in the religious texts. As the scholars neither mentioned their names nor the time of recomposing the texts,[97] the interpolations remained indistinguishable in the texts for the rest of the period.

The hunch is that the earlier interpolations might have been rather inadvertent as a result of scholars' intention to understand the deeper significance of the texts. The latter interpolations in the texts (such as *Bhagvad Gita, Mahabharata, Yog-Sutra, Manusmriti,* etc.) were probably caused by the mindset that also composed and recomposed the *Purans*. *Puranic* literature was distinctly different from the earlier texts and scriptures. The mindset was driven by the claim that Brahmins knew everything in the universe including the people in it and could communicate with the divine and regulate the supernatural forces to change the destiny of the people. The *Paurans*, while referring to the Vedas, Upanisads, and Brahmanas as their original sources, were quite down to earth in creating a mythology that equipped Brahmins to act as the path-finders of the people stricken by the state of scarcity, oppression, insecurity, and anxiety arising out of the unsettling economic and political conditions.

Instead of enabling the people to confront their problems directly and cultivate capabilities to solve them, Brahmins put them on the mercy of supernatural forces (gods and goddesses, planets and stars, and the destiny) on which the people had no control. They depended on Brahmins to play the via-media and regulate those forces on their behalf. Brahmins suggested ways and means by referring them to the *Pauranic* mythology and prescribing them chanting prayers, reciting *mantras*, undertaking *vrat*, and conducting *pooja* and *yagya* even for the mundane issues such as getting cured of a serious illness or escaping from death, getting out of extreme poverty and scarcity, achieving success in whatever people fantasized or endeavour, selecting marriage partner, undertaking a voyage, and so on.

The mythology was replete with the stories that backed what Brahmins made people to believe and practice. Let me cite just a few examples. An elephant was caught by a crocodile that was pulling it into the water. The elephant was resisting with its full force and yet was losing to the crocodile. It fought hard for a while, and then it gave up completely and helplessly called god Narayan. He rushed to rescue it. The message was that it is useless to fight against an adversary, and wiser to submit to a god. A whole life sinner, Ajamil, called and called his son, Narayan, at the time of his death, but god Narayan thought that he was helplessly calling Him and came rushing to take him to heaven. Savitri extracted his dead husband from the jaws of Yamaraj (death god) because she had performed a particular difficult *vrat*. Eclipses were believed to be caused by Rahu and Ketu grabbing sun and moon, the grief of which people were prescribed to share by conducting themselves in specifically restricted ways, lest they get into untoward problems.

The result was that people lost their capacity to think rationally and act forcefully to cope with exigencies. They lost their agency, self-confidence, "creative genius" and "creativity.[98] They got burdened with heaps of superstitions, taboos, restrictive practices, and social evils such as girl child marriage, *sati pratha,* discrimination of women, lower castes, untouchables, and *devadasi pratha*[99] (in the South).

Such a crippling condition was created despite the glorious legacy of advance technology, pioneering scientific knowledge, sophisticated schools of philosophical thoughts, and deep concern for spiritual realization. Even Adi Shankaracharya (788-820 AD) could not reverse the downslide of the mindset. Adi Shankaracharya was a charismatic religious leader. He integrated the essential ideas of Upanishads, *Brahma Sutra,* Buddhism, and other texts into the philosophy of *Advaita Vedanta,* which was a module for individual's inner development of the highest order.[100] However, it had hardly any effective drivers for getting people out of their quagmire. Rather, he preferred to preach for the *bhakti marg* (devotional path) in order for the people to get solace by being emotionally and passionately devoted to Shiva, Vishnu, Ganesh, Surya, and Devi. *Bhakti marg* was surely a solace to aggrieved people, but certainly caused excessive dependency on powerful others. Further, Adi Shankaracharya, taking cues from Buddhism, established four *mathas* (monasteries) at the four corners of the country so that people could pilgrimage to them and get integrated religiously that hardly helped them to think and act proactively.

Neither Jainism nor Buddhism was able to rescue the people from their morass. Both were fragmented into the orthodox and unorthodox streams. The extreme asceticism of Jainism precluded its potential for initiating any mass movement for development against Brahminism. Buddhists had also withdrawn from direct and daily interactions with the people. Their monasteries had accumulated substantial wealth and the ownership of large tracts of arable land where the monks lived comfortably. They did not have to go out daily and get alms for living. They had sufficient time to devote to refinement of their philosophical ideas and ascetic idealism that turned them as elites, but alienated from the people. This collective withdrawal not only constrained them from rescuing people from the clutches of Brahminism but also resulted into their collapse in India.[101]

In sum, the fragmented State politics welcomed Brahminism to exert overwhelming power and influence on the life of the kings-to-commoners. As a result, Brahminism over-grew and framed itself into a highly ritualistic, dogmatic, and *daan-dakshina* oriented religion that sapped people's energy and destroyed their capabilities to confront problems, think rationally, and act forcefully to steer through the difficult time. People were crippled by blind superstitions, restrictive habits and practices, and numerous social evils, which weakened them internally to Islamic assaults.

ISLAMIC IMPACT

Islamic invasions and rules changed the political, religious, and social landscape of the country adversely impacting its development.[102] Islam and State power were combined closely in assaulting Hinduism and Buddhism. Like Brahmins in Gupta and Rajput courts, Ulemas were enormously influential in Muslim regimes. They advised the rulers to follow *Shariat* in their administration, discharged judicial roles as Qazis, and also defined what Muslim masses must believe, practice, dress and, appear in public. Following *Quran,*[103] they preached the masses to obey the God, the Prophet, and the even the oppressive rulers. Then, there were luxury-seeking Sufi Mashaikhs close to the rulers who, besides engaging in devotional music, often flattered, lived in luxury, and enjoyed the favour of the rulers. Some of them were opportunists like Amir Kusaro,[104] "who changed with changing time and turned with shifting wind".[105] However, there were exceptions. Pious Ulemas and Sufi saints, for example, lived in poverty. A few rulers ignored Ulemas and were more accommodative to Hindu nobles and religious practices. Akbar (1542-1605) and Jahangir (1605-1627), particularly Akbar was very considerate. He appointed Rajput chieftains on important positions and disallowed *Jiziya* and other discriminative practices. His new religion, *Din Ilahi,* drew from Islam, Buddhism, Hinduism and other religious thoughts and aimed at unifying Hindus and Muslims into an integrative national community. *Din Ilahi* in fact was a socio-religious association of like-minded intellectuals and saints, but unfortunately, it could not get deep into the people's mind and disappeared with Akbar. Throughout the medieval period, it was the State and Islam that combined together to reign over the people (except during the Maratha Empire, 1674 – 1818

CE, when the Brahmin Peshawas fostered Hindu traditions and practices).

The people were not only reigned over, but were also victimized. Buddhists had already been victimized by Rajput kings. As their monasteries were demolished by the Muslim invaders and rulers, they fled into Nepal and Tibet resulting into the disappearance of Buddhism from India. Hinduism was on its back foot. Some Rajput kings gave their daughter in marriage to a Muslim king in order to retain their kingship. Some caste Hindus indeed got converted to get lucrative positions. Many lower castes feeling dejected by the higher castes' discrimination and artisans, and craftsmen who were dependent for their livelihood on the Muslim nobles also accepted. Islam But the majority of Hindus did not convert as religion was an inextricable part of their lifestyle. "The fact that they [the converts] remained in minority indicated that the majority of Hindus were not so desperate to get converted".[106]

However, they indeed were struggling for their existence by resorting to three defence mechanisms. First, there were efforts to establish a unified philosophy of Hinduism that could stand in face of Islam and thereby sustain Hindu's belief in their cultural superiority. There was already an ancient in-built tendency in the Hindu thought of "blurring of philosophical distinctions"[107] and accommodating new religious practices. During the earlier medieval period, Adi Shankaracharya, for example, integrated thoughts from many sources ranging from the Vedas, Upanishads, Buddhism and preached *bhakti-marg*. This trend continued by the medieval philosophers. It was particularly accentuated by the presence of Islam. Contrasting with Muslims, Hindu philosophers and scholars were "self-defining Hinduism"[108] by synthesizing the various schools of Indian philosophy into a coherent worldview without sacrificing the complexity of Hindu's divergent views and numerous deities.[109] Hindu worldview was shown to be much more elaborate and encompassing than the simplistic worldview of Islam. However, this was an exercise by the elite Hindu thinkers, which was hardly tangible enough for the Hindu masses with a sinking feeling to hold on and remain floating.

So, the second defensive measure was to hang on the heaps of superstitions, religious rituals, rigid caste hierarchy and other social evils, which Brahmins had already provided since the Gupta period. They were now the defining characteristics of being Hindus in contrast to Muslims who did not subscribe to caste hierarchy, idolatry, or most of the other religious beliefs and practices of Hindus. Hindus clung to them desperately. *Sati Pratha* (wife burning on the pyre of her husband), child marriage, and *Devadaasi Pratha* (girls dedicated to a temple), which were prescribed earlier, were now practiced more widely.[110] Hindu girls and women were protected from the evil eyes of Muslims by putting them in *purda* (veil) and discouraging them from going outside the house. However, the regressive beliefs and practices were not strong enough shielding them against the Islamic assault. They needed a higher order power to salvage them.

The higher order power was discovered in the third defence mechanism: *Bhakti-marg* (devotional path) that aimed to obtain the blessings (*kripa*) of gods and goddesses. *Bhakti-Marg* was first prescribed in *Shri Bhagvad Gita,* later glorified in the *Bhagavata Purana,* practiced widely in the South, then popularized further by Adi Shankaracharya, and was now adopted by a series of saints in the South as well as the North. They moved away from the abstract concept of *Brahman* and preached cultivating passionately devotional dependence on and total surrender to more accessible gods like Krishna and Rama and goddesses like Durga and Shakti wishing to be salvaged from existential crisis.[111] Ramanuja in the South taught it in the language of the common people. His disciple, Ramananda (1300 – 1385[112]), carried his Guru's teachings to the North. He also preached people to get rid of superstitious rituals, practices, and social evils. Similar reformative devotional approach was preached by Guru Nanak (1469 – 1538) as he formulated the Sikh religion and Chaitanya Mahaprabhu (1485–1534) in his pure Krishna *bhakti.* The most popular among the saints was Tulsidas (1497/1532–1623 CE[113]), whose *Vinay-Patrika* (Prayer Book) is an exemplary model of how a devotee must demean and denigrate himself and prostrate before his deity (e.g., Ram and Hanuman) in order to be relieved from all sufferings and sins. *Bhakti-Marg* was indeed a great solace to the people who were feeling miserable by being badly impoverished and victimized by an alien religion and the oppressive State. However, instead of enabling Hindus to introject the power of gods and goddesses, it inculcated excessive dependency on gods and goddesses for salvaging them.

The *bhakti-marg* resonated with Sufism that aimed to spread Islam through devotional approach. *Bhakti-marg* and Sufism had similar philosophy as well as practices. Monism was the core of Sufism that signified striving to get in union with Allah. Sufi saints also combined breathing exercises with meditation and contemplation to gain intuitive insights and intense spiritual experiences in order to induce altered states of consciousness.[114] They recited like Hindus divine names and their *qawwali* was quite similar to hindu *kirtan* in its collective emotionality in praying god. Hindus, like Muslims, respected Sufi saints and worshipped at *mazars* (Sufi shrines).[115]

Hindu and Muslim masses also maintained overlapping patterns of living[116] and borrowed rituals and practices from each other. Their domestic ceremonies and rituals pertaining to birth, marriage, and death were gradually got mixed. Converted Muslims retained the rituals that they had earlier, while Hindus accepted those of the Muslim's that they regarded to be auspicious.[117] However, the religious practices of Hindus and Muslims remained distinctly different, particularly in temples and mosque.[118] There was also remarkable convergence in various arts forms. Hindus had a tradition of promoting all forms of liberal arts, including music, poetry, dance, dramatics, painting and sculpture which naturally permeated into the luxurious life styles of the nobles and got blended into the Muslim art forms. Persian miniature paintings and Urdu poetry, for example, started adopting Hindu mythological themes such as love drama and dances (*rasa lila*) of Radha and Krishna often performed in the Kathak style. Kathak was originally a purely religious dance form, but was blended with Persian dance form for courtly entertainment. Similarly, *qawwali* was given a romantic twist. Hindustani classical music developed as a complex and sonorous blend of Vedic notions of *raga* and *tala* (notes and rhythm); ghazal singing became popular, and other instruments such as the sitar and santoor were invented. Urdu was developed by drawing on Persian and Arabic words mixed with local Hindi dialects and written in a modified Arabic script. Further, a new style of architecture was born out of the Indo-Islamic fusion resulting into the distinctive features of having domes, lofty towers or minarets, arches, lotus, and vaults.

Both Hindu and Sufi saints disregarded caste distinctions and attracted lower caste Hindus and Muslims who were still suffering from discriminations by higher caste Hindus and foreign born Muslim nobles (respectively). The disciples of Ramananda, for example, belonged to different castes: Kabir was a weaver, Sadhana was a butcher, Ravidas was a cobbler, and Sena was a barber. Another saint, Namadeva in Maharashtra was a tailor.[119] Caste discriminations continued even among Muslims, despite Islamic dictum against it. Foreign born Muslims were called *Ashrafs* (noble Muslims), who looked down upon Hindu converts from backward castes, *Ajlafs,* and the scheduled caste converts, *Arzals* (Singh Sikand 2006). *Ajlafs* and *Arzals* were called "*Pasmanda*" meaning (in Persian) "those who have fallen behind", "broken" or "oppressed".

Till the medieval period, it was not the caste, but the religion, which was the defining criterion of people. Castes remained functional categories for regulating social transactions through ritualized practices. Higher castes indeed discriminated the lower ones, which remained subservient to higher castes in their daily routines, but the State politics was not played in terms of castes, nor the State rewarded or punished on the basis of castes. "One of the surprising arguments of fresh scholarship, based on inscriptional and other contemporaneous evidence, is that until relatively recent centuries, social organisation in much of the subcontinent was little touched by the four *varnas*. Nor were *jatis* the building blocks of society".[120] Another observation was as follows:

> Until well into the colonial period, much of the subcontinent was still populated by people for whom the formal distinctions of caste were of only limited importance; Even in parts of the so-called Hindu heartland of Gangetic upper India, the institutions and beliefs which are now often described as the elements of traditional caste were only just taking shape as recently as the early eighteenth century—that is the period of collapse of Mughal period and the expansion of western power in the subcontinent".[121]

History tells us that whenever there was political turbulence and instability, people got anxious and insecure. Their rights and life were unpredictable and they sought security in the available social organizations such as caste and religion. Castes' norms were elaborated and petrified following the collapse of the Gupta period and the end of Harsha regime. But castes remained a flexible system of social stratification nested in Hinduism. As the Mughal Empire collapsed in the 18th century, groups of diverse religious, geographical, and linguistic background started exerting their power,[122] and were recognized as distinct caste entities. But it was the British who turned castes into political groups. We shall return to it in the next chapter.

CONCLUSIONS

State politics plays a critical role in mediating how social formations positively or negatively impact development process. Originally, king's wellbeing was believed to be dependent on subjects' wellbeing. Hence, kings were naturally predisposed to contribute to their subjects' wellbeing. Both were bound by religion and the State patronized and supported both Brahminism and Buddhism. The State also supported guilds, in which castes emerged as a function of occupational differentiations, skills development, and social transactions. With the royal support, religions and guilds did not only created enormous wealth, but also developed philosophy, science, arts, and technology, which were far ahead of those of the rest of the world. Indian culture and civilization, trade and commerce, religions and philosophies spread to a major part of Asia.

However, as the centrally and well-administered States broke into small kingdoms, small kings, ambitious chieftains, and invading warriors suffered from their existential anxieties. They colluded with Brahmins for mutual support. Brahminism got ritualized and oppressive weakening of both the State and the people. Muslim rulers were committed to spreading Islam. Ulemas preached[123] that the masses must obey the god, the Prophet, and, even the oppressive, rulers. Lords and Ulemas lived in luxuries and were engaged in ostentatious display of wealth by exploiting people who were badly impoverished and socially degraded. Hinduism became subdued, ritualized, more orthodox, and devotional by way of escaping the harsh reality.

The story from the ancient to the medieval period is an account of the shift from collaboration to collusion of the religion and the politics devolving the spirit of development from the well being of all to the stinking richness of and a vulgar display by a few. The State favoured Islam, but did not focus on castes in distributing patronage. Consequently, castes remained social in nature perpetuating discriminations and preserving a life loaded with rituals, superstitions, and social evils.

Notes

1. Alechina, 1982, p. 19.
2. Rajni Kothari, 1995.
3. http://www.thehindu.com/thehindu/quest/200206/stories/2002060801940300.htm
4. Srinivas, 1962, p. 225.
5. Singh, 1977.
6. Nehru, 1946/2001.
7. Thaper, 1972, p. 37.
8. Nehru, 1946/2001, p. 85.
9. Gupta, 2000, pp. 190-191.
10. B.M. Sinha, 1992, p. 1.
11. Thapar, 1972.
12. Hiltebeitel, 2011.
13. Sinha, B.M.1992.
14. Hopfe & Woodward, 2009, p. 79. The term, Hinduism, was started being used in the medieval period.
15. Sinha, B.M., 1992.
16. Pande, 2003, p. 317
17. Warder, 1998; Wiley, 2004.
18. Radhakrishnan, 1960, p. 341.
19. Sen, 2006, p. 15, 189.
20. Joshi, 2008.
21. Chinchore, 2007; Gethin, 1998.
22. http://1stholistic.com/prayer/hol_Jainism.htm on 22.09.2011.
23. Brahminism is a composite of all that Brahmins preached, practiced, and theorized about religion by drawing on Vedas, Upanishads, and *Brahmanas*, etc. It was later on labelled as Hinduism.
24. Nehru, 1934/2004.
25. See Nehru, J. (1934/2004). *Glimses of world history*, also available at http://www.oocities.org/rsr_sam/HARSHA.htm, retrieved on 04.12.2014.
26. Thapar, 1972, p. 86.
27. Nehru, 1934/2004.

28. Thapar, 1972, p. 131.
29. Cohen, 2001, p. 12.
30. See Sinha, 2014, pp. 128-129.
31. For example, about 150,000 captives of the Kalinga war (262–261 BCE) were put to clear forests and develop wastelands for new settlements in Magadha.
32. Kumar and Sethi, 2005.
33. Kautilya's *Arthashatra* cited by Kamat, 2004.
34. Gupta, 2000. p. 212.
35. The word, 'caste' is derived from the Portuguese word, '*casta*', meaning 'race, lineage, unmixed breed, etc.', *Oxford English Dictionary*.
36. Megasthenes identified seven castes the Maurya period: philosophers, farmers, soldiers, herdsmen, artisans, magistrates, and councillors. Thapar, 1972, p. 79.
37. Ghurye, 1932/1969.
38. Dumont & Pocock, 1961.
39. Thapar, 1972, p. 121.
40. Lannoy 1971/2008, p. 233.
41. McKnight, 1977, p. 12.
42. http://www.ancientindia.co.uk/staff/resources/background/bg12/bg12pdf.pdf
43. Thapar 1972, p. 124.
44. Nehru, 1946/2001, p. 221; present tense changed into past to suit the text.
45. Thapar, 1972, 149.
46. Historian, R.C. Makumdar, cited by Nehru, 1946/2001, pp. 202 & 203 respectively
47. Thapar, 1972, p. 151.
48. Based on Nehru, 1946/2001, p. 223.
49. Ancient Indian schools of philosophy are mainly identified as *astika* (orthodox) or *nastika* (heterodox) depending on whether they regard the Vedas as the major source of knowledge. The orthodox schools are *Nyaaya, Vaisesika, Saankhya, Yoga, Purva Mimaamsa* and *Vedanta*. The heterodox schools are Jain, Buddhist and Charvaka.
50. Thapar, 1972.
51. Nehru, 1946/2001, p. 216.
52. Nehru, 1946/2001, p. 222; present tense changed into past to suit the text.
53. Nehru, 1946/2001, pp. 222, 223, & 224 respectively present tense changed into past to suit the text.
54. Thapar, 1972, p. 166.
55. Thapar, 1972, p. 261.
56. Ingold, 1994, p. 1026.
57. Thapar, 2003, p. 487.

58. Inden, 1998, p. 67.
59. Nehru, 1946/2001, p. 120.
60. Thapar, 1972, p. 133.
61. Nehru, 1934/2004.
62. Thapar, 1972, p. 233.
63. Reddy, 2009.
64. https://en.wikipedia.org/wiki/Samanta
65. Thapar, 1972, p. 235.
66. Thapar, 1972, pp. 138-139.
67. McKnight, 1977.
68. Thapar, 1972, pp. 244-245.
69. Sinha, 2014, pp. 4-5.
70. *Puran* means Old.
71. Bailey, 2003, pp. 162-167.
72. Wendy, *Doniger*, 1980.
73. Klostermaier, 2000, pp. 83-84.
74. Thapar, 1972, p. 133.
75. According to the *Bhavishya Purana* (Wendy *Doniger*, 1980).
76. Champakalakshmi, 2011.
77. Nath, 2001, p. 31.
78. *Wendy Doniger, 2010.*
79. The following description is sourced from Kulke & Rothermund, 2016.
80. Drekmeier, 1962.
81. Blau, 1964.
82. Chakraborty, 1987, p. 167.
83. *Manusmriti* cited by Olivelle, 2005.
84. *Padma Purana* cited by Dubois 1821/1924.
85. *Manusmriti*, (Verses IX, 90, 94; *Brahma Purana* (95.7); *Padma Purana* (II.85.62-66); and *Vishnu Purana* (3.10) respectively. Available at https://www.quora.com/When-did-child-marriage-start-in-India, retrieved on October 8, 2016.
86. Hawley, 1994.
87. Altekar, 1956.
88. Eraly, Abraham, 2011, p. 370.
89. *Vishnu Smriti, 25.14.*
90. *Garuda Purana 1.107.29.*
91. O'Flaherty 1971.
92. *Manusmriti*, 5.51.
93. *Manusmriti* cited by Olivelle, 2005, pp. 31-32.
94. *Bhagavad Gita*, 9.34.
95. Minor, 1986.
96. *Bhagavata Purana*, XI.14.20).
97. Nakamura, 1964.
98. Nehru, 1946/2001, pp. 224.

99. Several *Puranas* recommended it. Iyer, 1927; also available at https://en.wikipedia.org/wiki/Devadasi
100. Rambachan, 1991.
101. Fogelin, 2015, p. 33.
102. Wink, 1991.
103. Quran, IV, 59.
104a. Historian, a musician, a poet, a litterateur, a Sufi Shaikh.
105. Mirza, 1935, p. 177.
106. Thapar, 1972, p. 289.
107. Burley, 2007, p. 34.
108. Lorenzen, 2006, pp. 24–33
109. Nicholson, 2011.
110. Basham 2007, p. 65.
111. Basham, 1999.
112. Uncertain dates.
113. Uncertain dates.
114. Miller, 1986, p. 21.
115. See Sinha, 2014, pp. 14-16.
116. Thapar, 1972, p. 289.
117. Thapar 1972, p. 300.
118. Aggarwal, 1978; Joshi et al., 2003.
119. https://en.wikipedia.org/wiki/History_of_Hinduism.
120. Metcalf & Metcalf, 2012, p. 24.
121. Bayly, 2001, pp. 3-4.
122. Bayly, 2001, pp. 29-30.
123. Following Quran IV, 59.

REFERENCES

Aggarwal, P. (1978). *Caste and social stratification among Muslims in India.* New Delhi: Manohar.

Alechina, I. (1982). The contribution of United Nations system in formulating development concept. In UNESCO (ed.), *Different theories and practices of development.* UNESCO, Paris, pp. 9-68.

Altekar, Anant S. (1956). *The position of women in Hindu civilization: From prehistoric times to the present day.* Delhi: Motilal Banarsidass.

Bailey, Gregory (2003). The *Puranas.* In Arvind Sharma (Ed.), *The Study of Hinduism.* Columbia, SC.: University of South Carolina Press.

Basham, A.L. (1999). *A cultural history of India.* New Delhi: Oxford University Press.

Basham, A.L. (2007). Medieval Hindu India. In A.L. Basham (Ed.), *A cultural history of India* (pp. 53–65). New Delhi: Oxford University Press.

Bayly, S. (2001). *Caste, society and politics in India from the eighteenth century to the modern age*. Cambridge: Cambridge University Press.

Blau, P.M. (1964). *Exchange and power in social life*. New York: Wiley.

Burley, Mikel (2007). *Classical Samkhya and Yoga: An Indian metaphysics of experience*. London; New York: Routledge, Taylor & Francis Group.

Chakraborty, S.K. (1987). *Managerial effectiveness and quality of work life: Indian insights*. New Delhi: Tata McGraw Hill.

Champakalakshmi, R. (2011). *Religion, tradition, and ideology: Pre-colonial South India*. New Delhi: Oxford University Press.

Chinchore, M.R. (2007). *Buddhist conception of man and human emancipation*. Delhi: New Bhartiya Book Corporation.

Cohen, S.P. (2001). *India: Emerging power*. New Delhi: Oxford University Press.

Drekmeier, C. (1962). *Kingship and community in early India*. Stanford: Cal.: Nalanda University Press.

Dubois, A.J.A. (1821/1924). *Hindu manners, customs, and ceremonies* (Edited H.K. Beauchamp). Oxford, U.K.: Clarendon Press.

Dumont, L. and Pocock, D. (1961). *Contributions to Indian sociology* (Vol. 5). Paris: Hague: Mouton.

Eraly, Abraham (2011). *The first spring: The golden age of India*. New Delhi: Penguin.

Fogelin, L. (2015). *An archaeological history of Indian Buddhism*. New York: Oxford University Press.

Gethin, R. (1998). *The foundations of Buddhism*. London: Oxford University Press.

Ghurye, G.S. (1932/1969). *Caste and race in India* (Fifth Ed). Bombay: Popular Prakashan.

Gupta, Dipankar (2000). *Interrogating caste: Understanding hierarchy and difference in Indian society*. New Delhi: Penguin Books.

Hawley, J.S. (1994). *Sati, the blessing and the curse: The burning of wives in India*. New York: Oxford University Press.

Hiltebeitel, Alf (2011). *Dharma: Its early history in law, religion, and narrative*. New Delhi: Oxford University Press.

Hopfe, L.M., Woodward, M.R. (2009). *Religions of the world*. Pearson Education.

Inden, Ronald (1998). Ritual, authority, and cycle time in Hindu kingship. In J.F. Richards (Ed.), *Kingship and authority in South Asia*. New Delhi: Oxford University Press.

Ingold, T. (1994). *Companion encyclopedia of anthropology*. London: Routledge.

Iyer, L.A.K. (1927). Devadasis in South India: Their traditional origin and development. *Man in India*, Vol. 7, No. 47.

Joshi, A.P., Srinivas, M.D. and Bajaj, J.K. (2003). *Religious demography of India*. New Delhi: Centre for Policy Studies.

Joshi, L.M. (2008). Brahminism, Buddhism, and Hinduism: An essay on their origins and interactions. The Wheel Publication No. 150/151. Online Publication available at—https://store.pariyatti.org/Brahmanism-Buddhism-Hinduism-WH150-1_p_1573.html

Kamat, Jyotsna (2004). Guilds in Ancient India. Updated on June 28, 2016 and retrieved on June 26, 2016. http://www.kamat.com/kalranga/ancient/guilds.htm.

Klostermaier, K.K. (2000). *Hinduism: A short history*. London: One World Publications. pp. 83–84.

Kothari, Rajni (1995) (Ed.). *Caste in Indian politics*. New Delhi: Orient Blackswan.

Kulke, H. and Rothermund, D. (2016). *A history of India* (6th Edition). London: Routledge.

Kumar, R. and Sethi, A. (2005). *Doing business in India*. New York: Palgrave Macmillan.

Lannoy, R. (1971/2008). *The speaking tree: A study of Indian culture and society*. New Delhi: Oxford University Press.

Lorenzen, David N. (2006). *Who invented Hinduism: Essays on religion in history*. New Delhi: Yoda Press.

Majumdar, R.C., Raychaudhuri, H.C. and Datta, K.K. (1960). *An advanced history of India*. London: Macmillan.

McKnight Jr. and J. Michael (1977). Kingship and religion in India's Gupta Age: An analysis of the role of Vaisnavism in the lives and ideology of the Gupta kings. *Journal of the American Academy of Religion*, Volume XLV (2), p 227.

Metcalf, B. and Metcalf, T. (2012). *A concise history of modern India*. Cambridge: Cambridge University Press.

Miller, E. (1986). Forward: Sufis-the mystical muslims. In M. Lings (Ed.), *What is Sufism* (pp. 17–23)? London: George Allen and Unwin.

Minor, R.N. (1986). *Modern Indian interpreters of the Bhagavad Gita*. New York: SUNY Press.

Mirza, M.W. (1935). *Life and Works of Amir Khusrau*. Calcutta: Idarah-i Adabiyat Delli.

Nakamura, H. (1964). *Ways of thinking of eastern people: India, China, Tibet, and Japan*. Honolulu: East West Center Press.

Nath, Vijay (2001). From 'Brahmanism to Hinduism: Negotiating the Myth of the Great Tradition, *Social Scientist*: 19–50.

Nehru, J. (1934/2004). *Glimpses of world history*. London: Penguin Books.

Nehru, J. (1946/2001). *The discovery of India* (3rd Edition). New Delhi: Oxford University Press.

Nicholson, Andrew J. (2011). *Unifying Hinduism: Philosophy and identity in Indian intellectual history*. Delhi: Permanent Black.

O'Flaherty, W. (1971). *Asceticism and eroticism in the mythology of Shiva*. London: Oxford University Press.

Olivelle, P. (2005). *Manu's code of law.* New Delhi: Oxford University Press, pp. 31-32.

Pande, Rohini (2003). Can mandated political representation increase policy influence for disadvantaged minorities? Theory and Evidence from India. *American Economic Review,* 93 (4).

Radhakrishnan, S. (1960). *Occasional speeches and writings: October 1952 – February, 1959.* New Delhi: Publications Division, Government of India, 337-346.

Rambachan, A. (1991). *Accomplishing the accomplished: Vedas as a source of valid knowledge in Sankara.* Honolulu: University of Hawaii Press.

Reddy, K. (2009). *Indian history.* New Delhi: Tata McGraw-Hill.

Sen, A. (2006). *The argumentative Indian: Writings on Indian history, culture and identity.* New York: F Picador, Farrar, Straus, and Giroux.

Singh, H. (1977). *Caste among non-Hindus in India.* New Delhi: National (Original from University of California).

Sinha, B.M. (1992). Religion's Place in the Politics of Ancient India. Magazine Web Edition, January 1992. http://www.hinduismtoday.com/modules/smartsection/item.php?itemid=891. Retrieved on June 27, 2016.

Sinha, J.B.P. (2014). *Psychosocial analysis of the Indian mindset.* New Delhi: Springer.

Srinivas, M.N. (1962) *Caste in Modern India: And other essays* Asia Publishing House, Bombay.

Thapar, R. (1972). *A history of India.* London: Penguin Books.

Thapar, R. (2003). *The penguin history of early India: From the origins to AD 1300.* New Delhi; Penguin.

Verma, Bhagawati Charan (2009). *Chitralekha.* Delhi, Raj Kamal Prakashan.

Warder, A.K. (1998). *Lokayata, Ajivaka,* and *Ajnana Philosophy". A Course in Indian Philosophy* (2nd Ed.). Delhi: Motilal Banarsidass Publishers.

Wendy Doniger, (1980). *The origins of evil in Hindu mythology.* Oakland, CA: University of California Press.

Wendy Doniger, (2010). *The Hindus: An alternative history.* New Delhi: Oxford University Press.

Wiley, K.L. (2004). *Historical Dictionary of Jainism.* Lanham, Maryland: Scarecrow Press.

Wink, A. (1991). *Al-Hind: the making of the Indo-Islamic world* (Volume 1). Boston, MASS.: Brill Academic Press.

4
Politicizing Castes and Religion

COLONIAL POLITICS OF EDUCATION AND RELIGION

Gateways for Colonial Intrusion

Education and religion were the gateways for British intrusion into the Indian landscape. Englishmen, irrespective of whether they were policy-makers, administrators, Indologists, ethnographers, or Christian missionaries, had a sense of racial superiority over Indians. They all believed that Indians were backward. Hence, it was their "white man's burden" to intervene actively in education in order to help Indians come out of their backwardness. Religion, because of its pervasiveness, was the first target. However, their approach to education and religion varied depending on their prime objectives and orientations. The policymakers and administrators were guided primarily by the imperative to form a sufficiently large native cadre in order to be able to run the administration of a vast country with a small number of expatriates. Macaulay represented this British interest with a blend of contemptuous beliefs about the native people, their languages and literature. He advocated discontinuing the prevailing practice of the State supporting Sanskrit and Persian languages and the traditional forms of education:

> ...for printing books which are of less value than the paper on which they are printed while it was blank; for giving artificial encouragement to absurd history, absurd metaphysics, absurd physics, absurd theology.... Who

> could deny that a single shelf of a good European library was worth the whole native literature of India and Arabia... all the historical information which has been collected from all the books written in the Sanskrit language is less valuable than what may be found in the most paltry abridgements used at preparatory schools in England.[1]

Sanskrit and Persian languages, therefore, were naturally considered to be irrelevant and in fact useless for creating a cadre of native administrators who were required to learn English as well as to acquire the Western worldview in order to govern the natives:

> We must at present do our best to form a class who may be interpreters between us and the millions whom we govern; a class of persons, Indian in blood and colour, but English in taste, in opinions, in morals, and in intellect. To that class we may leave it to refine the vernacular dialects of the country, to enrich those dialects with terms of science borrowed from the Western nomenclature, and to render them by degrees fit vehicles for conveying knowledge to the great mass of the population.[2]

The result was the English Education Act (1835) by the Council of India (London)[3] that accordingly set the State's objectives and obligations to higher education. Three universities were set up in Calcutta, Madras, and Bombay Presidencies (1857), which "did little to promote analytic capacity or independent thinking and produced a group of graduates with a half-baked knowledge of English, but sufficiently Westernized to be alienated from their own culture".[4] The lower order native functionaries that the universities produced worked under the civilian officers who were exclusively British till 1920 when Indians were allowed to compete for the ICS (Indian Civil Services). These indoctrinated "baboos" [Indian Civil Servants] indeed turned into "pliable" and "plastic" partly from "a servile wish to please the White *Shahib's* [boss's] tongue, and partly from a desire to obtain a government appointment"[5] and, as stated earlier, copied the white bosses in sporting English language, tastes, dresses, life styles, and aloofness from the native population. The new urban middle class male professionals also emulated them to a great extent.

Indologists of the colonial era were primarily interested in unveiling the distinctiveness of Indian culture and society expecting, implicitly or explicitly, that such an understanding would help the colonial rulers in their governing process. They believed that language and literature of a people were the sure way to know the way they lived, thought, and behaved, which could enable the rulers to regulate them properly. They learnt Sanskrit and accessed into the ancient Indian religious texts. Philologists such as Sir William Jones established the Asiatic Society (1784) and got a number of ancient Sanskrit texts translated into English. He in fact found that Sanskrit, Greek and Latin languages had a common root, and that they might all be further related to a common linguistic source. Sanskrit in fact was found to have an edge over Greek and Latin:

> The *Sanscrit* language, whatever be its antiquity, is of a wonderful structure; more perfect than the *Greek*, more copious than the *Latin*, and more exquisitely refined than either, yet bearing to both of them a stronger affinity, both in the roots of verbs and the forms of grammar, than could possibly have been produced by accident...[6]

The common linguistic source was also believed to be related to a common cultural heritage and shared knowledgeu:—some indications of which were found in the ancient Indian texts. For example, "the fundamental tenet of the Vedanta school" showed that "existence and perceptibility are convertible terms".... "It is not denying the existence of matter, that is solidity, impenetrability, and extended figure (to deny which would be lunacy), but in correcting the popular notion of it, and in contending that it has no essence independent of mental perception..."[7]. That is, the objects and their subjectivity are inseparable—a preposition which was made much later in the 17th century by the famous French philosopher, Rene Descartes, who said that "I think, therefore I am", that is, matter exists because our mind senses it[8].

Some Indologists were later labelled as "orientalists" and were accused of their "patronizing representations" of the East and having all their "academic knowledge about India and Egypt...

somehow tinged and impressed with, violated by, the gross political fact"[9] and servile attitude to colonial power: "the Orientalist poet or scholar, makes the Orient speak, describes the Orient, renders its mysteries plain for and to the West".[10] They translated the ancient Indian texts to explore Indian thought and found it full of romantic otherworldly mystical wisdom, but were textualized, static, and stagnant, and therefore earnestly needed Western agency, rationality, and scientific knowledge.[11] A ground for the need of such worldview was provided by the ethnographic studies painting Indians as "... abusive of women, hopelessly backward, ridden with weird notions of caste, dowry, *sati* etc. and ruled by some very strange-looking half animal gods...".[12] Therefore, there was a case to expose the inner contradictions of the Indian culture and society by aligning them with European humanitarian thoughts through a literature that retained the native spirit and forms but contained the seeds of modernization. Max Muller was the most articulate advocate among the orientalists.[13] He suggested:

> India has been conquered once, but India must be conquered again, and that *second conquest should be a conquest by education* [Italic added]. Much has been done for education of late, but if the funds were tripled and quadrupled, that would hardly be enough... A new national literature may spring up, impregnated with western ideas, yet retaining its native spirit and character... A new national literature will bring with it a new national life, and new moral vigour. As to religion, that will take care of itself. The missionaries have done far more than they themselves seem to be aware of.[14]

Max Muller was interested in showing how Indian society and culture had degenerated by contrasting their present with the one enshrined in the most ancient Indian text, the *Rigveda,* which was the root of the people's religion. He believed that all religions decay over time: "Whenever we can trace back a religion to its first beginnings, we find it free from many blemishes that affected it in its later states".[15] In order to show it happening in case of India, he persuaded the East India Company to enable him to translate the *Rigveda* that he did in 25 years (1849–1874).[16] He argued,

> The translation of the *Veda* will hereafter tell to a great extent on the fate of India, and on the growth of millions of souls in that country. It is the root of their religion, and to show them what the root I feel sure, is the only way of uprooting all that has sprung from it during the last 3,000 years.[17]

He argued that uprooting religious beliefs of Indians would facilitate a process of 'Restoration' like the one that Christians had in Europe. In other words, highlighting the tenets of Vedic religion was meant to underline the degenerative beliefs and practices that Hindus had acquired since the ancient time, and that in turn would usher them into Christianity—an Indian form of Christianity "without being Roman Catholics, Anglicans, or Lutherans"[18]. He hoped and encouraged Brahmo Samaj to engender it.

It was not what the **Evangelicals** wanted. They were aggressively committed to 'civilize' the 'barbarians' and convert them into the Christianity of their kind. Christianity might or might not have been brought in to India as early as 52 AD by Thomas the Apostle, but was certainly established in the South by the 6th century, and was further popularized by a flow of Catholic and Protestant missionaries since 1500 AD. Of them, the most dominant Protestants were the Evangelicals.[19] They were critical of orientalists for being too generous in their view of Indian culture, society, and Hinduism. Hinduism, according to them, was full of social evils and devoid of morality. One of them, for example, Charles Grant, an employee and subsequently a director of the East India Company, wrote a harshly critical treatise in 1792 on Hindu religion and customs justifying for a free hand from the East India Company to spread Christianity. There were others writing petitions and mounting pressures on the Company to back them.

Box 4.1: How India was denigrated

The West tried its best to persuade India that its philosophy is absurd, its art puerile, its poetry uninspired, its religion grotesque and its ethics barbarous.

— S. Radhakrishnan[20]

However, the Company was not fanatic in spreading Christianity.[21] It was first of all a trading company meant for making money, and then had the need to rule over a highly polarized religious people. It did not want to antagonize Hindus and risk its business interests. It moved as expediently as it could. Further, while some of its officials were supportive to missionaries, there were others who were exposed to the rising secularism in Europe, according to which public policy and State functions were required to be cleansed of religious views and discriminations allowing people to indulge in earthly pleasures and use their intellect and follow their dispositions to live the way they wanted to live. Accordingly, the East India Company treaded cautiously adopting a policy of free exercise of religion.[22] One of its judges, Sir William James, compiled personal laws of Hindus and Muslims, which were customary from the Mughal days, and framed them within the British judicature.[23] The Company took the view that its subjects were Hindus, Muslims, and tribal people, each having their own traditions, practices, and rituals, which they should be allowed to follow so long they did not violate the British legal norms. Such an accommodative stance, however, got increasingly precarious over time.

Box 4.2: The White Man's Burden

The missionaries asserted that since God laid upon Britain the solemn duty of evangelizing India, the Government should not hesitate to throw its weight into the struggle. They demanded above all open Government patronage of Christian education and vigorous warfare upon the abuses associated with Hindu religion.

—Claudius Buchanan[24]

Pressures kept mounting by the combined campaigns of the missionaries in India and their supporters in England. As a result, the Charter Act of 1813 made provisions to allow the missionaries to expose Indians' superstitious rituals and beliefs and persuade or press them to replace them with the thoughts and practices of Christianity.[25] The subsequent Charter Acts of 1833 and 1853 were the decisive steps to help the missionaries spread Christianity aggressively.[26] They realized that education was the best way to do so. They believed that the European science and Christianity were supportive to each other: If people were educated into science, they would learn to think and behave rationally, and that in turn would make them discard their religion and accept Christianity, which will then turn them loyal to the British Raj. In order to get easy access to the masses, they opted for vernacular languages linking them with English. Schools and colleges were established. By this time printing presses were available for publishing books, magazines, and pamphlets that exposed the social evils, superstitions, and religious rituals in Hinduism and thus tended to induce people to embrace Christianity. The Bible was translated into many languages and distributed freely among people. Many upper class *bhadralok* (elites) of Bengal indeed took English education and accepted Christianity. However, many did react sharply; not for promoting vernacular education, but against demeaning Hinduism and denigrating people by way of imposing Christianity.

Hindus, particularly their elites, felt threatened. They felt that the missionaries had to be resisted and retorted by re-establishing the sanctity of ancient wisdom and cultural heritage. Of course, they all agreed that the superstitious beliefs and rituals and social evils had to go. So, they opposed missionaries, but supported the Raj to initiate a number of social reforms (1820s to 1850s). For example, the State outlawed infanticide and *sati pratha* (ritual burning of widows), abolished slavery that was customary from the Mughal days, eliminated dacoits in forms of religious *thugs*, legalized remarriage of widows, and enforced a penal code for equitable punishment across castes.[27] However, the Hindu elites knew that the acts were not enough; the real issue was a revitalization of the degenerated society in order to restore the self-respect of the nation. This led to religious renaissance that prepared the ground for the sprouting of Hindu nationalism.

Movements for Religious Renaissance

Confrontations and collaborations between the missionaries and the emerging urban educated Hindu elites led to create a space where it became possible to imagine and argue for designing a new Indian society. Missionaries aimed to design it by converting Hindus into Christians and imparting them western knowledge of science and technology. Hindu elites agreed the need to gain from European science, humanitarianism, and Christian thought, but preferred to draw on their glorious ancient past to revitalize the Indian society.

The glorious past of India, which the orientalists retrieved for contrasting with the deplorable present hoping to convert Indians into Christianity, in fact transformed some of the orientalists themselves. Max Muller (1883), while growing from his sixties into seventies, for example, realized that India could teach the Europeans in a number of ways:

> If I were to look over the whole world to find out the country most richly endowed with all the wealth, power, and beauty that nature can bestow—in some parts a very paradise on earth—I should point to India. If I were asked under what sky the human mind has most full developed some of its choicest gifts, has most deeply pondered on the greatest problems of life, and has found solutions of some of them which well deserve the attention even of those who have studied Plato and Kant—I should point to India. And if I were to ask myself from what literature we, here in Europe, we who have been nurtured almost exclusively on the thoughts of Greeks and Romans, and of one Semitic race, the Jewish, may draw that corrective which is most wanted in order to make our inner life more perfect, more comprehensive, more universal, in fact more truly human, a life, not for this life only, but a transfigured and eternal life—again I should point to India.[28]

Such laudable expressions must have enthused and inspired all those Indians who were deeply concerned with degraded conditions of the people and were looking for a source of inspiration to revitalize them. Swami Vivekananda was one of them. He visited the transformed Max Muller and experienced the following:

> That little white house, its setting in a beautiful garden, the silver-haired sage, with a face calm and benign, and forehead smooth as a child's in spite of seventy winters, and every line in that face speaking of a deep-seated mine of spirituality somewhere behind; that noble wife, the helpmate of his life through his long and arduous task of exciting interest, overriding opposition and contempt, and at last creating a respect for the thoughts of the sages of ancient India—the trees, the flowers, the calmness, and

> the clear sky—all these sent me back in imagination to the glorious days of ancient India, the days of our *brahmarshis* and *rajarshis*, the days of the great *vanaprasthas*, the days of Arundhatis and Vasishthas. It was neither the philologist nor the scholar that I saw, but a soul that is every day realizing its oneness with the universe.[29]

The potential of the ancient Indian religio-spiritual thoughts to transform human beings was thus validated in Max Muller. On the other hand, the superiority of modern science and technology, rationality, and statecraft was also quite recognized[30] and the impact of the Christian ideology was "significantly" and "consequentially" felt by the Indian elites.[31] The interplay of these three sets of forces led to three religious movements, which aimed at revitalizing the Indian society and people by reviving the Vedic and Vedantic thoughts and drawing or distancing from Western modern and Christian influences. They were Brahmo Samaj, Arya Samaj, and Ram Krishna Mission.

The Brahmo Samaj was established by Raja Ram Mohan Roy (1772 – 1833) in 1828. Raja Ram Mohan Roy was a Brahmin who worked for the East India Company (1803-1815) while still pursuing the vocation of a *pundit*. However, he vehemently opposed to his family's orthodoxy, idolatry, polytheism,[32] superstitious rituals, and social evils like the *sati-pratha* (widow burning). It is said that he had two houses—one having fully Western ambience where he was the only authentic Indian and another one with all Indian fixtures where he was the only odd Western man. He knew many languages and drew primarily on the Vedas, Upnishadas, and Vedant-Sutra to believe in *Brahman*—the Supreme Reality and the single source of all virtues and moralities. Hindu *samaj* (society), he thought, had to reflect these attributes, which could be the foundation for restoring Hinduism to its original, pure, rational, and ethical version[33]. And yet, he greatly respected ethical Christianity and subscribed to Western humanitarianism. He favoured liberal-minded discourses on Hinduism and Christianity and their rational interpretations in order to promote collaborations rather than conflicts.

At heart, Raja Ram Mohan Roy was a nationalist who was the first to estimate that around one-half of the total revenue of the British India was driven out to Britain. Yet he never wanted to oust the British. For example, he preferred the 'civilized British' over their 'tyrannical' Muslim predecessors. He believed that colonial rule was not hostile to religious reform; for "the greater our intercourse with European gentlemen, the greater will be our improvement in literary, social, and political affairs".[34] In ideals, he was a Vedic Hindu, but in practices, he kept getting so close to Christians that the *Brahmo Samaj* was admired and supported by Unitarian Christians, but was perceived by the orthodox Hindus as a threat to the Hindu identity. They strongly reacted to this attempt to "Christianize' Hinduism".[35] One of the close associates of Raja Ram Mohan Roy, Bhabani Sharan, dissociated from him and started a newspaper, *Samachar Candrika,* that became a rallying ground for defining Hinduism in terms of beliefs and rituals by drawing on the traditional *karm-kand,* weaning out those rituals and practices that were discordant with the core ones, and thus reinforcing a tangible framework for Hindus to cope with the Christian threat by remaining faithful to traditional Hinduism.[36] Further, *Chandrika* retrieved and highlighted a core traditional Hindu value: tolerance of other religions, which, instead of fighting Christianity, allowed Hindus to ignore and insulate Christian influences into small sized Bengali elites and eventually render them insignificant in the societal landscape.

The Arya Samaj was founded by Swami Dayananda Saraswati (1824 – 1883) in 1875 as a purist movement that aimed to resurrect the Vedic society by cleansing the present one of all the social evils, superstitious beliefs and rituals, and religious distortions that had seeped into Hinduism since the Vedic days. It advocated the doctrine of *karma* and reincarnation and emphasised the ideals of *brahmacharya* (chastity) and *sanyasa* (renunciation). It rejected all non-Vedic beliefs and practices such as idolatry, animal sacrifices, ancestor worship, pilgrimages, priestly rituals, offerings made in temples, caste system, untouchability and child marriages. The Arya Samaj had a missionary zeal to counteract both Christianity and Islam and to spread the Vedic Hinduism to the whole world.[37] Swami Dayanand did not only launch a scathing theological attack on the validity of Christian scripture and its inferior teachings, but argued for the superiority of his own doctrine of Vedic Hinduism and the superiority of the Vedas.[38] The Arya Samaj started schools to teach his principles and practices, set up missionaries to spread Vedic Hinduism both inside and outside India, and even established rules and procedures for *shuddhikaran* (purification) of those who were converted into Christianity and Islam in order to get them back into the Hindu fold. The assertive stance of the Arya Samaj attracted many, particularly those who had nationalist temper and were seething with a desire to resist the alien rules. Punjab became the stronghold of the Arya Samaj, its influence, however, spread to most of the Northern India and reached even to the deep South in Tamil Nadu.[39]

The Ramkrishna Mission, established on 1 May 1897 by Swami Vivekanand (1863 – 1902), was posited on three pillars of thought: Advait Vedanta, Yoga, and nationalism.[40] Advait Vedanta, for Vivekananda, was the one universal religion, which was inclusive of all religions and an ultimate expression of Hindu spiritual supremacy.[41] Christianity and Islam too could be subsumed in the Vedantic framework, despite their dualistic faiths, which were the aberrations caused by specific cultures in historic times.[42] Vivekanand opposed Christian conversion as it meant an exploitation of the poor and the lower castes, which were already oppressed by the higher castes. Christian schools too turned young ones into the heaps of useless mass.

Box 4.3: What Christianity Does to an Indian

The child is taken to [missionary] school and the first thing he learns is that his father is a fool, the second thing that his grandfather is a lunatic, the third thing that all his [previous] teachers are hypocrites, the fourth that all his sacred books are a mass of lies. By the time he reaches sixteen, he is a mass of negation, lifeless, and boneless... —Swami Vivekananda[47]

The Advait Vedanta, on the contrary, helps realize full human development. Every soul is potentially divine and hence manifestation of the same Supreme Being. So, there is unity of souls in the whole universe. In other words, every person is capable of feeling being one with the universe at some moments in their life and expresses it as love and sympathy for others, which is the basis of all ethics and morality. However, individuals have to realize this divinity by controlling their impulsive nature, modifying the conditions in which they live, and relating with others with love and sympathy. That they can do by practicing yoga including *karm-yoga*. *Karm-yoga* means doing one's work diligently and discharging one's duties to others faithfully. Further, individuals can also realize divinity through worship or meditation, or can do all these faithfully—their work, duties, worship, and meditation. "This is the whole of religion. Doctrines, or dogmas, or rituals, or books, or temples, or forms, are but secondary details".[43] Yoga for him was a science of supra-consciousness and an ancient wisdom that was beneficial not only to Indians but all humankind.[44] Realizing divinity by large number of individuals also amounted to nation building; for love and sympathy for each other unite diverse people into a nation. The Ramkrishna Mission was the social instrument to reach out to the poorest and to bring noblest ideas to the doorstep of even the meanest.[45] It was the means to forge people into a nation.[46] Nation building was a prominent theme in Vivekanand's thoughts; Advait Vedanta and Yoga were the means.

CO-EVOLVING NATIONALISM WITH COMMUNALISM

Hindu Nationalism

Nationalism of different intensities remained as undercurrents in the three religious movements. The movements were not manifestly against the colonial rule, nor did they overtly seek support and patronage of the State. They aimed to revive the ancient glories through retrieving the Vedic and Vedantic thoughts, reforming Hindus by cleansing them of the social evils and superstitious beliefs, and thereby constructing a new vibrant Hindu society. However, those who joined the movements later on felt disenchanted, frustrated, and in fact angered by the exploitative nature of the colonial rule. The blend of the three—the fantasy of the glorious past, the degradation of the present, and the exploitative colonial rule—produced a fertile ground for the sprouting Hindu nationalism. Hindu nationalism, by default, excluded other religious communities, particularly Muslims. Probably at the back of the mind of the Hindu nationalists was the historical experience of being harassed and degraded by the Muslim rulers in the medieval period. In other words, Hindu nationalism was not only anti-colonial but was also exclusive of Muslims.

For instance, Bankim Chandra Chattopadhyaya (1838-1894) was a thought leader in the Brahmo Samaj tradition. He was convinced of the material superiority of the West. However, he believed that the spiritual superiority of Hinduism was capable of leveraging it.[48] Despite his being an officer in the British administration for over 30 years, he nursed a strong urge for the independence of the country from the British—an urge that got expressed in his famous novel, *Anandmath,* which also contained the famous national song, *Vande Mataram*. The novel and the song were intensely national, essentially religious, but also anti-Muslims.[49] Swami Vivekanand, on the other hand, was cognizant of Indian diversity:

> Here have been the Aryan, the Dravidian, the Tartar, the Turk, the Mogul, the European—all the nations of the world, as it were, pouring their blood into this land. Of languages, the most wonderful conglomeration in here; of manners and customs there is more differences between two Indian races than between the European and the Eastern races.[50]

And yet, he argued that his Advait Vedanta was inclusive enough to provide a common platform for building nationalism. He posited the following:

> The one common ground that we have is our sacred tradition, our religion. That is the only common ground and upon that we shall have to build [our nation]....The unity in religion, therefore, is absolutely necessary as the first condition of the future of India".[51]

Bengal in the mid-nineteenth century was in the vanguard in religious renaissance that prepared ground for the sprouting of Hindu nationalism. Two persons, Raj Narain Basu (1826-1899) and Nabha Gopal Mitra (1840–1894), were the conspicuous among those who vehemently promoted Hindu nationalism. Basu formed *Bharat Dharma Mahamandal,* a precursor of *Hindu Mahasabha,* that aimed to establish an Aryan nation.[52] His dream was not only to liberate the country, but to enlighten the whole world: "I see this rejuvenated nation again illuminating the world by her knowledge, spirituality, and culture, and the glory of Hindu nation again spreading over the whole world".[53] Nabha Gopal Mitra was surely anti-Muslim. He started Hindu–Mela for inculcating nationalism that was exclusive of Muslims, thereby "Nabha Gopal forestalled Jinnah's theory of two nations by more than half a century".[54] Sri Aurobindo (1872-1950), the grandson of Basu, and "the poet of patriotism and prophet of nationalism"[55] made it quite clear that the vision of nationalism was constructed by the tenets of Hinduism:

> I say no longer that nationalism is a creed, a religion, a faith; I say that it is the *Sanatan Dharma* which for us is nationalism. This Hindu nation was born with the *Sanatan Dharma*, with it, it moves and with it, it grows. When the *Sanatan Dharma* declines, then the nation declines, and if the *Sanatan Dharma* were capable of perishing, the nation would perish.[56]

Muslim Political Consciousness

Hindu nationalism inevitably put pressure on the elites of the Muslim community to assert their religious identity and to protect their interests by resorting to political means. There had already been a cleavage between Hindus and Muslims running from the medieval period.[57] The Census since 1871 had sharpened this cleavage by transforming the various local religious communities into the national political communities of minority Muslims and majority Hindus.[58] A minority community universally experiences competitive anxiety that was probably aggravated in the case of Muslims by the rising political activism of Hindus. The British further aggravated this competitive anxiety by resorting to "divide and rule"[59] that others preferred to call "balance and rule".[60]

Initially, the East India Company was not positive to Muslims. It had fought *nababs* and Muslim rulers and destroyed their aristocracy. As a fallout, it started believing that "the race [Muslim] is [was] fundamentally hostile to us, and therefore, our true policy is [should be] to conciliate the Hindus".[61] Hence, The East India Company "followed the deliberate policy of keeping the Muslims away from all positions of importance and strength and had increasingly depended upon the support and loyalty of the Hindus".[62] The three major policy decisions of the Company, the Permanent Settlement Act (1793), Resumption Regulation Act (1820), and replacing Persian by English as the official language (1835) vindicated the Company's policy.[63] Massive land transfer occurred from Muslim landed gentry to Hindus while virtually closing the door of landlordism to Muslims.[64] More Muslims than Hindus lost their free gifted land (*lakaraj*) because they had more such land and did not have proper title deeds. Further, Muslims thought it against their religion to learn English[65] while Hindus did not have any such qualms. In fact, indologists had established affinity between Sanskrit and the European languages. Hence, Hindus quickly grasped this opportunity to learn English and get Company jobs. As a result, Muslims between the years 1867-1887 had only two to five percent while Hindus got over 50 per cent of jobs in the British administration paying higher salary of Rs. 75 or above.[66] In 1901, only 22 out of 10,000 Muslims knew English while the corresponding number for the Hindus was 114.[67] The first war of independence (1857) had already reinforced British animosity against Muslims. Although the war was fought jointly by Hindus and Muslims, but, because the Mughal Emperor, Bahadur Shah Zafar, was the declared leader, the British construed it as a revolt by Muslims. This led to their further distrust of Muslims and inclination towards Hindus. The rise of educated Hindus and the downslide in the Muslim community were the hallmark of the Company regime.

However, the situation changed towards the end of the nineteenth century when the rise of educated Hindus turned into Hindu nationalism, particularly in Bengal which was the centre of the Company rule. Some of the nationalist organizations were militant engaging in violent attacks on the British. The British were now weary of Hindus and turned to Muslims to counteract this rising militant nationalism. And, the Muslims needed jobs and patronage from the British. They both needed each other. This was the genesis of the rise of Muslim political consciousness.

Sir Syed Ahmad Khan (1817-1898), Muslim elite from an aristocratic background, was the pioneer in cultivating political consciousness of Muslims. He strongly advocated that Muslims must learn English and science in order to be able to compete for jobs in the British administration. Further, they must prove their complete loyalty to the British in order to turn them receptive to Muslims' interests. He started a number of educational schemes, associations, and institutions including the Anglo-Muhammadan Oriental College (1875) that later on, with a liberal assistance of the British, developed into the Aligarh Muslim University (1920).

Aligarh became the centre of rising Muslim consciousness and identity leading to what was called the Aligarh Movement.[68]

Sir Syed was initially committed to the Hindu-Muslim harmony. In a speech in Patna on Janyuary 27, 1883, he said:

> ... we [Hindus and Muslims] both belong to the same country, we are a nation, and the progress and welfare of the country, and both of us, depend on our unity, mutual sympathy, and love, while our mutual disagreement, obstinacy, and opposition and ill-feeling are sure to destroy us".[69]

But just after three years in 1888, he was worried that who—Hindus or Muslims—will rule over India, should the British leave. "Will they share power? Certainly not. It is necessary that one of them should conquer the other. The hope that both could remain equal is to desire the impossible and the inconceivable";[70] for Sir Syed believed, "Muslims and Hindus will not put their hearts in any venture together" and that "there will be an ever increasing hatred and animosity" between them.[71] Since then, he was totally committed to promote Muslim interests, remain loyal to the British, and denounce whatever the British did not approve. His *Muhammadan Educational Conference* (1886) was a precursor of the formation of the All India Muslim League in 1906.[72] The League had twin objectives that were set long before by Sir Syed: To cultivate Muslim's loyalty to the British and to seek preferential treatment in allocation of jobs and separate electorates and seats to Muslims. It was later on that the League pledged to split the country and got it partitioned.[73]

Secular Nationalism of the Congress

In the meanwhile, a third force of secular national movement was in the making that was distinctly different from both Hindu nationalism and Muslim political movement. It was the Indian National Congress (1985). Sir Syed denounced it as Hindu dominated body while Hindu nationalists disliked it because it was too close to the British, It indeed was originated by a retired British civil servant, Allan Octavian Hume. Hume, with the approval of the British Raj, invited a group of educated and anglicized professionals in dialogues and debates with the government for providing constructive suggestions and legitimacy to the Raj. The Congress indeed was dominated by Hindus, but it also had Muslims, Sikh, Parsees, Christians, Scottish, and Irish men, among others of varied background and orientations.

Indeed some of the early Congress leaders, such as Sarankan Nair and B.N. Dar, subscribed to the colonial ideology—eulogizing the Raj, professing to be loyal, collaborating, and competing with the British for their power and privilege.[74] They were the "mimic men".[75] However, the Congress also had leaders like Dadabhai Naoroji and Pherozeshah Mehta, who were loyalists, but did not fail to ask the British to treat Indians not like slaves, but the British citizen entitled to civil rights and the opportunities of conducting fair trade and establishing new industries. It had revolutionaries like Lokmanya Bal Gangadhar Tilak (1856-1920), who proclaimed that "*swarajya* (self-rule) is my birthright and I shall have it!" by violent means, if necessary. It also had the reformists like Gopal Krishna Gokhale (1866 –1915) who insisted to serve people's interest by working with the British Government and adopting the constitutional means.[76] It had Rahimtulla Sayani (1896) who ardently advocated for harmony among all communities in order "to develop and consolidate sentiments of national growth and unity, to weld them together into one nationality...".[77] It had Muhammad Ali Jinnah who had campaigned for Dadabhai Naoroji in England and later on took Gokhale for his role model. He in fact aspired to be "a Muslim Gokhale". It had Annie Besant from the Theosophical Society who united a diverse set of prominent leaders such as Joseph Baptista, Muhammad Ali Jinnah, Bal Gangadhar Tilak, G.S. Khaparde, Sir S. Subramania Iyer to form a national alliance demanding *Home Rule* (self-government). The Congress in essence emerged as an inclusive and secular movement in direct response to "... the existence of a common oppression by a common enemy and the struggle against it which provided important bonds uniting the Indian people".[78]

However, it was secular only in its policy and intention. Secularism anzd inclusion were neither culturally rooted nor were the deep structures in the leaders' mind. The religious renaissance of the nineteenth century had already laid out the foundation in terms of Hindu nationalism. Secular and inclusive nationalism of the Western origin could be built only as a super-structure on the foundation of Hindu nationalism. The edifice of nationalism, as a result, had varying shades of secular as well as communal beliefs, thoughts, and actions. Some of the Congress leaders were staunchly secular containing their Hinduism effectively while others were manifestly Hindus in their beliefs and behaviour.

They were manifestly secular in their action programmes against the British. But whenever they started mobilizing the mass, Hindu symbols, imageries, and mythology spontaneously came alive in their minds. Tilak, for example, popularized a family deity, Ganesh, for public celebrations in order to arouse nationalist spirit of Hindus of Maharashtra and Gujarat. He used Shivaji's resistance to Mughal oppression for justifying direct action against the British, which was often construed as his anti-Muslim sentiment. Tilak believed that India was "united as a great nation" during the Vedic period, was degraded during the Muslim rule, and needed to revive its ancient Vedic glory by the nationalist movement.[79]

Even Gandhi, who was totally committed to secular and inclusive nationalism, had a Hindu at the core of his thought: "Most of the central categories of Gandhi's political philosophy such as *ahisma, satya,* and *moksha* were derived from traditional Hindu thought and remained intelligible to a predominantly Hindu audience although he redefined and established new relations between them in the light of his borrowings from other religious traditions".[80] His vision of *Ram-rajya,* though was elaborated in a non-religious and compassionate form, resonated with the Hindu's nostalgia of the *Satyayug.* Although he was particular to include other religions in his discourse, a Hindu variant was central to Gandhi's political thought. Jawaharlal Nehru once commented that Mahatma Gandhi was "essentially a man of religion, a Hindu to the inner-most depths of his being";[81] his secularity was faithfully superimposed on his commitment to nationalism. Other prominent Congress leaders such as Madan Mohan Malaviya (1861–1946) and Lala Lajpat Rai (1865–1928) had a Hindu lens to view their nationalism. Malaviya was three times Congress President (1909, 1918, and 1932), but left Congress in 1934 to join the Hindu Mahasabha. He established Benaras Hindu University (1916). Lala Lajpat Rai was a devotee of Arya Samaj. He believed that "Hindus are a nation in themselves because they represent a civilization all of their own" and shared "a common name, a common ancestry, a common religion, a common language and a common future".[82]

In contrast, Nehru was a model of secular and inclusive leadership in the best of the European tradition. India, in his view, was "a geographic and cultural entity, a cultural unity amongst diversity, a bundle of contradictions held together by invisible threads".[83] It belonged to all communities and people. Hence, the national movement had to include diverse communities and people. He saw to it that the Country remained constitutionally secular after independence—people observing own and respecting others' religions. But his Deputy Prime Minister, Vallabhbhai Patel had plenty of Hinduism in him that often surfaced in his public appearance.

It is true that the majority of Congress leaders were Hindus and most of them had varying shades of Hinduism at the core of their identity. And yet, it also true that they were able to contain their ethno-religious pressures to the extent that the Congress remained the mainstream of secular and inclusive nationalism focused first on the home-rule and then on the struggle for full independence of the country. The basic premise was that the country belongs to diverse groups of individuals who hold different beliefs, values, and practices, and they all have to come together and remain united to seek national freedom in order to prosper in their own ways. Of course, there would be differences and clash of self and group interests, but they can be moderated and subordinated to the common goal of getting freedom and building a nation.

Sir Syed's led Aligarh movement was based on a different premise of irreconcilable differences and interests of Hindus and Muslims. It was a false belief in primordiality. That is, "Hindus and Muslims constituted in pre-modern times distinct civilizations destined to develop into separate nations once political mobilization took place.... Hindus and Muslims in nineteenth century India were separate religious communities predisposed towards, if not necessarily pre-ordained as, separate national groups". The counter-argument was that "... the cultural and religious differences between Hindus and Muslims were not so great as to rule out the creation of either a composite national culture or at least a secular political union in which those aspects of group culture that could not be shared would be relegated to the private sphere". It was further pointed out that "Muslim separatism was not pre-ordained, but resulted from the *conscious manipulation* of selected symbols of Muslim identity by *Muslim elite groups* in *economic and political competition* with each other and with elite groups among Hindus" (Italics added).[84] In order words, Muslim elites, because of their self and group interests, deliberately turned religious identity into an ideology[85] to instigate a separatist movement. It was indeed the result of "a narrow group mentality basing itself on a religious community but in reality concerned with political power and patronage for the interested group".[86] Power politics was the main drive.

The British indeed played a critical role in this politics. They were getting weary of the increasingly anti-British stance of the Congress and so started playing Muslim communalism card against the Congress. Three measures were taken, the partition of Bengal (1905), the Minto-Morley (1909), and the Montagu-Chelmsford Reforms (1919), that aggravated the discord between Muslims and Hindus.[87] The carving out of Muslim majority eastern Bengal for special care of the less developed Muslims was construed as a conspiracy to undermine the supremacy of the upper caste Hindu elites of the western part of Bengal. While Muslim elites favoured the partition, and in fact got together at Dhaka (in 1906) to form the League, Hindus opposed it vehemently causing a rift from Muslims.[88] Sir Hebert Hope Risley, a British ethnographer and officer, was quoted reporting "the agitation against Partition has resolved itself into a condition of general ill feeling between Hindus and Mohemadens... All we can do is to wait and see".[89] In 1909, Muslims were granted separate electorates, which meant that candidates of either religion had to distribute patronage and freebies to the members of their own community in order to get their votes. Ten years thereafter, Central and State assemblies were expanded and Muslims, who already had the privilege of separate electorates, got over-representation, as result of which they were in a position to bestow favours to their own electorates, woo them, and cultivate communal base for winning election.

Forming of the Sangh Parivar. The proposed partition of Bengal and separate electorates to Muslims lifted the spirit of the Muslim League and reinforced the belief that Hindus and Muslims were separate entities sharpening the cleavage, and increasing the animosity between them.[90] Hindu elites were already suspicious when the League was formed (in 1906). In reaction, Lala Lajpat Rai, a prominent Congress leader, formed the Punjab Hindu *Sabha* in 1909 for safeguarding the interests of "the entire Hindu community".[91] Its first session was presided by no other than another prominent Congress leader, Pandit Madan Mohan Malviya. The Punjab Hindu Sabha expanded into the All India Hindu Sabha in 1915 affiliating State level *Sabhas*, which in 1921 became the Akhil Bharatiya (All India) Hindu Mahasabha—a federal organization of Hindu-minded leaders, some of which were also in the Congress. Despite the formation of the Hindu Mahasabha, there was some semblance of Muslim-Hindu unity following the massacre of Jalhianwala Bagh (1919) and during the Khilafat movement that lasted till 1922. Thereafter, communal animosities escalated and riots occurred at several places (including 91 in UP alone), and the number of Muslim delegates to the Congress decreased sharply from 11 per cent in 1921 to under 4 per cent in 1924.[92]

The Congress since 1920s grew enormously as the mainstream of nationalism. Under the leadership of Mahatma Gandhi, it launched nation-wide mass-based *satyagrah (assertion of truth)* and *savinay avagya* (civil disobedience) *andolan* (movement). Gandhi attracted a large number of leaders including Jawaharlal Nehru who mobilized the whole country for its independence. And yet, they could not completely contain the Hindu and Muslim communal forces.

Some of the Congress leaders were quite unhappy with Gandhi for overstretching the Congress to outreach Muslims. They got more involved in the Hindu Mahasabha. Hindu Mahasabha was now organized into "... an enlarged and more comprehensive edition of the Arya Samaj".[93] It marked a "qualitative change" from the earlier form of Hindu nationalism.[94] Savarkar provided it a more sharply defined philosophical base of *Hindutva* for promoting the rights and interests of (the ethnic entity of) Hindus, their culture (*sanskriti*), and their nationalism (*rashtriyata*).[95] *Hindutva* signified the totality of the characteristics of Hindus. Hindus were defined as those who were born of *Aryans* and belonged to the religions (Hinduism, Buddhism, Jainism, and Shikhism) that originated in India excluding those who believed in Christianity, Judaism, and Zoroastrianism. A more extreme view was later advocated, "Those [Hindus] only are nationalist patriots, who with the aspiration to glorify the Hindu race and nation next to their heart are prompted... to achieve that goal. ... The rest are "traitors and enemies to the national cause."[96] An active Congress leader, K.B. Hedgewar, was not only displeased with the Congress but also unhappy with the Hindu Mahasabha for the way they were responding to the communal riots in 1920s. He broke away from the Hindu Mahasabha to form a more assertive organization, *Rashtriya Swayamsevak Sangh* (RSS: Association of National Volunteers, 1925) to raise a cadre of militant preachers (*pracharaks*) to promote *Hindutva*. The RSS abstained from direct participation in party politics, but created a fertile ground for the proliferation of a number of outfits, which constituted the *Sangh Pariwar* complementing the activities of each other within the overarching framework of *Hindutva*. They all opposed to the policies and programmes of the Congress.

On the other side was the Muslim League that claimed the total allegiance of the Muslims. Attempts to forge its united front with the Congress had ended by the early 1920s. Muhammad Ali Jinnah, who was instrumental in making such attempts, was frustrated to resign from the Congress and had left for England. Now the League opposed all policies and programmes of the Congress.[97] The riots of 1920s and 1930s had provided it with the opportunity to nurse its separatist moves more vigorously. Every riot was used for advocating separate rights and privileges for Muslims. The leadership of the League was taken over by more radicals like Sir Muhammad Iqbal, who in 1930 demanded a separate Muslim majority state by combining the North-West Frontier Province, Baluchistan, Punjab, and Sindh. Though Iqbal did not ask for a sovereign State, this was the idea that led Choudhary Rahmat Ali in 1933 to envisage Pakistan.[98] Jinnah was back to India as a changed person. Now he was a staunch advocate of a separate State for Muslims. In 1940, he finally paved the way for parting of Muslims and Hindus when he proclaimed the "Two-Nation Theory" at the League conference in Lahore:

> Hindus and the Muslims belong to two different religions, philosophies, social customs and literature.... It is quite clear that Hindus and Muslims derive their inspiration from different sources of history. They have different epics, different heroes and different episodes.... To yoke together two such nations under a single state, one as a numerical minority and the other as a majority, must lead to growing

> discontent and final destruction of any fabric that may be so built up for the government of such a state.[99]

The rest is well known: The country was divided accompanied by massive displacement of people, unprecedented massacre of Muslims and Hindus, desperate attempts by Mahatma Gandhi to restore communal harmony, and his assassination by a fanatic Hindu who claimed that he did it for protecting the Hinduism and the Hindu *Rashtra*. This was the historical experience that later on turned into a fountain of flourishing communalism.

AWAKENING OF CASTE CONSCIOUSNESS

As we know, castes originated from the hierarchical *varna* system as functional differentiation for skills specialization, and then kept on proliferating as a function of new occupations, waves of immigration, and the changing socio-economic and geographical settings. Over the centuries, it got more and more top-down oppressive. But it was never a major part of State politics, nor was the hallmark of people's total identity till the end of the medieval period. In fact, "until well into the colonial period, much of the subcontinent [India] was still populated by people for whom the formal distinctions of caste were of only limited importance".[100] Actually,

> ... it was under the British that 'caste' became a single term capable of expressing, organising, and above all 'systematising' India's diverse forms of social identity, community, and organisation. This was achieved through an identifiable (if contested) ideological canon as the result of a concrete encounter with colonial modernity during two hundred years of British domination. In short, *colonialism made caste what it is today* (Italics added)[101].

Let us see how it happened. The British viewed Indians being Hindus, Muslims, or tribal. The Hindus were most conspicuously clustered into castes. So, the colonial rulers found castes as a handy mechanism for an administrative advantage. This led to caste Census starting from 1871. The British, however, could not appreciate the unique features of castes and their complex relationships. For them the primary concern was their use for administrative convenience. So, the Census adopted simplistic zoological and botanical principles to classify people into standardized categories and sub-categories of castes. Later on in 1901, Sir Herbert Hope Risley, who was heading the Census, introduced a racial bias in ranking the superiority of castes on the basis of purity of rituals, occupational origin, and collective moral worth.[102] The ranks were used for granting administrative jobs to upper castes and excluding members of the other castes. All administrative jobs and senior appointments during 1860-1920 were granted to the upper castes.[103] Even the tax rates were different for differently ranked castes. At the lower end of the ranks were the castes, which were considered to be criminal and rebellious by birth, and therefore unreliable and unfit for any government job.[104] Even those who were only suspected of indulging in criminal activities, violence, acting against the State, or obstructing in tax collection process, or their forefathers were traced to act against the State during the Mughal period were labelled as criminals and rebellious and unfit for government job. Hundreds of lower end castes were brought under the Criminal Tribes Act (1871). Even the intermediate castes of Ahir, Gurjar, and Jat were listed as criminals.[105] By 1931, 237 castes and tribes were recorded as criminals in the Madras Presidency alone.[106] There were other measures such as the Land Alienation Act (1900) and Punjab Pre-Emption Act (1913), through which criminal and rebellious castes were prevented from owning land and property rights and their lands and properties were liable to be confiscated by the State.

Ranking of castes rigidly, aligning caste ranks with job and other opportunities, and stigmatizing castes led to the "hardening of caste identities".[107] It stirred caste consciousness as had never happened before. The consciousness took a political colour overnight. People compared their caste ranks, strived to improve their rank in order to maximize their opportunities and benefits, and were envious and hostile to those castes which were ahead of them.[108] To these ends, they formed caste *sabhas* (associations), which transformed the traditional caste-*panchayats*. Caste *panchayats* were location-specific custodians of codes of conduct for regulating social transactions within and between castes. Caste *sabhas*, on the other hand, enrolled membership on the basis of ancestry alone having profound implications. Caste *sabhas* were now larger regional blocs incorporating many formerly discrete sub-castes located at several places. As a result, the members were free from the ascriptive obligations allowing them to behave toward other castes as they wish without fear of losing caste standing. While different castes could still claim equivalence or superiority to each other, but there was no transactional norms to corroborate that claim.[109] Caste rankings were somewhat blurred. And, caste *sabhas* functioned as primarily a utilitarian political instrument, which their leaders used to improve the image of their caste as well as to impress upon the colonial authority to upgrade castes' rankings, mobilize the members politically, and or serve their own and collective interests.

The caste *sabhas* had formal structure and constitutions with procedures for the elections of officers, the holding of annual sessions, the handling of funds, and the affiliation of local groups. Their leaders were well-off urban and educated elites who aspired to gain political power and the economic benefits that political power brought to them.[110] While the leaders of the upper castes used their *sabhas* to expand their power base for playing politics, the leaders of the intermediate and lower caste *sabhas* were focused to realize the following:

- To move politically by submitting petitions to the colonial authority demanding new and more honourable name, and hence, better ranking for their castes, and
- To refurnish their castes by engaging in social and cultural activities that enabled the castes to gain upward mobility and proximity to the higher castes.

Among the social and cultural activities, the one that was quite striking was the *sanskritization*.[111] Because a caste's ranking was based on the socio-religious rituals (for example, wearing sacred thread, vegetarianism, etc.) that Brahmins were practicing, some of the lower and intermediate castes adopted them, including those (such as child marriage, prevention of widow remarriage, etc.) that were social evils. *Sanskritization*, they thought, elevated their social status by gaining proximity to upper castes.

Furthermore, castes worked now as ethnic groups engaged in mobilizing their members to raise their political consciousness that led to make claims for a better standing in the eyes of the colonial authorities. Petitions to the colonial authorities were the reflections of this ethnic activism. Petitions started being submitted immediately after the ranking was introduced in 1901 Census. It increased from 27 in 1901, though 55 (1911) and 67 (1921), to 113 in 1931 (the Census year after which caste entry was discontinued). An upsurge in people's political consciousness and actions were reflected in the increase of submitting petitions from 16.2 per cent (1901) to 31.15 per cent (1931) of all the castes in the Census.[112] Education certainly played a significant role in elevating political consciousness. Only 10.85 per cent of the castes having very low (i.e., less than 1%) literacy rate while 20.83 per cent of castes having very high (i.e., more than 40%) literacy rate submitted petitions. However, more revealing was the evidence that the largest (29.22%) per cent of all castes having the literacy rates in-between (i.e., 1.00 to 40%) submitted petitions. It was not the most highly educated, but moderately educated castes which aspired to upgrade their caste identity politically. The highly educated upper castes had already a lion's share in the high paying government jobs and high political visibility. For example, out of 1,000 Biharis, the numbers of literates within upper, intermediate and low castes were the following: 372 Kayasthas, 195 Brahmins, 136 Bhumihars, and 120 Rajputs, but only 40-50 Kurmis and Yadavs, and 52 Telis.[113] The most highly educated Kayasths in Bihar had only 1.20 per cent of the state population in 1911, but had 32.50 per cent of the gazetted civil service positions and constituted 47.90 per cent of the State delegates to the Indian National Congress. It did not need to submit any petition.

Interestingly, it was not only the intermediate literacy rates, but the intermediate levels of castes, which were politically most sensitized to submit petitions by way of improving their status and image. They had a greater expectancy to mobile upward. Only 18.37 per cent of Dalits submitted petitions compared to 27.50 per cent of the backward castes and 21. 52 per cent of the non-Brahmin forward castes. Only 2.50 per cent of Brahmin castes ever submitted any petition to the colonial authority.

Brahmins were already privileged from the early days of the East India Company. They knew Sanskrit and Persian, and were quick to start learning English and getting high positions in the British administration, which brought to them power and affluence. They were believed to be the custodians of the ancient religio-philosophical heritage. The Census confirmed their superiority. But now that some of the lower castes were trying to catch up with them through *sanskritization,* the upper castes preferred to get westernized. That is, they tended to acquire certain Western values and practices that were consonant with their proximity to the ruling class[114] and allowed them an easy access to politics. They did not need to make narrow ethnic appeals; rather they preferred to employ a broader rhetoric of class, religion, or nation to appeal to the larger masses across castes. On the other hand, Dalits were too deprived and depressed to exert politically at the national level. It was the intermediate castes, which were economically not so deprived and in many cases somewhat well-off, which were now getting some education that fired their political aspirations. Their leaders were not able to compete with the upper castes and had the compulsion to focus on a narrow ethnic identity to gain politically.[115]

The decade of 1920s was of great social unrest.[116] Access to school education, missionary works, social reform movements, and mass based political activism of Gandhi had raised political consciousness to a new height. The middle and lower castes were getting restless complaining against the British policy of favouring only upper castes in administration. The British, as result, was re-aligning their policy accommodating middle and lower castes. Hence, the castes dynamics was taking a sharp turn. Depending on the history of their relationship with the upper castes and the local contexts, the middle and lower castes either competed and conflicted with the upper castes exerting their autonomous identity or collaborated with them while retaining their ethnic identity in order to claim political space, and to use it for gaining greater access to economic gains and social mobility.

Dravidian Movement

The most conspicuous caste conflict was witnessed in the South where the Non-Brahmins challenged Brahmin's supremacy. The Non-Brahmin movement with its epicentre in the Tamil land was a product of socio-economic and political changes that accompanied the advent of the British. Earlier till the fourteenth century, Brahmins and Non-Brahmins lived in peace. In the South there were no caste labels of Kshatriyas or Vaisyas. So, the British following Vedic theology, categorized all castes as either Brahmins, Shudras, or Untouchables. However, the land-owning castes such as the Vellalas, Nairs, Reddis, Chettiars, Kammas, and similar others were non-Brahmins but otherwise forward. People did not view them as Shudras. A sizable part of the land in the Madras Presidency was held by them.[117] In addition, some of them were employed in government services as village revenue collectors or were engaged in trade and commerce. They were affluent rural elites along with Brahmins. They donated to Brahmin temples, were welcome there on special occasions, and invited Brahmins to perform pooja and other rituals on religious and domestic occasions. So, there was inter-dependence and cooperation between them. In fact, they both considered themselves superior to other castes and untouchables and maintained distance from them.[118]

The relationship, however, changed drastically during the British Raj. Brahmins, as elsewhere in the country, were favoured by the colonial authorities. But in the South, this led to their disproportionately high dominance over others in education, administration, as well as politics.[119] They constituted only 3.20 per cent of population, but many more Brahmins than Non-Brahmins occupied higher positions of Deputy Collectors (55.00 versus 21.50%), Sub-Judges (82.30 versus 16.70%), and District Munsifs (72.60 versus 19.50%) in the government.[120] While only 18 to 22 per cents of Non-Brahmins received Bachelor of Arts degrees between 1870 and 1918, the corresponding percentages for Brahmins were 67 to 71. According to the 1911 Census, 1,094 Brahmins but only 163 Non-Brahmins got a teaching degree. They dominated politics too. The Congress was led by Annie Besant. She was a charismatic personality who never missed any opportunity to highlight the glorious ancient Indian tradition of religio-spiritual thought in her lectures. She passionately called upon people to be proud of their glorious past. Her most companions and supporters, besides theosophians, were Brahmins. Together they controlled the nationalist movement in the South.[121]

Non-Brahmins felt aggrieved and agitated, particularly those who belonged to the land-owning castes, moved to urban centres, got educated and aspired to get high positions in the government and urban pursuits. They were deprived of new opportunities and discriminated not only by the British but also by Brahmins. To add insult to their injury, Brahmins often called them Shudras. Men, who were proud landlords in villages and were educated now, had lost their status in cities. This was because the Census officials did not understand the intricate caste equations between the various castes, and blindly followed the *varna* categories (having only three options of Brahmin, Shudra, and Untouchable) to dump the forward Non-Brahmin castes as Shudras. But it was too much for non-Brahmins. They reacted sharply.

Thus, self-interest and personal hurt were the chief initiators of Non-Brahmin's movement against Brahmins. They viewed *varnashram* as the root cause of their deprivation and discrimination. Hence, they negated *varnashram* and sought its replacement by the indigenous Dravidian culture. In other words, the Non-Brahmin movement turned into Dravidian movement aimed to restore Non-Brahmin's self-esteem, demolish Brahmin's claim of superiority, and widen Non-Brahmin's access to new opportunities in the government and elsewhere in the South.[122] Interestingly, the process of retrieving Dravidian culture was initiated by Europeans. Like the orientalists in the North, Christian missionaries in the South were the first to show that the Tamil language and literature preceded and developed independent of Sanskrit. Similarly, the people in the South had their own culture and traditions of unity and integrity without having sharp caste differentiations.[123] It was "the Aryan Brahmin colonialits" who brought Sanskrit "with it a peculiar type of Hinduism..."[124] in order to dominate Dravidians. While addressing the graduates of the University of Madras in 1886, the British Governor of Madras pointed out, "It was these Sanskrit speakers, not Europeans, who lumped up the Southern races as *Rakshusas* – demons. It was they who deliberately grounded all social distinctions on Varna, Colour."[125]

Box 4.4: Brahmins were Perceived to be Colonialits

The Brahmins are also foreigners to India as are the British. The English have been ruling India for the last one century and a half. The Brahmins, coming into India from Central Asia three thousand years ago, put down the ancient inhabitants of the country, have created disaffection among them by bringing into racial, religious, and caste differences, and have been commanding the Indians ever since (*Nyaya Dipsika*, January 25, 1923).

Thus, it was established that that non-Brahmans were Dravidians—the original civilizers of the South, while Brahmins were the "Aryan invaders" from the North. This separatist view, fuelled by Non-Brahmins self-interest and personal hurt, led them, particularly the Tamils, to see themselves not as part of the nation (as one of the collective of many ethnic groups), but *a nation with an intrinsic ethnic legitimacy of its own"* (Italics added).[126] This cultural foundation gave a momentum to the movement that took a concrete shape in form of the South Indian Liberal Federation (SILF), which later became the Justice Party. The Justice Party obviously was seeking justice from the oppressive dominance of Brahmins. It had both reformist and political agenda. A Manifesto was formulated declaring opposition to the Brahmins, the Congress, and its leader Annie Besant, who at that time championed the Indian Home Rule movement. The Home Rule, according to the Manifesto, would result in the rule by the Brahmins who controlled the Congress. So, Non-Brahmins must oppose the Home Rule and any other measures that could undermine the influence and authority of the British; for only the British could balance the interests of different castes and communities and maintain unity and solidarity of the country. Without the British rule, the country, according to the Manifesto, was likely to break into "mutually exclusive and warring groups".[127] The Justice Party won the general election in 1920, but lost to the Congress in 1937. Unfortunately, the Congress imposed Hindi as a compulsory subject in schools that, along with the growing popular discontent over agrarian and urban economic problems, gave a handle to the Justice Party to ask for a separation from the country in 1938. The movement continued with its ups and downs but never died out because of the cultural roots that it established. Eventually it led in 1949 the formation of a political party of the Dravida Munetra Kazhagam (DMK).[128]

Middle Castes Rising Consciousness

The caste conflicts elsewhere in the country were not so sharp due to several reasons. First of all, the castes were not trichotomized into Brahmin, Shudra, and Untouchable. The Non-Brahmins were not necessarily called Shudras. Both Brahmins and Non-Brahmins were in fact finely differentiated further into a variety of upper, middle, and lower castes, which had varying nomenclatures of being forward, backward, other backward, and extremely backward castes. The ranks within the categories were often blurred and contested preventing the castes' from polarizing sharply. At places, a Non-Brahmin caste was more educated and privileged than Brahmin. For example, the Kayashthas in Bihar were non-Brahmin, but at the top in education, administrative jobs, as well as professional services. Secondly, the Congress being the main nationalist party tended to appropriate whenever and wherever protest movements of any kind either against a local tyrant or the British cropped up. Hence, it grew as an amalgamated body accommodating diverse and even incongruent groups of different castes, which were united on the political platform under Gandhi for fighting against the British. The rest of the time they functioned often at cross purposes, in-fighting, playing power politics, but still rubbing shoulders within the Party framework. Finally, although the Congress was dominated by upper castes, their leaders, tended to expand their support base by looking out for emerging elites of the other, including backward and lower, castes, who were not quite politically conscious. They co-opted such elites and groomed them as the second or third line of leaders. Gradually, the third and second line leaders started mobilizing their caste men and creating their own power base, standing on their own, bringing submerged castes in the "the vortex of politics",[129] and playing politics. Thus, the castes were not polarized into upper versus middle castes. It was not unlikely that the two rival leaders of from upper castes picked up and groomed rival subordinate-leaders from an intermediate or lower caste and thereby caused cliques formations across castes. As a result, the leaders formed alliances and counter-alliances across castes creating a complicated web of inter-related as well as competing, but not necessarily confronting, political relationships that were both vertically as well as horizontally structured. The leaders, irrespective of being first or second or third line, cultivated an elitist mindset by advertently or inadvertently drawing on the ethos of the medieval mindset permeated with the impulse for power and privileges.

Dalits Movement

The poorest and the most illiterate were the untouchables who were also called *Harijans* (children of god) on compassionate ground[130] and Dalits (Oppressed)[131] for their being depressed, struggled, and defiant. Dalits were outcastes and excluded from *varnashram* and therefore had the legitimate grudge to revolt against the caste Hindus. They did. In 1920s, a number of Dalits movements sprang up at different places in the country. They were either directed to remove the stigma of being untouchables, refuse performing their caste-based undignified roles, defy restrictions on their dress codes or entry into temples, ponds, wells, and other places of public utilities, strive for education and job, or emulate caste Hindu's rituals for upward mobility (*sanskritization*), or combination of all these. They had a common "Adi" theme. That is, Dalits believed that they were once the original, united, and egalitarian inhabitants of the land whereas Aryans were the invaders who imposed on them and forced them into undignified roles. They strived to get united with the Non-Brahmin movements in the country in order to organize a joint front against the Caste Hindus. But it did not work. There were a number of reasons.[132]

First of all, Hindu reform movements invariably co-opted Dalits movements by taking up their causes and thereby diluting their impulse to fight against caste Hindus. All three religious movements—Brahmo Samaj, Arya Samaj, and Ram Krishna Mission—were committed to eliminate untouchability by getting the untouchables back into the Hindu fold. Arya Samaj had a purification programme for them. However, Dalits were ambivalent about them. While they appreciated their stance, they did not believe that caste Hindus could sincerely think and do good to them. Their "Adi" theme was pre-Brahminic where the religious movements were entrenched in the *varnashram dharma,* which in fact was the basis of their discrimination. They did not like the paternalistic attitude of the Hindu reformers. They wanted to stand on their own, and in fact fight them out.

To that end, they preferred to join the Non-Brahmin movements that were strong in Maharashtra and the South. But a large number of Non-Brahmins from Maharashtra joined the Congress. Although Congress had already added social reforms to their political agenda as back as 1917 asking for of "removing all disabilities imposed upon the depressed people", it was still dominated by upper castes and the conservatives among them were not only indifferent, but often resistant to the causes of Dalits. Similarly, educated Dalits joined the Justice Party in the South, but when the Party came into power in 1920, it did not give them due representation. Dalits felt left out in both cases believing that the Non-Brahmin leaders too had the Brahminic mindset and were guided more by their self-interests than by their common interests.

Another weakness of the Dalit movements was the lack of national level leaders of their own, except Dr. B.R. Ambedkar.[133] Ambedkar had a high national stature. He got from the British a communal award of separate electorates whereby certain number of seats in the State and Central legislative assemblies were allotted to Dalits who were to be elected by the Dalit voters only. Gandhi vehemently opposed resorting to fast unto death. He argued that Harijans were very much Hindus and could not be separated from them. Ambedkar yielded. Their Poona Pact (1932) paved way for The Government of India Act (1935) reserving seats for Dalits who were to be elected by all eligible voters. The arrangement, however, allowed the locally influential persons of the dominant castes to get their favourite Dalits elected. In this respect, the Congress having mass contacts had an advantage. Their Dalit candidates won handsomely. Gandhi also made the Harijan a central concern of the Congress and formed the Hanjan Sevak Sangh to address them. Consequently, Dalits indeed received various concessions (for example, reservations in education, in jobs, and in the government, besides welfare benefits), but the Dalits movement was turned into a concession seeking outfit, and the Dalits leaders were absorbed into the elite group of high caste Non-Dalit politicians, rather uprooted from their own mass.

CONCLUSIONS

Castes categorization and ranking, on the basis of which the colonial authorities offered jobs to the natives, certainly transformed the castes from social into political entities, competing and conflicting or collaborating for an edge over each other. The cleavage between Brahmin and Non-Brahmin castes in the South at one point was so sharp that it threatened the integrity of the country. Elsewhere castes competed for societal resources and political dominance more than they conflicted with each other. The major cleavage in the country was of religious nature. The Muslim League on the one hand and the Hindu Mahasabha on the other hand tended to exploit religion while the Congress, under Gandhi's leadership, provided an over-arching bridge that accommodated both Hindus and Muslims. Religious animosities, despite the Congress efforts, kept on escalating resulting into the partition and blood bath.

Castes have always been nested in religion. Both the Muslim League and the Congress were composed of regional groups having diverse castes and religious identities, which prevented the League from gaining an undivided hold on all Muslims and the Congress from having a single blended nationalism of all castes.[134] However, during riots, caste identities were subjugated to the religious identities and they all fought as either Hindus or Muslims.[135] Caste interests generally yielded to the national movement for freedom against the British, particularly whenever it passed through a high time. Otherwise, caste rivalries kept simmering, despite the caste system being denounced by the leaders such as Vivekanand, Gandhi, and Ambedkar.[136] Rivalries assumed a complex dynamics where the Dalits were not strong enough to demand parity and compromised with concessions and reliefs; the high caste leaders tended to groom second or third line leaders from the OBCs (Other Backward Castes) and Dalits who were economically not-so-weak, were now getting education, and nursing political ambitions. As a result, the caste politics was gathering strength to storm the country's landscape.

Notes

1. Cited by Maddison, 2013, p. 5.
2. Cited by Maddison, 2013, p. 10.
3. https://en.wikipedia.org/wiki/English_Education_Act_1835.
4. Maddison, 2013, p. 12.
5. Carter & Harlow, 2003 cited by Nilekani, 2008, p. 334.
6. William, Sir Jones, 1824, p. 28.
7. William, Sir Jones, 1824, p. 164.
8. http://www.spaceandmotion.com/Philosophy-Rene-Descartes-Philosopher.htm
9. Said, 1978, p. 11.

10. Said, 1978, p. 21.
11. Cohn, 1996.
12. Malhotra, 2014, p. 267.
13. https://en.wikipedia.org/wiki/Max_M%C3%BCller
14. A Letter to the Duke of Argyll. Oxford, December 16, 1868. Available at http://www.encyclopediaofauthentichinduism.org/articles/35_max_muller.htm
15. Waardenburg, 1999, p. 87.
16. According to a journal, *Scientific American,* December 8, 1900, he usurped the credit which was due to an unnamed German by paying for the translation.
17. Bryant, 2001, p. 289.
18. Sugirtharajah, 2003, pp. 60-61.
19. https://en.wikipedia.org/wiki/Christianity_in_India
20. cited by Oswald Spengler, 1926/1991 p. 13.
21. Maddison , 2013, p. 1.
22. Carson , 2012.
23. Introduced by Warren Hastings in 1772.
24. Yasumasa, 2001, p. 38.
25. https://selfstudyhistory.com/2015/10/23/christian-missionary-activities-in-india/
26. Palsetia, 2006, p. 616.
27. Maddison, 2013, p. 4.
28. A lecture, " What India Can Teach US " at the University of Cambridge, Project Gutenberg. Available at https://en.wikipedia.org/wiki/Max_M%C3%BCller . Retrieved on March, 10, 2017.
29. Nikhilananda, 1953, p. 106.
30. Chatterjee 1993, p. 6.
31. Palsetia, 2006, p. 616.
32. Jones, 1989:p. 31.
33. Jones, 1989, p. 31.
34. Parekh, 1989, p.48.
35. Bhatt, 2001, p. 23.
36. Pennington, 2001, p. 581.
37. Metcalf, 1992, p.236.
38. Kenneth W. Jones, 1992, p. 64.
39. Kenneth W. Jones 1992, p. 53.
40. Georg, 2002 , p. 600.
41. Jones, 1989, p. 46.
42. Raychaudhuri 1998, p. 3.
43. Vivekanand cited by Jackson, 1994, pp. 33–34.
44. Van der Veer, 1994.
45. Bharathi 1998, p. 37.
46. Miller 1995, p. 181; Thomas, 2003, p. 44.

47. Yasumasa, 2001, p. 41.
48. Chatterjee, 1986, p. 50.
49. Islam, 2017.
50. Seshadri cited by Islam, 2017, p. 160.
51. Islam, 2017, p. 161.
52. Tara Chand, 1992, p. 493.
53. Gupta, 1972, p. 103.
54. A famous historian, R. C. Majumdar cited by Islam, 2017, p. 155.
55. Described by C. R. Das who defended him in the Alipur bomb case, cited by Islam, 2017, p. 162.
56. In his Uttarpara speech on May 30, 1909 available at http:// intyoga.online.fr / uttaspch.htm.
57. Bayly, 1985; Van der Veer, 1994; among others.
58. Shani, 2005, p. 3.
59. Kabir, 1969; Islam, 2017, p. 153.
60. Bayly, 1985.
61. Lord Ellenborough cited by Gupta, 1973, p. 25.
62. Gupta, 1973, p. 25.
63. Kabir, 1969.
64. Hardy, 1972.
65. Khalidi, 2006.
66. Seal, 1968.
67. Ray, 1977.
68. Hasan, 1985.
69. Prasad, 1941, p. 45.
70. Syed Ahmad Khan cited by Sharma, 1998, p. 20.
71. Hali, 1993 citedein https://en.wikipedia.org/wiki/ Syed_Ahmad_Khan. Retrieved on May 2 , 2017.
72. Kahn, 2007.
73. Azad, 1988.
74. Seal 1968.
75. Bhabha, 1994.
76. Wolpert, 1962, pp. 158-160.
77. https://en.wikipedia.org/wiki/Rahimtulla_M._Sayani
78. Chandra, 1984, p.210.
79. Tilak in 1919 cited by Bhatt, 2001, p. 36.
80. Shani, 2005, p. 16.
81. Nehru, 1945/ 2003, p. 362.
82. Rai cited by Bhatt, 2001, pp. 50 & 52.
83. Nehru, 1945/2003, p. 562.
84. Brass, 1994, cited by Islam, 2017, 150.
85. Thapar, 1989, p. 209.
86. Nehru, 1945/2003, p. 382.
87. Mehta & Patwardhan, 1942, Sahoo, 2008.
88. McLane, 1965.

89. Tara Chand, 1992, p. 346.
90. Hardy, 1972; Hasan, 1980.
91. Prasad, 1941, p. 45.
92. Brown, 1994, p. 228.
93. V. D. Savarkar cited by Prakash, 1952, p. xvii.
94. Jaffrelot, 1996, pp. 32.
95. Savarkar, 1923/1989.
96. Golwalkar, 1939/2007 quoted in Panikkar 1993, pp. 24 –25.
97. Embree & Carnes, 2015.
97. https://en.wikipedia.org/wiki/All-India_Muslim_League
98. Ali, 1942/1944.
99. Embree & Carnes, 2015.
100. Bayly, 2004 , pp. 3-4.
101. Dirks, 2001 , p. 5.
102. Bayly, 200 4 , pp. 125-127.
103. Burguière & Grew, 2001, pp. 215-229.
104. Raheja, 1999.
105. Rawat, 2011, pp. 26-27.
106. Yang, 1985.
107. Corbridge & Harriss, 2000, p. 243.
108. de Zwart, 2000, p. 235.
109. Barnett & Barnett, 1973.
110. Chandra, K. 2012; 1986.
111. Srinivas, 1956.
112. Unless otherwise indicated, the statistics cited in this paragraph were taken from Lee, 2015.
113. Misra, 1961 cited by Roy, 1995, p. 219 based on 1931 Census.
114. Srinivas, 1956.
115. Lee, 2015, p. 8.
116. Burguière & Grew, 2001, pp. 215-229.
117. Grave, 1979, pp. 12-13.
118. Stein, 1967-1968.
119. Subramaniam, 1969.
120. *Census Report*, 1921, Madras, Vol. II cited by Reddy, 2011.
121. Grave, 1979, pp. 14-15.
122. Grave, 1979.
123. Irshchick, 1969, p. 276.
124. Robert Calwell cited by Irshchick, 1969, p. 278.
125. Irschick, 1969, p. 280.
126. Barnett, 1972.
127. Reddy, 2011.
128. Irschick, 1986.
129. Roy, 1995, p. 236.
130. by Gandhi in 1933 : https://en.wikipedia.org/wiki/Harijan
131. by Dr. B. R. Ambedkar

132. Omvedt & Patankar, 2014.
133. Moon, 1995
134. Reetz, 1993, p. 110.
135. Bandyopadhyay, 2004.
136. Ambedkar, 1968; Gandhi cited by Mondal, undated; Vivekananda, 1952.

REFERENCES

Ali, Choudhary Rahmat (1942/1944). *The Millat and the mission.* Cambridge: Pakistan National Movement.

Ambedkar, B.R. (1968). *Annihilation of caste with a reply to Mahatma Gandhi and castes in India: Their mechanism, genesis, and development.* Jullundur City: Bheem Patrika Publications.

Azad, Maulana Abul Kalam (1988). *India wins freedom.* Hyderabad: Orient Blackswan.

Bandyopadhyay, Sekhar (2004). *Caste, culture and hegemony: social Dominance in Colonial Bengal,* New Delhi: Sage.

Barnett, Marguerite Ross (1972). The Politics of cultural nationalism: The DMK in Tamil Nadu, South India. Ph.D. Dissertation, University of Chicago.

Barnett, Marguerite Ross and Barnett, Steve A. (1973). *Contemporary peasant and post-peasant alternatives in South India: The ideas of a militant untouchable·* New York: Annals of New York Academy of Sciences.

Bayly, C.A. (1985). The pre-history of 'Communalism'? religious conflict in India, 1700–1860. *Modern Asian Studies,* 19 (02), 177–203. Berkeley, CA: University of California Press.

Bayly, Susan (2004). *Saints, goddesses, and kings: Muslims and Christians in South Indian society, 1700-1900.* Cambridge: Cambridge University Press

Bhabha, H. (1994). *The location of culture.* London: Routledge.

Bharathi, K.S. (1998). *Encyclopaedia of eminent thinkers: the political thought of Vivekananda,* New Delhi: Concept Publishing Company.

Bhatt, C. (2001). *Hindu nationalism: Origins, ideologies and modern myths.* Oxford: Berg.

Brass, P.R. (1994). Elite composition and nation-formation. In John Hutchinson and A.D. Smith (Eds.), *Nationalism.* Oxford: Oxford University Press.

Brown, J.M. (1994). *Modern India: the origins of an Asian democracy.* Delhi & New York: Oxford University Press.

Bryant, Edwin (2001). *The quest for the origins of Vedic culture: The Indo-Aryan migration debate.* Delhi & New York: Oxford University Press.

Burguière, A. and Grew, R. (2001). *The construction of minorities: Cases for comparison across time and around the world.* Ann Arbour: University of Michigan Press.

Carson, P. (2012). *The East India Company and religion, 1698-1858* (Worlds of the East India Company). Martlesham, Suffolk, UK: Boydell Press.

Carter, M. and Harlow, B. (Eds.) (2003). *Archives of empire* (Vol. 1). Durham: Duke University Press.

Chand, Tara (1992). *History of freedom movement in India* (Volume 3), Delhi: Publications Division, Government of India.

Chandra, Bipin (1984). *Communalism in modern India,* Vikas: New Delhi.

Chandra, Kanchan (2012). *Constructivist theories of ethnic politics.* New Delhi: Oxford University Press.

Chatterjee, Partha (1986). *Nationalist thought and the colonial world.* London: Zed Books.

Chatterjee, Partha (1993). *The nation and its fragments.* Princeton: Princeton University Press.

Cohn, B.S. (1996). *Colonialism and its forms of knowledge: The British in India.* Princeton: Princeton University Press.

Corbridge, S. and Harriss, J. (2000). *Reinventing India: Liberalization, Hindu nationalism and popular democracy.* Cambridge: Polity Press.

de Zwart, Frank (2000). The logic of affirmative action: Caste, class and quotas in India. *Acta Sociologica,* 43 (3), 235–249.

Dirks, Nicholas B. (2001). *Castes of mind: Colonialism and the making of New India.* Princeton: Princeton University Press.

Embree, A.T. and Carnes, M.C. (2015). *Defining a nation: India on the eve of independence, 1945.* New York: W.W. Norton & Company.

Georg, F. *(2002). The Yoga tradition.* Delhi: Motilal Banarsidas.

Golwalkar, M.S. *(1939/2007). We or our nationhood defined. In C. Jaffrelot (Ed.), Hindu Nationalism—A Reader. Princeton: Princeton University Press.*

Gupta, D.C. (1973). *Indian national movement and constitutional development.* Delhi: Vikas

Gupta, Manmath Nath (1972). *History of the Indian revolutionary movement.* Mumbai: Somaiya Publications.

Hardgrave, Robert L. (1979). *Essays in the Political Sociology of South India.* Delhi: Usha Publication.

Hardy, P. (1972). *The Muslims of British India.* London: Cambridge University Press.

Hasan, M. (1980). Communalism in the provinces: A case Study of Bengal and the Punjab, 1922-26. *Economic and Political Weekly,* 1395–1406.

Hasan, M. (1985). Nationalist and separatist trends in Aligarh, 1915–47. *Indian Economic and Social History Review,* 22 (1), 1–33.

Irshchick, E.F. (1969). *Politics and social conflict in South India: The Non-*

Brahmin movement and Tamil separatism, 1916-1929: Berkeley and Los Angeles: University of California Press.

Irschick, E.F. (1986). *Politics and social conflict in South India and Tamil revivalism in the 1930s*. Madras: Cre-A.

Islam, Shamsul (2017). *Hindu nationalism and Rashtriya Swayamsevak Sangh*. Delhi: Media House.

Jackson, C.T. (1994). *Vedanta for the West: the Ramakrishna movement in the United States*. Indianapolis: Indiana: Indiana University Press.

Jaffrelot, C. *(1996). The Hindu nationalist movement and Indian politics*. C. Hurst & Co. Publishers.

Jones, Kenneth W. (1989). *Socio-Religious Reform Movements in India*. Cambridge: Cambridge University Press. 1-47.

Jones, Kenneth W. (1992). Swami Dayananda Saraswati's critique of Christianity. In Kenneth W. Jones (Ed.), *Religious controversy in British India: Dialogues in South Asian languages* (pp. 52-74). Albany: SUNY Press.

Kabir, Humayun (1969). *Muslim politics, 1906-47: And other essays*. Calcutta: Firma KL Mukhopadhyay.

Kahn, A.R. (2007). All India Muhammadan Educational Conference and the Foundation of the All-India Muslim League. *Journal of the Pakistan Historical Society*, 55, 1/2, 65–83.

Khalidi, Omar (2006). *Muslims in Indian economy*. Gurgaon: Three Essays Collective.

Laitin, D. (1986). *Hegemony and culture*. Chicago: University of Chicago Press.

Lee, A. (2015). The origins of identity politics: Caste in colonial India. file:///C:/Users/Jai/Documents/Caste%20Identity%20%20Origin.pdf. Retrieved on May 15, 2017

Maddison, A. (2013). *Class structure and economic growth: India and Pakistan Since the Moghuls*. Oxford, New York: Taylor & Francis. Available at http://www.ggdc.net/maddison/articles/moghul_3.pdf. Retrieved on January, 17, 2017.

Malhotra, Rajiv (2014). *Indra's net: Defending Hinduism's philosophical unity*. New Delhi: Harper Collins.

McLane, J.R. (1965). The decision to partition Bengal in 1905. *Indian Economic and Social History Review*, 2 (3), 221–237.

Mehta, Asoka, and Patwardhan. Achyut (1942). *The communal triangle in India*. Allahabad: Kitabistan.

Metcalf, Barbara D. (1992). Imagining community: Polemical debates in colonial India. In Kenneth W. Jones (ed.), *Religious controversy in British India. Dialogues in South Asian languages* (pp. 229-240). Albany: SUNY Press.

Miller, Timothy (1995). *The Vedanta movement and self-Realization fellowship: America's Alternative Religions*, Albany, New York: SUNY Press.

Misra, B.B. (1961). *The Indian middle classes: Their growth in modern times.* London: Oxford University Press.

Moon, V. (1995). (Ed.) *Dr. Babasaheb Ambedkar. Writings and Speeches* (Vol. 14/1). Mumbai: Education Department, Government of Maharashstra.

Mondal, P. (2017). Mahatma Gandhi Views on Caste System! Available at http://www.yourarticlelibrary.com/caste/mahatma-gandhi-views-on-caste-system/38494/. Retrieved on August 20, 2017

Nehru, J. (1945/2003). *Discovery of India.* New Delhi: Oxford University Press.

Nikhilananda, Swami (1953). *Vivekananda: A biography* (PDF), New York: Ramakrishna-Vivekananda Centre.

Nilekani, N. (2008). *Imagining India: Ideas for the new century*. Allen, Lane: Penguin.

Omvedt, G. and Patankar, B. (2014). The Dalit liberation movement in colonial period. https://www.facebook.com/notes/obed-manwatkar/the-dalit-liberation-movement-in-colonial-period-by-gail-omvedt-and-bharat-patan/10201552341642917. Retrieved on May 20, 2017.

Oswald, Spengler (1926/1991). *The decline of the West.* In Arthur Helps & Helmut Werner (Eds., Trans. by Charles F. Atkinson. Preface Hughes, H. Stuart). New York: Oxford University Press, p. 13.

Palsetia, Jesse S. (2006). Parsi and Hindu traditional and non-traditional responses to Christian conversion in Bombay, 1839-45. *Journal of the American Academy of Religion,* 74 (3), 615-145.

Panikkar, K.N. *(1993).* Culture and communalism. *Social Scientist, 21 (3/ 4), 24–31.*

Parekh, B. (1989). *Colonialism, tradition and reform: An Analysis of Gandhi's political discourse*. London: Sage.

Pennington, Brian K. (2001). Constructing colonial dharma: A chronicle of emergent Hinduism, 1830-1831. *Journal of the American Academy of Religion,* 69 (3), 577-603.

Prakash, I. (1952). *A review of the history and work of the Hindu Mahasabha and the Hindu sangathan movement*. Delhi: Hindu Mahasabha.

Prasad, Beni (1941). *The Hindu-Muslim question*. Allahabad: Kitabistan.

Raheja, G.G. (1999). The Illusion of consent: Language, caste, and colonial rule in India. In Peter Pels and Oscar Salemink (Eds.), *Colonial subjects: Essays on the practical history of anthropology* (pp. 120–122). Ann Arbor: University of Michigan Press.

Rawat, R. (2011). *Reconsidering untouchability: Chamars and Dalit history in North India*. Bloomington: Indiana University Press.

Ray, Anil Baran (1977). Communal attitudes to British policy: The case of the partition of Bengal 1905. *Social Scientist*: 34–46.

Raychaudhuri, Tapan. (1998). Swami Vivekananda's construction of Hinduism. In William Radice (Ed.), *Swami Vivekananda and the modernization of Hinduism* (pp. 1-16). New Delhi: Oxford University Press. 1-16.

Reddy, G.S. (2011). Caste, politics, and social conflict. *Social Science* December 30, 1-14.

Reetz, D. (1993). Ethnic and religious identities in colonial India (1920s-1930s): A conceptual debate. *Contemporary South Asia,* 2(2), 109-122.

Roy, R. (1995). Caste and political recruitment in Bihar. In Rajni Kothari (Ed.), *Caste in Indian politics* (p. 215-244). New Delhi: Sage.

Sahoo, S. (2008). Ethno-religious identity and sectarian civil society: A case from India. *Studies in Ethnicity and Nationalism,* 8 (3), 453–480.

Said, Edward W. (1978). *Orientalism.* New York: Pantheon Books.

Savarkar, V.D. (1923/1989). *Hindutva.* Bombay: Veer Savarkar Prakashan.

Seal, Anil (1968). *The emergence of Indian nationalism: Competition and collaboration in the later nineteenth century.* Cambridge: Cambridge University Press.

Shani, G. (2005). Indigenous Modernities: Nationalism and communalism in Colonial India. *Ritsumeikan Annual Review of International Studies,* 4, 87-112. Available at http://www.ritsumei.ac.jp/acd/cg/ir/college/bulletin/e-vol4/shani.pdf. Retrieved on March 14, 2017.

Sharma, H.D. (1998) (Ed.), *100 best pre-independence speeches, 1870-1947.* NOIDA, UP: Harper Collins.

Srinivas, M.N. (1956). A note on sanskritization and westernization. *The Far Eastern Quarterly,* 15 (4), 481-496.

Stein, Burton (1967-1968). Brahmin and peasant in early South Indian history. In *Dr. V. Raghavan Felicitation Volume of the Adyar Library Bulletin,* 31-32.

Subramaniam, T.V. (1969). The Tamil Brahmins: Some guidelines to research on their emergence and eclipse. *Economic and Political Weekly,* p.1.

Sugirtharajah, S. (2003). *Imagining Hinduism: A post-colonial perspective.* London: Routledge.

Thapar, Romila (1989). Imagined religious communities? Ancient history and the modern search for a Hindu identity. *Modern Asian Studies,* 23 (2), 209-231.

Thomas, W. (2003). *Hinduism invades America 1930.* Kessinger Publishing.

Van der Veer, Peter (1994). *Religious nationalism: Hindus and Muslims in India.* Berkeley, CA: University of California Press.

Vivekananda, Swami (1952). *The complete works of Swami Vivekananda* (Vol. 5). Calcutta: Advait Ashram. pp. 25–30.

Waardenburg, J. (1999). *Classical approaches to the study of religion: Aims, methods, and theories of research* (Volume 1). New York: Walter de Gruyter.

William, Sir Jones (1824). *Discourses delivered before the Asiatic Society and miscellaneous papers, on the religion, poetry, literature, etc., of the nations of India.* London: C.S. Arnold.

Wolpert, S. (1962). *Tilak and Gokhale: Revolution and reform in the making of modern India*. Berkeley: University of California Press.

Yang, A. (1985). *Crime and criminality in British India*. Tucson, AZ: University of Arizona Press.

Yasumasa, Sekine (2001). Religion and Politics in Contemporary India: The Complexities of Secularism and Communalism. Institute for Conflict Management, South Asia Terrorism Portal (SATP), New Delhi.

5
Politics Playing Havoc

DENTED IDEALISM AND INCOMPLETE SOLUTIONS

Pre-independence was the Gandhian era known for the mass movements for freedom, concern for communal harmony, and emphasis on social reforms particularly accepting *Harijans* into the main Hindu stream. Caste differences were coming up, but were covered up by the nationalism, and communal conflicts were occurring but were contained to some extent. The next twenty years (1947–1967) witnessed the unchallenged rule of the Congress under the overwhelming charisma of Nehru; then, a new phase ensued that witnessed eroding integrity and polluting politics under the leadership of Indira Gandhi.[1] Nehru was essentially a philosopher king of virtues and wisdom[2], who was committed to democracy, secularism, and modernization, which majority of Congress men and women by and large shared. The country, which he led, faced existential threat of getting disintegrated. Hence, he has to accommodate diverse views and pressures in order to keep the country intact and to move ahead. He thus made compromises with his idealism and settled for incomplete solutions that did not eliminate the forces of casteism, communalism, and corruption, which only remained suspended for a while.

Reservation: Demanded and Denied

Nehru believed that although the caste system persisted for centuries as a symptom of people's backwardness, it will disappear soon "That is not chiefly because of some powerful urge to reform itself which has arisen in Hindu society... nor is it because of ideas from the west...The change that is taking place before our eyes is due essentially to basic economic changes which have shaken up the whole fabric of Indian society and are likely to upset it [caste system] completely".[3] Being an accommodative visionary, he invited Ambedkar, a non-Congress Dalit leader, to head the Law Ministry and the Committee, which drafted the Constitution. The Constitution was indeed quite progressive and ideal. It prohibited discrimination based on religion and caste (Article 15) and declared the practice of untouchability illegal (Article 17). Later on in 1955 the Untouchability (Offences) Act was passed. Among the Dalits, the Scheduled castes (SCs) were offered 15 per cent and the Scheduled Tribes (STs) 7.50 per cent reservations in government jobs and educational institutions. Subsequently, 15.47 per cent seats for the SCs and 8.66 per cent seats for the STs were reserved in the Parliament as well in the State Assemblies, and local bodies.[4]

Reservations for the SCs and STs provided a ground to the intermediate level castes to demand similar affirmative action for them. Their political consciousness and aspirations were already rising sharply from the late colonial period. Now, the universal suffrage granted in the Constitution highlighted their numerical strength. The three factors—reservations for SCs and STs, rising political consciousness and aspirations, and numerical strength—led a movement to grant reservations also for the castes that were backward. Nehru conceded the backwardness of the intermediate level castes and gave it a name, Other Backward Classes (OBCs), while ignoring their caste identity[5] and refusing to extend the advantages of reservations that were extended to the SCs and STs. However, an opening was allowed through the Article 16(4) of the Constitution stating that "Nothing in this article shall prevent the State from making any provision for the reservation of appointments or posts in favour of any backward class of citizens which in the opinion of the State, is not adequately represented in the services under the State." Further, Article 340 stipulated that the President was entitled to appoint a commission for identifying the socially and educationally backward *classes* and suggesting measures to improve their condition. Hence, a commission under Kaka Kalelkar was constituted in 1953. The Commission submitted its Report in 1955.[6] It identified four main criteria for social backwardness—a degraded status, lack of education, under-representation in the civil service, and secondary and tertiary sectors—all came down to one common denominator: Belonging to lower castes: OBCs (Other Backward Castes[7]). The Commission prepared a list of 2,399 OBCs representing 32 per cent of the population.[8] It recommended 70 per cent quota for admissions of OBCs in vocational training institutions, 25 to 40 per cent reservation in the civil services, and higher percentages in the lower grades.

Nehru conceded that SCs and STs deserved reservation. It was a policy decision of the Congress before Independence. It did not encroach significantly on the elitist turf of the Indian politics and administration. But, OBCs were likely to disrupt the upper castes dominance. The elites were against it, so was the modernist Nehru. He wrote to the Chief Ministers of the States:[9]

> I react strongly against anything which leads to inefficiency and second rate standards. I want my country to be a first class country in everything. The moment we encourage the second rate, we are lost. The only way to help a backward group is to give opportunities for good education.... Everything else will be providing them (backward groups) some kind of crutches which don't add to the strength or health of the body.... But if we go in for reservation on communal and caste basis, we swamp the bright and able people and remain second rate or third rate. I am grieved to learn of how far this business of reservation has gone based on communal consideration....This way lies not only folly, but disaster.

G.B. Pant, Home Minister, echoed Nehru. He rejected the Commission's Report by concluding that development efforts through the first Five Year Plan would lead to "the establishment of our society on the socialist pattern" evolving into a state in which "social and other distinctions will disappear".[10] That is, backwardness of lower castes was to be eliminated, not through reservation, but by the socialist mode of development.

It was an elitist vision of development that was planned to be realized by grandiose such as heavy industries, big dams, ivory towers of management, technology, and higher education, and so on. There was no realization that the backwardness of the people can be alleviated by enabling them to acquire basic capabilities to try on their own and achieve what they aspire for. Instead of grandiose, what the country needed most was to prioritize stabling well-equipped institutions for primary and secondary education and health care, income generating skills, and for cultivating democratic values. As backwardness was not directly targeted, the backwards had only one avenue—politics—open to fight back.

They were led by the *Samyukt* Socialist Party (SamSoPa). It passed a "Socialist Programme" in 1959 demanding 60 per cent reservation for the backwards (*SanSoPa ki yeh hai maang, pichhare paiye sau mein satth*) proportionate to their percentage in the population[11]. A socialist ideologue, Ram Manohar Lohia (1910-1967), argued that caste, much more so than class, was the basic unit of Indian society and that Nehru's version of socialism would not be enough to combat inequalities. For, nationalizing industries and collectivizing land would never lead to revolutionizing the social order, simply because the upper castes would continue to find ways, on the basis of their skills inherited from generations, to dominate the backwards "for thousands of years". So, the backward castes needed reservations not only of socio-economic redistribution but also to shed their feelings of inferiority[12]. But *SamSoPa* did not have enough political clout to make a dent in the policy. So, nothing happened on the ground for the time being.

Coexistence of Hindu Code and Personal Law

Nehru was a staunch secularist in the European tradition who wanted to modernize Indians by eradicating their outdated traditions, rituals, and religious practices. He believed that religion, like caste, is the vestiges of old tradition and would disappear with the socialist form of economic development. As back as in the 1930s, he wrote, "Personally, I am not interested in religious labels and I am sure that they will soon disappear, or, at any rate, cease to have any political significance".[13] He in fact "felt angry with Bapu [Gandhi] at his religious and sentimental approach to a political question.... And his frequent references to God—God has made him do this—God even indicated the date of the fast...What a terrible example to set!"[14]. He was also angry and quite cynical about the Muslim and Hindu leaders who fanned religious differences for serving their selfish or sectarian interests: "There is no religious or cultural conflict in India. What is called the religious or communal problem is really a dispute among upper-class people for a division of the spoils of office for representation in a legislature".[15] He kept on believing that

> Communalism is one of the obvious examples of backward looking people trying to hold on to something that is wholly out of place in the modern world and is essentially opposed to the concept of nationalism. In fact, it splits up nationalism into a number of narrower nationalisms.[16]

Having such a worldview in support, Ambedkar drafted the Constitution that promised that "the State shall endeavour to secure for the citizens a uniform civil code throughout the territory of India" (Article 44). However, the Constitution also guaranteed freedom to free profession, practice and propagation of religion (Article 25), manage religious affairs (Article 26), pay taxes for promotion of any particular religion (Article 27), and to attendance at religious instruction or religious worship in certain educational institutions (Article 28). The Constitution also protected the interests of minorities (Article 29) and their 'right...to establish and administer educational institutions (Article 30). It also recognised distinctly different personal codes (Entry 5 in Article 44) of the various religious communities. By implication, the State was to respect the personal codes of the people of different faith.

Here was the dilemma: How could the State allow freedom to different religious communities to follow their distinctly different personal laws while still being bound by a uniform civil code? There had to be a demarcation line separating religious from civil rights and obligations. Ambedkar was quite straightforward about it:

> Coming to the question of saving personal law...The religious conceptions in this country are so vast that they cover every aspect of life, from birth to death. There is nothing which is not religion and if personal law is to be saved, I am sure about it that in social matters we will come to a standstill. I do not think it is possible to accept a position of that sort. There is nothing extraordinary in

> saying that we ought to strive hereafter to limit the definition of religion in such a manner that we shall not extend beyond beliefs and such rituals as may be connected with ceremonials which are essentially religious. It is not necessary that the sort of laws, for instance, laws relating to tenancy or laws relating to succession should be governed by religion.[17]

In other words, Ambedkar advocated to have a uniform code for the rights of property, order of succession, maintenance, marriage, divorce, and similar other issues of individual civil rights leaving socio-religious rituals, practices, and ceremonies to be based on the personal laws. There were others of different background such as K.M. Munsi (a Hindu minded Congress leader) and Minoo Masani (a socialist) who favoured a uniform civil code. However, only the Hindu Code was framed along these lines rectifying the retrogressive practices and aligning them with a modern set of secular laws. They were strongly opposed by the orthodox Hindu leaders on many grounds, particularly that the Hindu laws had divine origin and must not be tinkered with by the State. However, it was passed through, though as separated bills, watered down, and after going through slow grinding processes. But the opposition to the uniform civil code was even stronger by Muslim leaders.

Nehru wavered. He felt that Muslims were rather shaken by the partition and might feel further insecure by the imposition of a uniform civil code. So, he preferred to wait till they get mentally prepared to accept it. He believed they will eventually. Hindu Code Bills were a grand project of modernization where Hindus as the majority community were to set an example in the interest of building a secular society. Hindus were not totally transformed even after 60 years. Only those clauses could be implemented (e.g., polygamy) where the State was able to keep surveillance and punish the deviants, but the rest (e.g., dowry or equal share in property to sons and daughters) remained more in the books. Muslim elites successfully resisted any attempt to change their personal law. The opportunity to enforce a uniform civil code was lost in the 1950s when Nehru had the absolute majority in the parliament. In fact, his compromise created a legacy that was much difficult to break through in the following decades.

There was another lapse that later on proved to be a fountain of State instigated communalism. India had a long tradition where kings patronized and financed constructing buildings and running temples, monasteries, and mosques of the religion of their choice. A secular State, on the contrary, guarantees freedom to individuals to practice, profess, and preach the religion of their choice but refrains from any positive discrimination. Some of the Congress leaders in the government selectively followed the royal tradition rather than the secular norms. For instance, immediately after the princely State of Junagarh (where the old dilapidated Somanath temple was located) was annexed to India (1947), the Deputy Prime Minister, Sardar Vallabhbhai Patel, ordered the reconstruction of the temple and entrusted it to another Union Minister, K.M. Munsi. Gandhi was approached to bless the move. He did but suggested that the funds for the construction should be collected from the public, the temple should not be constructed by the State money.[18] The restoration was sponsored by the Government of India and was conducted through a Trust. The ruins of the dilapidated temple were removed and the mosque at that site was shifted few kilometres away. Dr. Rajendra Prasad, the first President of the Republic of India, presided over (May, 1951) the installation ceremony.[19] Nehru opposed both K.M. Munsi and Dr. Prasad fearing that the restoration might be misconstrued as Hindu revivalism. But they did not listen to him. Nehru himself, later on, got land donated for the construction of a Buddhist pilgrim's centre in Sanchi as well as for the restoration of Buddhist monastery at Sarnath. These and similar other instances created a precedence for the political leaders in power to use the State instrument to favour and discriminate individuals and communities on the basis of their religion. Their religious discriminations and favours were bound to cascade over the rest of the society, irrespective of how pious their beliefs and intentions might have been.

The Black Sheep: Corruption

Congress leaders were not immune to the vice of corruption, although they were armoured by Gandhian ethics, Nehru's idealism, and their own involvement in the nationalist movement. Mahatma Gandhi was anguished by the instances and allegations of corruption in the Congress.[20] He wrote as back as 1934, "The corruption in the Congress is preying on me as it has never before done".[21] A few years later when the Congress formed provincial governments (1937-1938), there were allegations of malpractices. Gandhi confirmed that "... in the Congress there are much corruption and jealousy, but they are confined to those few who run the machinery".[22] Towards the end of his life in 1947, he again lamented that, "I have it from very trustworthy sources that corruption is increasing in the country"[23]. Soon after Nehru was sworn in Prime Minister, Dr. Radhakrishnan called upon him to "destroy corruption in high places, root out every trace of nepotism, love of power, profiteering, and black-marketing....".[24] Steps such as the Prevention of Corruption Act, 1947 were taken immediately after Independence.

However, skeletons kept tumbling out the cupboards at the high places. There was a scam in the purchase of jeep for the Army in which one of the closest associates of Nehru, V.K. Krishna Menon, was indicted; the Finance Minister, T.T. Krishnamachari, and the Finance Secretary, H.M. Patel, had to resign because of their involvement in the LIC-Mundhra deal; the first Punjab Chief Minister, Pratap Singh Kairon, highly appreciated by Nehru, but, according to the Prime Minister Lal Bahadur Shastri, was consumed by the monster (of corruption) he had created in Punjab; so was the perception of Biju Patnaik. There were other numerous instances.

Government reports documented the presence of corruption in high places. It was reported that Ministers, Legislators and Administrators providing patronage based on communalism, sectarianism, nepotism and favouritism and found that "the public generally feel that anyone really influential can get away with anything."[25] There was corruption in the Railways[26] as well as at the higher levels of administration:[27]

> ... corruption has increased to such an extent that people have started losing faith in the integrity of public administration. We heard from all sides that corruption has, in recent years, spread even to those [higher] levels of administration from which it was conspicuously absent in the past (pp. 12–13).

Allegations of corruption were freely floating around, yet hard evidence to verify them was often difficult to find. However, people invariably believed the allegations to be true. They imagined widespread corruptions. It so happens that what many people imagine most others doing becomes a psychological reality, that is, a norm that legitimizes the act. It probably happened with corruption. Prime Minister Nehru observed that "merely shouting from the house tops that everybody is corrupt creates an atmosphere of corruption. People feel they are in a climate of corruption and they get corrupted themselves".[28]

Corruption was indeed creeping into the Nehruvian era, but it was still, by and large, contained. The top leaders certainly belonged mostly to upper castes and had an elitist mindset. But they had mass contact and a nationalist spirit ingrained through working for years in the freedom movement. They were enthused by the idea of socialist development under the leadership of Nehru. "Nehru never liked associating himself directly with any unscrupulous act, anything... immoral...".[29] It was rightly observed that

> "...there is no doubt that the top level of the Congress leadership was quite sincerely committed to a developmental agenda. Above all, Nehru's commanding presence in the cabinet ensured that such malfeasance as existed remained within limits. For all its shortcomings, the Nehru regime nevertheless evinced a degree of integrity that has been altogether absent in the regimes that followed".[30]

POLLUTING MILIEU AND ERODING INTEGRITY

Nehru died in 1964 and three years later (in 1967) the Congress lost its absolute majority in the Parliament that it had enjoyed since 1952, besides losing power or majority in several States. The Syndicate of powerful Congress leaders made Indira Gandhi the Prime Minister presuming that she would be a *Gungi Guria* (dumb doll) whom they would control easily. However, she turned into a tactful and tough politician. She herself accepted that "My father was a statesman, I am a political woman. My father was a saint. I am not". She was driven by her self-interest, but camouflaged it in socialist ideology. Never before she had shown any inclination towards socialism,[31] but now, in order to hedge the Syndicate, she made a common cause with the young socialists in Congress and got passed their 10-point Programme through the All India Congress Committee. The Programme sought nationalisation of banks, and later on steel, coal, oil, insurance, export, and import. Further, it asked for curbs on monopolies and concentration of economic power; limits on urban income and property; land reforms, and abolition of princely privileges and privy purses. She thus gained immense popularity and manoeuvred to consolidate her power and authority in both the government and the Party. She eased out those Congress chief ministers who were not loyal to her, imposed President rule in non-Congress ruled States, and even fired her Deputy Prime Minister, Morarji Desai, whom the Syndicate was planning to replace her with. She launched the 20-point populist programme, *Garibi Hatao* (Eradicate Poverty) that took her to a landslide victory in 1971 election. Riding on the tide of her popularity, she broke Pakistan to create Bangadesh, defied super-powers to get the first Indian nuclear device exploded, refused to yield to the USA for a food-aid, incorporated Sikkim, and aligned Nepal and Bhutan closely to India. When threatened to be convicted for an election fraud, she imposed Emergency that also got the notorious 42nd Amendment in the Constitution curtailing the power of the Supreme and High Courts to review the acts passed by the Parliament. There were similar other bold acts of forceful leadership that made her immensely popular among the people enabling her to cow down whoever came in her way. Atal Bihari Vaipayee, who later became a BJP (Bharatiya Janata Party) Prime Minister, called her "Durga"—the most powerful and aggressive goddess in the Indian mythology.

However, she was not a consensus builder like her father, Nehru. Rather she centralized all power in herself. It was often said in media that she was the only "Man" in her all male Cabinet. She openly asserted that "the PM (Prime Minister) is not bound to put everything before the cabinet". She neither consulted nor informed the Cabinet before declaring Emergency. In the first year of her office, she devalued rupees by 57 per cent without taking her Finance Minister in confidence. She was authoritative in her decision-making demanding personal loyalty[32] and placing the loyal ones on the crucial positions. One of her sycophants, Dev Kant Barua, was made the Governor of Bihar (1971-1973). He proclaimed (in 1974): "Indira is India and India is Indira", and was made the President of the Congress during Emergency (1975-1977)[33] in order probably to have an unquestioned support of the Congress Party.

She did not only personalize politics, but politicized the bureaucracy too. During Nehru's time, bureaucrats were shielded from politics. Their transfers, promotions, and other service conditions were decided within their own framework by following certain procedure and precedence. Now, they had to seek patronage of powerful politicians in the government who got them posted at privileged positions in return for personal loyalty and energetic implementation of their partisan agenda.[34] If they did not perform up to the mark and were pulled up by the superior, they were protected. In fact they did not only get scot free, but were able to turn the table on their superior[35] and harassed them. The officers with integrity were victimized and demoralized. The civil service was indeed sucked into the whirlpool of personalized politics.

Criminalization Spilling into Society

The whole paradigm of politics was indeed changed. Earlier, leaders' contact with and popularity among people were the primary consideration for being sponsored by the Congress to contest for positions in the party, the legislative assemblies, and the Parliament. Selections were made at the district and State levels. Now they were made in Delhi by those who were close to Indira Gandhi. The aspirants did not need people's support as much as they depended on Delhi's blessing. Naturally, the aspirants had to hang around the senior leaders and power brokers in Delhi. This gave them visibility in the corridors of power and opportunities to show their loyalty to those who mattered in deciding their political prospects. There was virtually no use wasting time in the constituency for cultivating mass support of the people, because the political aspirants' fate was decided in the *Delhi Darbar* (Royal Court).

Still elections had to be won, but not necessarily with genuine popular support. Money and muscle power substituted public support. The aspirants tended to hire local level influential persons who could serve as vote banks, can capture election booths and get the bulk of votes cast in their favour, and/or physically prevent the hostile voters from voting. These vote getters were mostly moneyed and muscle men or criminals. In return, the aspirants had to give them patronage, pull connections to get them favours from the State, and provide them safety and sanctuary, should the police keep looking out for them. Bureaucrats, as stated earlier, were already getting politicized. Hence, a nexus between the trio—bureaucrats, political bosses, and the vote getters–developed. The money and muscle men soon realized their potential to win elections and get elected themselves rather than getting others elected. They became politicians displacing many old style ones. How could they give up using muscle and money power that got them elected or how could they refrain from indulging in crime that added weight to their muscle and money power? So, they became criminal-politicians. Some of them won election even from a prison. Now, they did not have to seek protection and sanctuary, nor even to fear law and order authorities. In fact, they were the masters whom the armed security protected against their rivals. Bureaucrats appeased them to get favours in transfer and posting. Not all politicians of the older style were replaced. However, the new breed had enough of critical mass to create compulsions for the older type to make compromises and allow sufficient space to the criminal politicians. In sum, the whole architecture of politics deteriorated and kept on deteriorating in the following years.

A 10 years (2004-2013) survey showed the linkage between money, criminal charges, and participation in electoral politics[36]. All together 62, 847 persons contested for either Parliament or State Assemblies. Of them, 8,790 got elected. Of the elected ones, 29 per cent MPs (Members of Parliament) and MLAs (Members of the Legislative Assemblies) had criminal cases pending against them. In fact, 14 per cent were facing serious criminal cases. Among the 232 sitting Rajya Sabha (Upper House) members, 17 per cent admitted having criminal cases against them. Those who contested election had the asset of Rs. 1.37 crore. Elected ones had three times more: Rs. 3.83 crore. Those facing criminal charges had even more: Rs. 4.30 crore. And, those facing serious criminal charges were the richest with the asset of Rs. 4.38 crore. In other words, by their own admission to the Election Commission, the contestants for the Parliament and State Legislative Assemblies had more than 100 times the per capita wealth of Indians (Rs. 133,400 approximately in 2011[37]) suggesting that only the rich ones were able to contest elections. Further, the elected ones were three times richer than those who contested but lost election. Those facing criminal charges had on the average around Rs. 50 crore more in asset. And, those facing serious charges were the richest.

Up-to-dating its report (August, 2017), the ADR (Association for Democratic Reforms) examined the election affidavits of 774 of the 776 current Members of Parliament and 4,078 of the 4,120 MLAs from across India. Of these, about 32 per cent declared criminal cases against them, with 51 involved in cases of crime against women, including rape by four MLAs. Thirty five candidates for the Parliament and 294 for the State assemblies facing charges of crime against women were given tickets by the recognised political parties.[38] Out of 78 Union Ministers, 72 were corepatis, the average asset of the entire cabinet amounted to Rs. 12.94 crore. Twenty four Ministers were facing criminal charges.[39] A significant chunk of super-rich criminals were holding powerful positions in the politics.

There were variations in the criminalizing politics from place to place. It was at its full form, particularly in the places like Bihar. Here are the two accounts that aptly captured how criminal politicians ruled as back as in the 1990s.

> Sahabuddin, a Member of Parliament from Lalu's party, established complete hold over Siwan district. Tales of his gory crimes and terror often filled the pages of newspapers. Similar was the case of Bhagar Yadav who established his crime capital in the diara areas of West Champaran and was later successful in sending his younger brother to the State Assembly as an elected member. Another backward-caste RJD leader, Brij Bihari Prasad, known for his muscle power, ended the crime empire of the Congress leader Devendra Dube that spread from East Champaran to Muzaffarpur districts. Yadav criminals operating in Nalanda, Nawada and Patna districts regularly made it to the newspapers headlines by their unrelenting spate of kidnappings in the capital town of Patna.[40]

Another account from *The Republic of Bihar,*

> From Mohammed Suleiman's territory in Kishanganj through Pappu Yadav's domain in Purnea Madhepura, one can cross Bihar by passing through Anand Mohan Singh's area and then into the realm of Raghunath Pandey and 'Samrat' Ashok and further into the Gopalganj belt of Salaluddin and the Wild West of Champaran. Alternatively, one can go through Makhi Paswan's Khagaria, Kailu Yadav's region, into the Dularchand tal and then through Dilip Singh's land and on to the lawless Kaimur ranges crossing the realm of Surendra Yadav.[41]

These crime lords of politics had the hierarchy of associates who now constituted a large part of the political elites of Bihar. They freely captured public resources such as fishing ghats, diara lands, government lands[42], bossed over government functionaries, and started schools and coaching centres for making money and bullying local people.

Criminalization of politics, though started earlier, was conspicuous by the 1980s. It was observed that the country had become "a playground for growing corruption, criminalisation, repression and intimidation of large masses of the people". As a result, the State was distracted from its purpose of development. There was "discontent and despair in the air" with a belief that the society had deliberately turned indifferent to the impoverished and the destitute.[43]

Since the 1980s, the milieu kept worsening. Liberalization of the economy created many new opportunities, which tempted an increasing number of politicians, administrators, businessmen, and other powerful men and women to indulge in huge scams and scandals. The corrupt ones became the role models that the people emulated leading to the criminalization of the whole society. Even those who are not criminally disposed started committing crimes, often first time and at times even without being quite conscious of their seriousness. For example, otherwise innocent school children, housewives, house heads, and god-fearing persons are reported behaving the ways that are hard to believe what they did. In the present scenario, common people shout against corruption at the top of their voice, but are found breaking norms, adopting dubious practices, or committing crimes. There is a wide spread cynicism wondering whom to believe and trust. Blatantly crooks and criminals are found flourishing demoralizing others, distracting them from righteous conduct, and sliding down into criminal activities.

Box 5.1: Who will Believe?

- Five boys in the age range of 9 to 14 watched a porn on a mobile phone and two days after, they lured an eight year old girl into one of their houses and raped her.[44]
- A retired man killed his wife and younger brother who did not switch off the AC in a hot sweaty night, despite he had forbidden them to do so.
- In September 2017, a 16 year old boy killed a boy of 7th class in a Gurgaon school hoping to get the school closed in condolence and thus sparing him from taking an examination.
- A Swiss couple was attacked by three teenagers in the Fatehpur Sikri fort area without thinking why they did so. They were stalling the couple, wanted to have selfie with them, and then they without any provocation brutally attacked the couple.[45]
- When Aditya (19yrs) and his friends enraged Rocky (24 yrs) by taking over his SUV on a highway, Rocky chased them and then gunned Aditya down.
- Rocky's father, Bindi Yadav, was alleged to start with pretty crimes leading to bigger ones such as forgery, extortion, murder, theft, cheating, rioting, assault, and outraging modesty of women. Simultaneously, he became a government contractor taking up projects in many States. Like his MLA (Member of Legislative Assembly) wife, he nursed political ambitions too.[46]

Caste Politics

Indira Gandhi had tight control over the Congress Party and the Government. However, because of the Emergency, she lost power in 1977. There was political instability in the country.[47] Jai Prakash Narayan cobbled together an amalgam of Hindu-minded, socialists, and disgruntled Congress leaders into the Janata Party that formed the government (1977). The socialists revived their claim for reservation by constituting the B.P. Mandal Backward Classes Commission in 1978. Its Report (1980) reaffirmed that "Caste is also a class of citizens" and the socially and educationally backward castes constituting 52 per cent of the population deserved at least 27 per cent reservation in government jobs (considering that SCs and STs had 17.50 per cent and total percentage of reservation, according to the Supreme Court, should not exceed 50 per cent).[48] It conceded that the reservations would not make the OBCs forward. However, their backwardness had "to be fought in the minds of the backward people". Government jobs were looked upon as a symbol of prestige and power. By increasing the representation of OBCs in them would "elevate their immediate feeling of participation in the governance of this country". The material benefits would be limited to the members of their family. But the "psychological spin off of this phenomenon would be tremendous: The entire community of that backward class candidate would feel socially elevated" realizing that now it had its own men in the "corridors of power". This will act "as morale booster".[49]

As the Janata Party disintegrated and Indira Gandhi came into power (1980), the Report was thrown into a cold storage, but was quickly retrieved and implemented as soon as V.P. Singh, a socialist, became the Prime Minister (1989). In his independence day speech (August 15, 1990) from the Red Fort, he declared:

> We believe that no section can be uplifted merely by money. They can develop only if they have a share in power and we are prepared to provide this share. ...Bureaucracy is an important organ of the power structure. It has a decisive role in decision-making. We want to give an effective share in the power structure and running of the country to the depressed, downtrodden and backward people.[50]

There were sharp and violent protests, particularly by young from high castes. Again it was not driven by the actual loss of government jobs, but by the fear arising out of potential intrusion into the high castes' position of dominance. The fight was based on political power and for gaining power, not for number of jobs. The OBCs did not have power earlier. So, they were not listened to. Now, they were sensitized politically to get united and wrench that power by voting only for OBC contestants. They had the number. So, every political party, including the Congress and the BJP, now were wooing for OBC contestants for the Parliament, State legislatures, and local bodies. In northern India, the OBCs' elected representatives rose from 11 per cent (1984) to 25 per cent (1996) while the upper castes' dropped from 47 per cent to 35 per cent during the same period.[51] In Bihar, the percentage of upper castes MLAs (Members of Legislative Assembly) dropped from

46.00 in 1952 to 21.50 in 1995 while that of the OBCs increased from 19.30 to 43.60.[52] The scenario at other places was more or less similar. A silent revolution in the transfer of power was taking place.[53] The OBCs were dominating the country's political landscape and the upper castes were yielding.

An extreme case of this changing scenario was the State of Bihar.[54] Lalu Prasad Yadav came into power in 1990 and reigned for 15 years. He called himself Raja (king). He was very open in his motto: *Vikas nahi, samman chahiye* (we want dignity, not development). That is, empowerment of those (OBCs) who were till now powerless, but without improving the conditions of their living. This he did by granting them free access to him, visiting them in their villages, mingling freely with them, eating with them, and encouraging them to approach him for any redress or even when they were in situations of conflict with law. Naturally, the backward, poor, illiterate, rustics, and even those who were involved in crimes sought his patronage. He let the "laws, rules and procedures to be bent, stretched, overlooked or even defied" in order to protect and favour them on political ground. The OBCs felt exhilarated by his patronage and rallied around him. He even instigated them to defy government officers whom he humiliated in public gaze by calling them "servants" of people. In other words, it was a "case of governance by dismantling, or partially immobilising, the government".[55] As a result, Bihar had "democratically endorsed non-governance"[56] where "democracy thrived but governance collapsed".[57] This was the model that the rest of his colleagues emulated creating a milieu where the OBCs, howsoever, poor and depressed, were no longer afraid of the administration and were unrestrained in doing what they thought were their rights.

The higher level bureaucracy in Bihar at that time (in the year 2002) was dominated by higher castes. About 60 per cent of the IAS officers (133 out of 224) belonged to upper-castes with only seven of them, all promotees, (that is, inferior to the directly recruited ones) were OBCs[58]. Lalu demoralized them by frequent transfers and postings of them at his whim. He in fact humiliated them publically. During his visits to the rural areas, he used to stop at the middle of a road and asked the escorting DM (District Magistrate) to go to the roadside eatery and personally bring some (cheap) snacks, which he enjoyed publicly. Media carried the pictures of Lalu keeping his feet on the centre table in the lawn of his official residence while the officers either stood or sat in front facing his feet. There were also stories abound about how he spoke in rustic language with his officers that could hurt and humiliate any one in a civilised parliamentary system. He often overruled bureaucrats who gradually lost their courage to resist and started yielding to him. His colleagues took the same liberty to boss over their under officers. Decisions were made, not on merit, but mostly on political considerations.

Easy access to politicians, rising aspirations of youth, demoralized bureaucracy, and demolished governance resulted into a milieu where politics became a "lucrative vocation". Regular jobs were scarce and required schooling even under reservations quota. On the other hand, politics was an attractive possibility even for ill-educated youth so long as they had the patronage of a local politician. There were many ways to make quick money and establish a link with a local politician, preferably of one's own caste. Easy one was to find an insider in the block development office, police station, or local court in order to get needy persons help in their fair or foul matters; of course, for a brokerage fee that was to be shared with the insider. Another was to pick up a stick and extract money from passengers, buses, and other vehicles at a bus stand on the pretence of regulating their flow. Yet another was to put up roadside barricades for *chanda* (donation) for some frivolous causes or celebrations. The more enterprising ones had the opportunity to make money through petty crimes, smuggling, liquor business, and so on. Through all these activities, they proved their prowess in grassroot activism that got them in the notice of a local politician who used them for various errands. The connection thus established opened up the possibility of elevating the activities to the construction business. The patron-politician was a great help in this regard. Construction business has been quite profitable. It allowed cuts that benefitted the contractor, his patron-politician, and the administration. Now the contractor had money and muscle power as well as a connection with a politician to enter politics at the local and then at the State level. The more ambitious and aggressive among them turned into the criminal politicians who are profiled earlier in this chapter. This was by and large the most opted route for political entry and progression for a large number of mediocre youth who were otherwise unemployable anywhere else, but quite tuned to the political opportunities. They were from all castes. For them politics was a business for harvesting benefits through criminal activities and playing power games by juggling with caste groups rather serving the country or working for larger causes.

There was a fusion of caste politics and criminalization. In the 1980s, a number of caste-based private armies of land owners had sprung up to counteract the Naxal groups, which were fighting for the landless labourers mostly Dalits. There were Ranbir Sena of Bhumihars, Brahmarshi Sena of Brahmins, Kunwar Sena of Rajputs, Lorik Sena of the Yadavs, Bhumi Sena of the Kurmis, among others. Lalu tactfully assimilated some into his OBCs' politics and let the others fight out, massacre, and liquidate each other while he played his political game. "Chaos, cooption, indifference and inaction were his profound tactics even when the Dalits bled in the central plains of Bihar".[59] He was rather compulsive in destroying the elitist political culture, but not in replacing with a substitute that can take the State ahead. His main game was caste politics. He professed to advance the cause of the OBCs, but in fact nurtured the Yadav constituency mostly. Out of 57 per cent OBC MLAs (Members of the Legislative Assembly) in 1995, Yadavs got 38 per cent while the next dominant caste in the OBCs, Koeri, got just 8.40 per cent. The EBCs (Extremely Backward Castes) having 32 per cent of the population had less than 5 per cent of the MLAs.[60] "Kurmis resented against Lalu Prasad for his bias against the Kurmis when he appointed Yadavs as heads of important boards such as the Bihar Public Service Commission, the Bihar Secondary Education Service Commission, the Bihar State Electricity Board, and the Bihar State Development Corporation"[61]. Its leader, Nitish Kumar started the *Kurmi Chetna Rally* (1994), brought in his fold non-Yadav OBCs, and extremely backward Muslims as well as the disgruntled upper castes in order to checkmate Lalu and formed government with BJP (2005).

After a while Nitish left BJP to form the Grand Alliance (*Maha-gathabandhan)* with RJD to counteract the Juggernaut of BJP under the charismatic leadership of the Prime Minister, Narendra Modi. After a short while, he dropped RJD to return back to BJP where he is trying to retain rather precariously his secular image in the communal company. He is trying to form his own power bloc by wooing Dalits led by Ram Vilas Paswan who till recently was dead against him and Lalu, besides the other extremely backward castes and Maha-Dalits. The OBCs and Dalits are fragmented too creating a highly fluid milieu where they are aligning and realigning and cobbling howsoever fragile alliances. In such a setting very little energy could be spared for addressing the basic issues faced by the people, except for some glamorous high cost projects to create a facade of development and enhance personal image.

Reservations Claimed. There is, however, one ground on which they all—OBCs and Dalits—are completely united: Reservations in educational institutions, jobs, and elected bodies. No one is allowed to raise any question about it, although some evidence suggests that reservations are about "distributing spoils of State power" rather than creating "equal opportunity".[62] It only benefits the well-off within Dalits and OBCs. In fact, reservations do not really help even the beneficiaries in maintaining their self-esteem.

Reservations in jobs and elected bodies have socio-economically benefitted those who got them. But their impact beyond the direct beneficiaries is either none or very limited or uncertain. For example, a survey for the period 1960-1992, revealed that increasing the share of reserved seats in the elected bodies of the sixteen major States of the country reduced the poverty of the STs (Scheduled Tribes) significantly, but not of the SCs (Scheduled Castes). Further, the impact of the reservation for STs was greater on rural than on urban poverty.[63] Because a number of welfare measures launched during this period were specifically targeted to STs, who are located mostly in remote places, the impact of reservations reported in the survey could be compounded with the effects of the welfare measures. It may also be possible that the elected STs helped more effective implementation of the welfare measures.

Reservations in job have limited significance as the government jobs constitute only about two percent of the total workforce. Even within this tiny scope of opportunities, STs are less advantaged than the SCs.[64] The SCs indeed have increased their share in the senior jobs from 1.60 per cent in 1965 to 11.50 per cent in 2011. Their share in fact is larger for junior posts.[65] However, their benefits have accrued largely in the urban setting. STs have double disadvantages: they are located in remote places where educational facilities are extremely limited; as a result of which their educational attainments are very low depressing their chance in getting jobs even through reservations.[66]

In order to claim preference in jobs, Dalits (STs and SCs) and OBCs need to have minimally required levels of educational attainment. An all India survey conducted by the Ministry of Human Resource Development, Government of India (September 2012), revealed a steep rise in the Gross Enrolment Ratio (GER) of the OBCs from 15.00 per cent (in 2009-2010) to 27.10 per cent (in 2011-1012). However, the GER for SCs and STs remained abysmally low at 10.20 per cent and 4.40 per cent[67]. In fact, a review of the available evidence on the consequences of reservation policies as implemented over the past half century in admissions to higher educational institutions showed that although there had been an increase in SCs and STs representation from 7.00 and 1.60 per cents (respectively) in the late 1970s to 7.80 and 2.270 per cent (respectively) in the late 1990s (SC 7.8%; ST 2.7%), the increment is hardly enough even till 1981. Further, the performance of the reserved category students in the professional courses like engineering, medicine, and law was considerably poorer than that in the non-professional courses like arts and sciences restricting their access to more profitable occupations. The professional courses offer better chances of getting jobs, but also require greater academic attainment, which STs and SCs lacked.[68]

A systematic survey of the state of reservations in higher education revealed that the OBCs, compared to their share of population, are adequately represented at the middle and secondary school levels, but their attainment drops at higher secondary level. Further, their university level performance was inferior compared to the general category students. Dalits have only very marginally improved their share in higher education over the years. It still remains abysmally low. The worse is that reservations in educational institutions were reported to dilute the standard of scholarship.[69]

Reservations in elected bodies are less controverted as the contestants do not need to have any minimum level of education and the impact of reservations on socio-economic conditions of the people is confounded by the numerous welfare measures that most of the States as well as the Central governments have already adopted. On the other hand, reservations in jobs are politically explosive and emotionally charged. Job reservations were never meant to eradicate the backwardness of the depressed, downtrodden, and backward people, nor were they meant to radically change the socio-economic landscape of the country.[70] It is only the holders of job who have powerful positions that yield personal benefits to them. Reservations, however, were aimed to give the backwards a vicarious sense of power by identifying with their caste men in powerful government positions. Reservations also raised their expectations to get job without competing with more competent candidates. Thus, the backwards could derive a *sense* of empowerment without having the actual *state* of being empowered by improvement in their socio-economic or other capabilities. Feeling empowered without having power causes some backwards to aspire for jobs that they cannot have without reservations. Being empowered combined with high expectations led them to fan the emotion of their caste men to put pressure on the government to grant their caste reservation so that they too can elevate their status and make personal gains. In the volatile politics starting from the eighties, the pressure kept on building on the government, which too kept yielding accordingly. Thus, reservations were a result of political expediency under the pressure of the various castes and their vocal leaders, rather than being directed by any principled policy of the government to redress the backwardness of the various castes.

It was only the Supreme Court which was in a position to temper the political expediency for reservations. In 1992-193, the Supreme Court reiterated its 1963 verdict that reservations cannot exceed 50 per cent of the jobs and that the creamy layer (as the Sattanathan Commission[71] had pointed out in 1971) must be excluded from the benefits of reservations. Those in the creamy layer of the OBCs, but not of the STs and SCs, were indeed excluded, but, the extent of exclusion was somewhat diluted. The demarcation line for excluding creamy layer was increased many times. It was fixed first in 1993 at Rs. 1.00 lakh per annum for a family, which was raised to Rs. 2.50 lakh in 2004, Rs. 4.50 lakh in 2008, and Rs. 6.00 lakh in 2013, and now Rs. 8.00 lakh in 2017[72]. It may be noted that the average household income of Indians was about 5.00 lakh in 2016[73] and that the limit for taxable income was about 2.50 lakh. Hence, the ceiling of Rs. 8.00 lakh allowed many not-so-poor OBCS, SCs, and STs to avail of the benefits of reservations. Further, the self-reported incomes are often misleadingly low because people hide the part of their real income. Thus, even the not-so-poor OBCs as well as even the affluent SCs and STs are still likely to harvest the benefits of reservations leaving the extremely poor[74] among them high and dry. Reservations in reality become a power game of the caste leaders of OBCs, SCs, and STs, in which they tend to win by assuming an aggressive posture expecting that the "soft" State would yield.

The political expediency also took shelter under the demographic compulsions in order to dilute the Supreme Court's ceiling of 50 per cent reservations. For example, Arunachal Pradesh, Meghalaya, Nagaland, and Mizoram, which are predominantly tribal, have 80 per cent reservations for STs. Andhra Pradesh has 25 per cent reservations for OBCs, 15 per cent for SCs, six per cent for STs, and four per cent for Muslims[75]. Tamil Nadu granted 69 per cent reservations (30% to Backwards, 20% to Most Backwards, 18% to SCs, and 1% to STs, among others)[76]. Kerala Public Service Commission has provided 40 per cent quota for the OBCs including 12 per cent for Muslims and 10 per cent for SCs and ST.[77]

Box 5.2: Reservations as Poll Planks

Gujarat Government (April 30, 2016) passed an ordinance to grant 10 per cent quota in jobs and college admissions to Patidars thus exceeding the 50 per cent ceiling by the Supreme Court. It was quashed by the Gujarat High Court, but the government appealed to the Supreme Court.

Rajasthan Government (October 26, 2017) passed a bill to increase the OBCs quota from 21 to 26 per cent amounting to a total of 54 per cent reservations in government jobs.

Haryana and Punjab Governments (2016) got their High Court's nod to extend reservations to Jats and five other communities, but the Supreme Court put it on the hold.

Telangana Government (April 16, 2017) passed a bill to increase the reservations to OBCs, Muslims, SCs, and STs reaching the total reservations to 62 per cent.

Karnataka Chief Minister (2016) announced 100 per cent horizontal reservation for Kannadigas in all private industries, except the IT-BT sector, which received concessions from the government; failing which, they were to forefeit all concession.

This instigated the dominant and not-so-backward castes to agitate for reservations. The Jats in the northern States, Patidars in Gujarat, Marathas in Maharashtra, and Kapus in Andhra Pradesh are agriculture-based dominant communities, which are not backward either economically or socially. The Patidars in fact have many more professionals and businessmen than other peasant castes in the country.[78] But they still demanded and bended the government to give them a slice of the pie. It is no longer a matter that a caste is so backward that it legitimately deserves affirmative action, but it depends whether it has a clout to agitate, take the people and the system hostage, and bend the State government to its will. Some political leaders keep add fuel to the fire by promising and demanding reservations to not-yet-included castes and communities in the public sector and to extend reservations into the private sector jobs. The State governments often get desperate, buckle down, and pass the buck to the Supreme Court hoping that the latter will take the heat from them. Reservations are so caught in the game of power politics that there hardly exists any space for rational public discourse on their uses and abuses.

It is the Supreme Court again, which has tried to inject rationality by suggesting a need to move away from the caste-centric identification of backwardness,

> ... as [it is] a manifestation caused by the presence of several independent circumstances, which may be social, cultural, economic, educational or even political. New practices, methods, and yardsticks have to be continuously evolved, moving away from a caste-centric definition of backwardness. This alone can enable recognition of newly emerging groups in society, which would require palliative action.[79]

Here are two separate issues here. First is whether to move away from the caste-centric identification to more legitimate—social, cultural, economic, and educational bases of backwardness in order to grant the backwards an easy access to the State resources. The second, in fact more crucial, is whether backwardness of any kind should be addressed by reservations at the hiring points or right at its inception by initiating systemic measures in order to build up sufficient competency in people irrespective of castes so that they all can compete for the societal resources equitably.

It has been politically wise that the Central Government has extended reservations to the poor in upper castes, disregarding the 50 per cent limit set by the Supreme Court. It is true that a sizable percentage of people in upper castes are obviously poor and about one third of them are illiterate.[80] But can the country afford to keep extending reservations well beyond 50 per cent while raising the poverty line for accommodating politically powerful castes? Even more contentious is to entertain the possibility of shifting the criterion of backwardness from caste-centric to deprivation-centric bases while keeping the ceiling at 50 per cent. It causes storms. The issue is deflected into the accusations of upper castes trying to exploit and subjugate the "down trodden". Emotions are aroused high and threats are advanced to turn the world upside-down. Electoral politics hardly has guts to lull the storms and tolerate rational public discourse. As a result, the existing pattern of reservations remains sacrosanct and is perpetuated benefitting mostly to the relatively affluent members of the OBCs, SCs, and STs.

Reservations, even demands for unreasonable reservations, are politically attractive means to build vote banks. On the contrary, initiating measures to eradicate backwardness or even to reduce it significantly, at its inception are more arduous, time taking, with uncertain political fallout, and hence are far less acceptable proposition. This is despite the report that reservations in jobs have made "India's bureaucracy increasingly rotten—and it was already one of the country's greater burdens. An obsession with making the ranks of public servants representative, not capable, makes it too hard to sack dysfunctional or corrupt bureaucrats".[81] Not only in government, but also elsewhere in academic, health, and other administrations, employees nourish their caste identity and use it to shield their incompetence. Further, this sharpens the caste divides and the upper caste bureaucrats too form their groups. We hear of Rajput lobby, Brahmin lobby, Yadav lobby, Kayasth lobby, and so on. Politicians find in them a fertile ground to spread their tentacles by bestowing patronage and favour. The administration is fractured and is geared to prioritize sectarian interests over common ones.

The problem that is often less realized and hence remains unaddressed is how reservations affect relationships between the employees who are recruited through general competition and those through reserved quota, and the resultant impact on the latter's self-image, self-esteem, and hence their sense of wellbeing. The directly recruited ones often ridicule those who are recruited through reservation by pointing out, explicitly or implicitly, to their caste origin responsible for their inferior performance and uncouth behaviour. It happens more often if they have the experience of being classmates or contemporaries in college having uneven academic records. Those hired through reservation often detest and resent being so hinted, commented or treated. At times, they imagine being denigrated and misconstrue even genuine, though adverse evaluations. The worse happens when the one who was recruited through the reserve quota and now is promoted becoming the boss of the one who was earlier a brighter classmate and later a sarcastic co-worker (Parliament has granted reservation in promotion in 2012). Now the promoted boss has an authority to settle the score resulting into further downsliding of the relationship and adversely affecting the team work.

There is another side of the picture. It is often difficult for those availing of the reserved quota to digest the feeling that they got the job or the promotion without competing for it. Gains without competing for them cause uncertainty about their capabilities causing a chain of adverse consequences for them:

> ... people who doubt their capabilities shy away from difficult tasks which they view as personal threats. They have low aspirations and weak commitment to the goals they choose to pursue. When faced with difficult tasks, they dwell on their personal deficiencies, on the obstacles they will encounter, and all kinds of adverse outcomes rather than concentrate on how to perform successfully. They slacken their efforts and give up quickly in the face of difficulties. They are slow to recover their sense of efficacy following failure or setbacks. Because they view insufficient performance as deficient aptitude it does not require much failure for them to lose faith in their capabilities. They fall easy victim to stress and depression.[82]

Quite often such a state of mind resorts to the defence mechanism to assume an overbearing posture, justify getting the benefits, and accuse the system for being unfair to them. In such cases, their sense of self-efficacy suffers, the self-esteem gets eroded, and the sense of wellbeing is depleted. On the other hand,

> A resilient sense of efficacy requires experience in overcoming obstacles through perseverant effort. Some setbacks and difficulties in human pursuits serve a useful purpose in teaching that success usually requires sustained effort. After people become convinced they have what it takes to succeed, they persevere in the face of adversity and quickly rebound from setbacks. By sticking it out through tough times, they emerge stronger from adversity.[83]

In sum, reservations neither help to perform well, nor build positive relationships on job and in educational institutions, nor alleviate backwardness of castes, nor help in maintaining a sense of self-efficacy. They only create elites from the backwards who represent a symbolic empowerment of the backwards.

Rising Communalism

The communalism that is getting increasingly conspicuous since 1980s had its genesis in the communal politics of the 19th and early 20th centuries, which eventually led to the bloody partition of the country. The simmering continued after Independence, but was somewhat contained in the Nehru era, mainly because of the Congress policy and an absence of any political arm of either the VHP (*Vishwa Hindu Parishad*) or the RSS (*Rashtriya Swamsevak Sangh*) to realize the *Hindutva* agenda. It was only in 1951 that a political extension of the RSS, *Jan Sangh*, was launched by Shyama Prasad Mookherjee[84]. *Jan Sangh* remained low in profile for about two decades partly because of the overwhelming dominance of the Congress, partly because the stigma of assassinating Mahatma Gandhi by a VHP man (Nathu Ram Godse), and partly because its mentor, RSS, was primarily concerned with "cultural moulding of a unified Hindu ethos around upper caste ideals" that was incongruent with the nuts and bolts of the electoral politics and opportunistic tactical alliance in power sharing. The RSS wanted its political wing to remain clean and unscathed by rough and tough tumble of dirty politics.[85] The political milieu, however, started changing by the late 1970s. The OBCs were on rise and *Jan Sangh* could not afford to remain contended with upper caste ideals. It joined OBCs and other disgruntled leaders of the Congress to form the *Janata Party,* which took over power from the Congress (1977). *Janata Party,* however, got disintegrated soon and *Jan Sangh* took a new *avatar as* the BJP (*Bhartiya Janata Party*) in 1980 under the shadow of the RSS.

The 1980s was the period of political instability. The Constitution had committed the country to secularism under the overwhelming influence of Nehru, who did not relish Gandhi's deeply religious thoughts and practices.[86] Nehru's secularism was western in origin and was supposed to be cleansed of any religious taint. But he did not let Ambedkar to legislate for a uniform code for civil rights for all communities.[87] He allowed Muslims to retain their own personal laws. Since then, the Congress has been accused of appeasing Muslims. It was exemplified by the famous Shah Bano case in which the Congress used its absolute majority in the Parliament to dilute the Supreme Court judgement (1986) under the pressure from Islamic orthodoxy.[88] Neither the Congress nor the Communist (CPM) rule did anything substantial to alleviate Muslims' backwardness. It was recorded that Muslims, compared to other major communities, were the least educated, least integrated into the formal sector, and least likely to gain employment in the public sector. Even after thirty years of CPM rule, West Bengal's Muslims were among the worst off in the entire nation in health, education, and employment. Muslim representation in the Parliament and in many States, was the lowest since 1947.[89] It seemed that the Congress only wanted to keep a face of being the custodian of Muslim's cause expecting them to return the favour in terms of votes.

The BJP, on the other hand, was wooing OBCs and other smaller parties and harping on Hindu sentiments to broaden its support base. There were other factors that were evoking the cleavage between Hindus and Muslims. Historically cultivated trust deficit, discords arising out of local interests, and occasional riots were the fuels keeping the communal fire live. Pakistan was a continuing provocation. Three wars, cross-border terrorism, and continuing claims over Kashmir were stoking anti-Muslim sentiments in many Hindu minds. The rise of Islamic extremism in the Middle East added an additional legitimacy and potency.

Islamic extremism in the Middle East grew up as a result of the failure of secular Arab nationalism as well as that of the monarchies to address the basic problems of the people.[90] Similarly, the deteriorating political milieu in the country since the 1980s led the *Hindutva*-indoctrinated politicians to profess to take strong measures with the ultimate goal of building *Akhand Bharat* (Undivided India) by assimilating non-Hindu neighbouring countries into the Greater India. They suspected that Muslims were not patriotic to India, but could be put under the pressure of spirited patriotic Hindus to succumb and fall in line for the national interests. Over a dozen of militant groups of diverse nomenclature (for example, *Bajarang Dal, Yuva Vahini, etc.)* sprang up within what was known as the *Sangh Parivar*. The militant groups probably played a role in fanning the communal fire and instigating a number of severe riots between Hindus and Muslims (at Moradabad, 1980; Nellie, 1983; Bhiwandi, 1984; Gujarat, 1985; Meerut, 1987; and Bhagalpur, 1989[91]) that occurred during the period.[92] The BJP grew stronger out of the communal conflicts.

An extreme of communalism was reached on December 6, 1992 when some of the top leaders of the BJP and VHP organized a rally of about 1.50 lakh Hindu *kar-sevaks* (volunteers) in Ayodhya. The rally, as planned, got violent and demolished the Babri Mosque, which was built by the Moghul Emperor, Babur, by allegedly destroying the Hindu temple on the Ram *Janmabhumi* (birth place of Lord Ram)[93]. The demolition had a tacit support of the BJP Chief Minister of the UP State (who belonged to an OBC) despite his promise to keep law and order. The Hindu minded Congress Prime Minister, Narsimha Rao, did not care to take any preventive steps either. There were instant retaliations resulting into several months of riots between Hindus and Muslims. The riots enveloped cities such as Mumbai, Surat, Kanpur, Delhi, Ahmedabad, Bhopal and several others, causing over 2,000 deaths, maostly of Muslim.[94] Only the Mumbai riots (in December 1992 and January 1993) caused about 900 causalities and estimated property damage of about Rs. 9,000 crore.[95] The vicious cycle of retaliations continued unabated resulting into Bombay blasts and the burning alive of 58 Hindu *kar-sevaks* (volunteers) in a railway compartment at Godhra (Gujarat) in 2002. The carnage sparked another round of riots in Gujarat causing the deaths of 790 Muslims and 254 Hindus, injuries to 2,500 people, while more than 223 were reported missing.[96]

In the meanwhile, the BJP got stronger. It formed government at the Centre (1998), lost it (2004), formed it again (2014) allying with aspiring leaders from diverse castes of the SCs (e.g., Chamars), OBCs (e.g., Yadavs and Jats), and other politically active communities across North India.[97] It was playing caste politics cleverly balancing the castes' pressures and keeping in good humour their leaders. In the 2019 election, it got the absolute majority in the Lok Sabha (Lower House) and had overwhelming influence even on the parties, which so far were by and large secular, to pass legislatures of its choice.

As the BJP expanded into a mass national party of dominance, the criminal elements of the society claimed their share in the power and positions. In the year 2013, the BJP had 12 per cent MPs (Members of the Parliament) and MLAs (Members of Legislative Assemblies) who had admitted having criminal cases against them, some parties (for example, Congress) had less (8%), while others (Samajvadi Party, Janata Dal United, Rashtriya Janata Dal) had proportionately larger share of criminals.[98] The BJP had largest number of the MPs and MLAs having criminal cases against another minority: women.[99] And in the Bihar Assembly election (2015), the BJP had the largest number of candidates having criminal cases pending against them.[100] Variations in the share of criminal politicians, however, were coincidental. The reality is that criminalization of politics is rampant across party lines. The only difference is that communal violence is targeted against clearly identified minorities, particularly Muslims and is patronized by higher ups in the BJP.

The top leaders of the BJP still talk of development and probably are sincere in doing so, but the dominant narratives and actual practices are unequivocally communal. They are glorifying the ancient Hindu traditions, establishing mythic characters as real ones serving as role models for new generations of Indians, re-inventing yoga for the wellbeing of all human beings, pleading to accept *Sri Bhagavad Gita* as the national book, renovating religious shrines, imposing *Bande-Mataram* (worship Mother India) on school children, and celebrating religious festivals with unusual enthusiasm. For example, the Chief Minister of UP, Yogi Adityanath, was instrumental in celebrating Diwali in Ayodhya (2017) on a grand scale where 1.7 lakh earthen lamps were lit in on the banks of the river Sarayu and a State helicopter was refurnished as a mythic

Pushpak Viman for actors dressed as Ram and Sita returning to Ayodhya in a stunning spectacle. All these were meant to recreate the mythic scene for promoting Hindu ethos[101] and probably symbolizing the advent of a Hindu King incarnation of Lord Vishnu. Hardly there is any evidence that the same leaders are rejoicing in non-Hindu celebrations with equal enthusiasm.

The sycophants among the academia went out of the way to argue that ancient Indians knew all sciences and technologies that the West is now proud of. For example, they knew how to fly an airplane by a sheer wish (*Pushpak Viman*), transplant a head (of Lord Ganesh), and even produce test tube babies (the Kauravs). Some re-constructed history positing, for example, that Prithvi Raj defeated Akbar. The lesser ones were loud mouths who asked persons like Hamid Ansari, who was a Vice President, to go to and live in a country (such as Pakistan) where they would feel safe. They did not consider Taj Mahal as a reflection of Indian culture, rather "a blot" on it or "just a beautiful building" which was rebuilt on what, they claimed, was originally a Shiva temple. They denounced Muslims as unpatriotic and glossed over their victimizations. They adopted legal and illegal ways to silence any dissent to the new Hindu cultural activism. Many of them nursed an imagined threat perception from Muslims. While Hindus have vast numerical superiority (79.80%) over Muslims (17.22%), but the latter, they argued, were growing faster (24.60%) than Hindus (16.80%)[102] which, they feared, might create a condition causing another partition of the country. Inadvertently, they expose their belief in the two-nation theory.

The mistrust persists. The wounds of the partition are still raw and still make extremist Hindus angry and Muslims insecure. Many Muslims believe that the majority of Hindus suspect that Muslims are largely unpatriotic and a potential threat to the nation, and hence have to be carefully watched and contained. This perception of Muslims certainly alienates them from the main stream of the country, solidifies their communality, and induces them to adopt an aggressively self-defensive over-reactive posture, particularly at the places where they have sizable numbers and militant leaders. Some among them over react to imagined or minor provocation to which Hindu extremists retaliate with greater force. Even small irritants spiral into big conflicts widening the faultline between them.

Majority of Hindus, however, are not extremists. They are traditionalists, located mostly in rural areas, and are not sufficiently aroused "to take up an ideologically committed activist stance",[103] nor do they apprehend that Muslims are a threat to the nation. They are preoccupied in their traditional lifestyles full of religious beliefs, values, rites, and rituals. They have the traditional tolerant view of other faiths—accepting differences and respecting them all. They, for example, believe that Jesus Christ, Lord Buddha, and Mohammad were also *avatars* (incarnation) and must be worshipped; Christian priests, Sufi saints, Buddhist monks, and Sikh gurus are as respectable as Hindu saints and sages; and temples, monasteries, churches, mazars, and gurudwaras are equally pious as places of worship. Religion is blended in living relationships rather than a ground to hurt and get hurt by the devotees of other faiths.

About 30 per cent of the rural Hindus have moved to urban centres, got education and jobs, and were exposed to western cultural influences. They have adopted modern lifestyles. Their modernity and new lifestyles, however, have not replaced their traditional religiosity. In a typical Indian way, they have simply added the new to the old.[104] As a result, they still engage in traditional religious beliefs and practices, but are conscious of new opportunities and challenges of modern life. They compare and compete with others, make money and run for material things, savvy of Internet, mobiles and television, relish new tastes and branded fashion products, explore new places and activities, entertain modern values, and enjoy new comforts. Simultaneously, however, they also find time to participate, enjoy, and celebrate their *vrat* (fasting and worship), festivals, pilgrimages, *guru-darshana* (glimpse of the guru) and discourse with him, and regularly watch TV channels that broadcast religious programmes. Of course, they take short cuts in their *vrat*, rites, and rituals; go on pilgrimages but enjoy it like a holiday trip; celebrate religious festivals and generously pay offerings to gurus and temples, but partly to show off their affluence and status; and wear precious stones to regulate planetary forces as well as to display their monetary power. They are "flexible" Hindus[105]—living with a mix of traditionalism and modernity.

Neither traditional nor flexible Hindus are endemically hostile to Muslims or any other minorities, at least not the majority of them. They are indeed enamoured by the references of Lord Ram,

Ramrajya (regime of Lord Ram), mythological characters and events, and scriptures such as Gita, *Vedas,* and *Purans*. Urbanized educated among them are impressed by the worldwide popularity of yoga as unique Indian contribution to the world. More religious among them want to get the *Ram Janmbhumi* (birth place) temple built, and feel good that the State sponsors pilgrimages and conducts *yajna* (religious ceremony) and celebrates religious occasions such as *deepawali* (festival of lights) at its costs.

The flexible Indians, however, are more enthused by the promise of *ache din* (good days) than the ideas of promoting intense nationalism and patriotism. They expect to have more opportunities and better prosperity, and to hold their head high in the global community for the power and position of their country. If the *ache din* proves to be a mirage, they get disillusioned; and nationalism and patriotism sound empty to them. They change their mind about the party of their preference, and turn back to focus on their daily struggles, achievements and failures, pleasures and pains. They hardly drift into extreme communalism.

Communal are only the rowdy men at the grassroot levels who are ill-educated, unemployable or poorly employed, "semi-modernized, semi-westernized", "about 250 million", Hindus. They are fanatic enough to commit violence. They are located mostly in cities and villages close to cities and commit almost all (98% or more) communal riots.[106] These are the ones, who envy people around them enjoying comforts and glamour of the modern life, but do not have the competence to get good job or run successful business or achieve professional excellence by fair means. They feel frustrated. As we know, a well-established psychological law is that frustration leads to aggression, not necessarily against the sources of frustration, which could be too powerful to be aggressed, but against the weak, vulnerable, and soft targets.[107] Those who cannot get good job or succeed in business cannot fight against employer or the market, but tend to displace their frustration into aggression against the minorities, particularly Muslims who are around them. They fabricate excuses that range from land disputes, eve-teasing, mixed marriage, professional rivalry, to more recently, religious issues[108] like love-jihad, *gau-raksha* (protection of cows) or eating of or dealing with beef, moral policing, *ghar-wapasi* (conversion into Hinduism), and similar other pretext to harass, victimize, and even lynch Muslims.

Violence especially on religious issues lends them visibility that often paves their path to politics. It is truer for those who have affiliations with one of the members of the *Sangh Pariwar* (the hub of which is the RSS) than for other major political parties. The *Sangh Parivar* has an ideology to protect, for instance, *gau-mata* (mother cow) that symbolizes the motherland: India—beloved and revered by Hindus. Killing cows or eating beef is like outraging the sanctity of the motherland and is certainly anti-national. Hence, violence against those who engage in such anti-national activities becomes acceptable and is taken for their positive acts of patriotism. The BJP has open arms for such patriots. Having their feet established in politics, the communal activists continue committing other crimes, even the serious ones, in order to achieve position, power, and privileges that they were not able to achieve earlier. There are others who are already involved in criminal activities. They find it expedient to turn to communal violence in order to cover up their criminality under political acceptability that also grants them greater immunity from law. Both of them accumulate wealth as well as political weight through communal violence. Taken together, the BJP leaders and the cadre are creating a milieu that is intimidating the minorities. Some of the minority leaders have raised their voice. For example, a former Vice-President of India, Hamid Ansari has shown concern that "... a feeling of unease and a sense of insecurity among the Muslims in the country".[109] He wrote in the preface of his book that the widely accepted pluralist view of nationalism and Indianness is now being challenged by a viewpoint depicting "purifying exclusivism" through the idea of "cultural nationalism". Further,

> Three among these, namely promotion of harmony, preservation of composite culture, and development of scientific temper, seem to be challenged with particular frequency and ferocity; this is indicative of reservations about their meaning and intent.[110]

Box 5.3: Rising Economy While Receding Happiness

Peace and harmony prevails when [a] nation celebrates pluralism, practices tolerance, and promotes goodwill among diverse communities and we purge the toxin of hatred, envy, jealousy and aggression from our everyday lives.

— Pranab Mukherjee[111]

Archbishop Anil Couto wrote to all parish priests and religious institutions in Delhi that "We are witnessing a turbulent political atmosphere which poses a threat to the democratic principles enshrined in our Constitution and the secular fabric of our nation".[112] Another alarm was sounded by the Goa Archbishop, Fr. Ferrao, Who felt that "Human rights are under attack and democracy appears to be in peril. Minorities fear for their safety as respect for law is on decline."[113] Instead of taking cognizance of the threat perception of the minorities and trying to mitigate them, the BJP and Sangh Pariwar leaders are further intimidating them hinting that their allegiance lays to Pakistan and Vetican.

INTEGRATIVE THOUGHTS

Nehru was keenly conscious of the poverty, emerging caste politics, and persisting communalism. But he believed that they would disappear with the economic development by following the socialist model. His worldview, however, was elitist subscribing to grandiose plan to develop the country at the top and make is respectable internationally. He did not realize that a nation's sound and sustainable development needs the foundation of the masses of people who have access to the institutions that impart them education enabling to cultivate skills and take informed decisions, provide adequate health care, and open opportunities to live a productive life by earning stable livelihood. The bottom of the pyramid was neglected while the top was built up in grandiose.

This strategy produced a vast majority of people uneducated or ill-educated, in poor health, and in miserable conditions of living. Yet, they nursed high ambitions because of the sights and sounds of development in the country. Though incapable, they were impatient to have a share of prosperity, which made them vulnerable even to the flimsy promises of petty gains. Politics exploited their castes and religion. Politicians early, in the Nehruvian era were tempered by the freedom movement, Gandhian ideas, and Nehru's idealism. They were aware of rising caste consciousness and lurking communalism, but were by and large able to contain them. As the politics degraded since the 1980s into a naked pursuit of power, politicians reached out to the smarter ones among the young who were unfit for any other productive work except politics, which did not require any other competence except to employ any—even corrupt and criminal—means to gain power and privileges that they aspired for. The upstarts started dominating politics, sidelining the old timers, overshadowing any well-intentioned individuals, demoralizing bureaucrats, and colluding with greedy businessmen.

Electoral politics highlighted the importance of numerical superiority of OBCs (Other Backward Castes). Reservations for them were a power ploy to manage caste politics and create coteries of influence in bureaucrats and youth. Castes were fragmented by rival caste leaders who were driven by selfish interests and personally loyal unscrupulous followers. Communalism was a handy means to fan the passion and cultural revival was the slogan to flare people's nostalgia for the past. Increasingly market-oriented economy since the 1990s has created many opportunities to make quick money and to wield political power. They accumulated both—money as well as power. They are the new elites who exploit the rest of masses in the name of castes and religion. The masses are still uncared and unprepared to improve the quality of their life.

This is not the development that we envision. We have to find another vision—a wholesome wellbeing for all—and a paradigm change in the strategies to realize it.

Notes

1. Satô, 1989.
2. Gopal, 1984.
3. Nehru, 1985, p. 246.
4. Almost proportional to their percentage in population.
5. Jaffrelot, 2003.
6. The Kalelkar Committee Report , 1955.
7. Classes were changed into castes.
8. on the basis of the 1931 census, thereafter castes were not identified in the Census.
9. Cited by Bhardwaj, 2014; Source: Nehru, 1989, pp. 456-457.
10. Pant, Undated, p. 2.
11. Mohan, Sharma, Singh, & Sunilam (Eds.), 1997, pp. 258-259.
12. Lohia, 1964.
13. Nehru, 1934, p. 62.

14. Nehru cited by Gopal, 1932, p. 408.
15. Nehru, 1942, p. 20.
16. Nehru, 1961/1989.
17. Ambedkar cited by Moon, 1995, p. 405.
18. Gabriel, 1996.
19. https://en.wikipedia.org/wiki/Somnath_temple
20. Yadav, 2012t:
21. Letter to Mirabehn, August 7, 1934.
22. Gandhi , 1940, p. 357.
23. Gandhi , 1948, p. 58.
24. Cited by Mehra, 2000, p. 1.
25. The Gorwala Committee (1951).
26. The Kripalani Committee (1955).
27. The Santhanam Committee (1962).
28. http://jaago.indiaonline.in/corruption-in-india-65. Retrieved on September 07 , 2017.
29. Wolpert, 1996, p. 489.
30. Chibber, 2003, p. 249.
31. Guha, 2007.
32. Steinberg, 2008.
33. https://en.wikipedia.org/wiki/Devakanta_Barua
34. Guha, 2007.
35. A letter of a retired civil servant to the Prime Minister, cited by Guha, 2007.
36. The ADR (Association for Democratic Reforms) Report, May 13, 2013. http://adrindia.org / content/nexus-between-elections-crime-and-money-ten-years-election-watch
37. http : //www.x-rates.com/average/?from=INR&to=USD&amount=1&year=2011, accessed on May 19, 2014.
38. http://zeenews.india.com/news/india/72-crorepatis-in-pm-narendra-modis-council-of-ministers_1904991.html
39. http : s://www.adrindia.org/content/51-mpsmlas-charged-crime-against-women-adr
40. Jha & Pushpendra, 2012, p. 11.
41. Das, 1992, p. 136.
42. Jha & Pushpendra, 2012.
43. Kothari, 1984, p. 218.
44. *The Times of India,* Patna, July 18, 2018, p. 5.
45. *The Times of India,* Patna, October 28, 2017, p. 1.
46. *The Times of India,* Patna, May 11, 2016, p. 4.
47. Brass, 1995, p. 40.
48. Mandal Commission Report (1980), p. 21. However, Tamil Nadu exceeded the 50 percent limit set by the Supreme Court by granting 69 percent reservations for Scs, STs, and OBCs.

49. Quotes in the paragraph are from the Report of the Backward Classes Commission. First Part , Government of India, New Delhi, 1980p. 57; Present tense changed into Past tense.
50. Mohan, et al. , 1997, p. 361.
51. Jaffrelot, 2000.
52. Jha & Pushpendra, 2012 , Appendix 1.
53. Singh, 1997, pp. 316-317.
54. The account about Lalu Prasad Yadav is mostly from Jha & Pushpendra, 2012.
55. Jha & Pushapendra, 2012, p. 9.
56. Mitra, 2006, p. 103.
57. Hauser, 2004, p. 426.
58. Jeffrey, 2006, p. 23.
59. Jha & Pushpendra, 2012, p. 15.
60. Jha & Pushpendra, 2012, p. 20.
61. Chaudhary, 1999, p. 242.
62. http://www.economist.com/blogs/banyan/2013/06/affirmative-action
63. Chin, & Prakash, Undated.
64. Prakash, 2007.
65. Narasimhan, 2015.
66. Prakash, 2007.
67. Verma, 2013.
68. Weisskopf, 2004.
69. Parasuraman, 2009.
70. Lohia, 1964 , p. 21.
71. The Sattanathan Committee, 1971.
72. https://en.wikipedia.org/wiki/Creamy_layer. The National Commission for Backward Classes (NCBC) had proposed the ceiling of Rs. 15 lakh in 2015.
73. Calculated from the per capita income of US$ 1,670 (https://en.wikipedia.org/wiki/Income_in_India) multiplied by an average of 4.90 persons in the Indian family (Households data for India , Census of India 2011, Government of India, New Delhi, 2013).
74. Indian families falling below the poverty line (calculated on the basis of former RBI governor C. Rangarajan's Report) https://en.wikipedia.org/wiki/Below_Poverty_Line_(India) spent not more than Rs. 8,500 per annum
75. https://en.wikipedia.org/wiki/Reservation_in_India
76. Gazette of Government of Tamil Nadu. Web link http://www.tn.gov.in/acts-rules/law/act_10to12_131_07jun06.pdf
77. https://www.keralapsc.gov.in/index.php?option=com_content&id=199&Itemid=119.
78. Jaffrelot, 2003.

79. Cited by Narasimhan, 2015.
80. https://en.wikipedia.org/wiki/Forward_caste
81. http://www.economist.com/blogs/banyan/2013/06/affirmative-action
82. Bandura, 1994, p. 71.
83. Bandura, 1994, p. 71.
84. Graham, 1960.
85. Hansen, 1999.
86. Nehru cited by Gopal, 1932, p. 408.
87. Ambedkar cited by Moon, 1995, p. 405.
88. https://en.wikipedia.org/wiki/Mohd._Ahmed_Khan_v._Shah_Bano_Begum
89. The Sachar Committee (2006).
90. Antunez, 2015.
91. file:///C:/Users/Jai/Documents/Riots.html
92. Satô, 1989, p. 15.
93. https://en.wikipedia.org/wiki/Demolition_of_the_Babri_Masjid
94. Guha, 2007, pp. 582 –598.
95. Wilkinson, 2006, p.14.
96. file:///C:/Users/Jai/Documents/Riots.html
97. Hansen, 1999.
98. Percentage: BSP 18, SP 26, JDU 30, & RJD 33 as reported by the ADR (Association for Democratic Reforms). Available at http://www.indpaedia.com/ind/index.php/Criminals_in_politics:_IndiaParty-wise_sitting_MPs_.26_MLAs_with_criminal_cases_.282013.29 ; Retrieved on March 6, 2018.
99. ADR (Association for Democratic Reforms) Report cited by *The Hindustan Times,* August, 31, 2017.
100. http://www.thehindu.com/elections/bihar2015/bjp-tops-list-of-candidates-with-criminal-charges/article7720972.ece!
101. Mehta, 2017, p. 12.
102. The Census, 2011.
103. Kakar & Kakar, 2009, p. 141.
104. Sinha, 2014.
105. Kakar & Kakar, 2009, p. 146.
106. Ashis Nandy, 2004.
107. Dollard, et al., 1939.
108. Ashis Nandy, 2004.
109. https://www.ndtv.com/india-news/live-in-a-country-where-you-feel-secure-rss-leader-slams-hamid-ansari-1737107.
110. *The Times of India,* Patna, July 8, 2018, p. 6.
111. Mukherjee (Former President of India), 2018, p. 7.
112. Reuters, May 22, 2018.
113. *The Times of India* , Patna, June 6, 2018, p. 5.

REFERENCES

Antunez, E. (2015). The rise of Islamic extremism. *World News,* March 1. Available at https://intpolicydigest.org/2015/03/01/the-rise-of-islamic-extremism. Retrieved on February, 27, 2018.

Bandura, A. (1994). Self-efficacy. In V.S. Ramachaudran (Ed.), *Encyclopedia of human behaviour* (Vol. 4, pp. 71-81). New York: Academic Press. Available at https://www.uky.edu/~eushe2/Bandura/BanEncy.html.

Bhardwaj, H.R. (2014). *Nehru: Gazing at tomorrow.* New Delhi: Anuradha Charitable Trust. Also available at http://www.dnaindia.com/india/report-hr-bhardwaj-stirs-hornet-s-nest-quotes-jawaharlal-nehru-demanding-end-to-caste-based-reservation-2022355.

Brass, P.R. (1995). *The politics of India since Independence.* Cambridge: Cambridge University Press.

Chaudhary, S.N. (1999). *Power-dependence relations: Struggle for hegemony in rural Bihar*. Delhi: Har-Anand.

Chibber, V. (2003). *Locked in place: State-building and late industrialisation in India*. Princeton: Princeton University Press.

Chin, Aimee and Prakash, Nishith (Undated). The Redistributive Effects of Political Reservation for Minorities: Evidence from India. IZA Discussion Paper No. 4391. Available at SSRN: https://ssrn.com/abstract=1489214.

Das, Arvind N. (1992). *The republic of Bihar*. New Delhi: Penguin Books.

Dollard, J.; Doob, L.W.; Miller, N.E.; Mowrer, O.H.; and Sears, R.R. (1939). *Frustration and aggression*. New Haven, CT, US: Yale University Press.

Gabriel, Marie Cruz (1996). *Rediscovery of India, A silence in the city and other stories.* Orient Blackswan.

Gandhi, M.K. (1940). *The collected works of Mahatma Gandhi.* New Delhi, Publications Division Government of India, p. 357.

Gandhi, M.K. (1948). *The collected works of Mahatma Gandhi*. New Delhi, Publications Division Government of India, p. 58.

Gopal, S. (1932). *Selected works of Jawaharlal Nehru* (Vol. 5). New Delhi: Orient Longman.

Gopal, S. (1984). *Jawaharlal Nehru: A biography*. New Delhi: Oxford University Press.

Graham, B.D. (1990). *Hindu nationalism and Indian politics: The origins and development of the Bharatiya Jana Sangh*. New Delhi & Cambridge: Cambridge University Press.

Guha, Ramchandra (2007). *India after Gandhi: The history of the world's largest democracy.* NOIDA, India: Harper Collins.

Hansen, T.B. (1999). *The saffron wave. Democracy and Hindu nationalism in modern India*. Priceton: Princeton University Press.

Hauser, Walter (2004). From peasant soldiering to peasant activism:

Reflections on the transition of a martial tradition in the flaming field of Bihar. *Journal of Economic and Social History of the Orient*, 47(3).

Jaffrelot, C. (2000). The rise of the other backward classes in North India. *The Journal of Asian Studies*, February.

Jaffrelot, C. (2003). *India's silent revolution: The rise of the lower castes in North Indian politics*. New Delhi: Permanent Black.

Jeffrey, Witsoe (2006). Social justice and stalled development: Caste empowerment and the breakdown of governance in Bihar. In Francine Frankel (Ed.), *India in transition: Economics and politics of change*. Philadelphia, Centre for Advanced Study of India.

Jha, M.K. and Pushpendra (2012). Governing caste and managing conflicts: Bihar, 1990-2011. *Policies and Practices*, No. 48. Kolkata.

Kakar, S. and Kakar, K. (2009). *The Indians: Portrait of a people*. New Delhi: Penguin.

Kothari, Rajni (1984). The non-party political process. *Economic and Political Weekly*, 19 (5). February, 4.

Lohia, Ram Manohar (1964). *The Caste system*. Hyderabad: Rammanohar Lohia Samata Vidyalaya.

Mehra, Ajay K. (2000). Politics and corruption in India. Available at http://www.thehindu.com/2000/10/21/stories/05212524.htm. Retrieved on September 7, 2017.

Mehta, N. (2017). Agra versus Ayodhya for 2019. *The Times of India*, Patna, October 24, p.12.

Mitra, Subrata K. (2006). *The puzzle of India's governance: Culture, context and comparative theory*. London: Routledge.

Mohan, S. Sharma, H.D., Singh, V.P. and Sunilam (Eds.) (1997). *Evolution of Socialist Party in India*. New Delhi: Bapu Kaldate.

Moon, V. (1995) (Ed.). *Dr. Babasaheb Ambedkar: Writings and Speeches* (Vol. 14/1). Mumbai: Education Department, Government of Maharashtra.

Mukherjee, Pranab (2018). Speech at the National Conference on Towards Peace, Harmony, and Haapiness. The Pranab Mukherjee Foundation and The Centre for Research and Industrial Development, New Delhi. *The Times of India*, Patna, November 24, p. 7.

Nandy, Ashis (2004). Communalism and politics in India. Institute of Peace and Conflict Studies. Lecture # 1380, April 22, New Delhi. Available at file:///C:/Users/Jai/Documents/Communalism%20and%20Politics.html. Retrieved on March 3, 2018.

Narasimhan, Mridulya (2015). Affirmative action in India: Is backward the new forward? *Development in Action*, June 16. Available at http://www.developmentinaction.org/affirmative-action-in-india-is-backward-the-new-forward/

Nehru, J. (1934). *Recent essays and writings*. Allahabad: Kitabistan.

Nehru, J. (1942). *The unity of India*. London: Lindsay Drummond.

Nehru, J. (1985). *The discovery of India* (4th edition). New Delhi: Oxford University Press.

Nehru, J. (1961/1989). Letter on 27 June 1961. In J. Nehru, *Letters to the Chief Ministers*, 1947-1964, (Vol. 5). Delhi: Oxford University Press, pp. 456-457.

Pant, G.B. (Undated). *Memorandum on the Report of the Backward Classes Commission*, Ministry of Home Affairs, New Delhi.

Parasuraman, S., Srinivasan, K., Thakur, Sai, C.T. Saritha, Goyal, Jaya, Singh, D.P. and Thombre, Bharat. (2009). *Analysis of OBS reservation policy for higher education in India.* Tata Institute of Social Sciences, Mumbai, February 2009. Available at http://lawandotherthings.blogspot.in/2009/05/impact-of-obc-reservation-policy-in.html. Retrieved on May 8, 2016

Prakash, N. (2007). Impact of reserving jobs for minorities on labour market outcomes: Evidence from India. Department of Economics, University of Houston, Houston, USA.

Satô, Hiroshi (1989). Indo seiji e no joshô (Introduction to Indian Politics). In Satô et al., (eds.), *Motto shiritai Indo I* (translated: I Want to Know More about India), Tokyo: Kôbundô.

Singh, V.P. (1997). Power and equality: Changing grammar of Indian politics. In A. Prasad (Ed.), *Reservational justice to other backward classes.* New Delhi: Deep and Deep.

Sinha, J.B.P. (2014). *Psychosocial analysis of the Indian mindset.* New Delhi: Springer.

Steinberg, Blema S. (2008). *The women in power* (Indira Gandi, pp. 17-114).Montreal: McGill-Queens University Press.

The Gorwala Committee Report (1951) On Public Administration. Government of India, New Delhi.

The Kalelkar Committee Report (1955) of the Backward Classes Commission, vol. 1, Government of India, Delhi.

The Kripalani Committee Report (1955). *On Railways.* Government of India, New Delhi.

The Mandal Commission Report (1980). *The Report of the Backward Classes Commission.* Government of India, New Delhi.

The Sachar Committee Report (2006). Ministry of Minority Affairs, Government of India, New Delhi.

The Santhanam Committee Report (1962). *On Prevention of Corruption.* Government of India, New Delhi.

The Sattanathan Committee Report (1971). *The Tamil Nadu Backward Class Commission.* Government of Tamil Nadu, Chennai.

Verma, A. (2013). Caste-education syndrome: Impact of reservations on institutions of higher education. *International Journal of Social Science and Interdisciplinary Research*, 2 (6), 139-146.

Weisskopf, Thomas, E. (2004). Impact of reservations on admission to higher education in India. *Economic and Political Weekly*, 39 (39), Sept 25-Oct 1, pp. 4339-4349.

Wilkinson, Steven I. (2006). *Votes and violence: Electoral competition and ethnic riots in India.* Cambridge: Cambridge University Press.

Wolpert, S. (1996). *Nehru: At tryst with destiny*. Oxford: Oxford University Press.

Yadav, Yogendra (2012). Corruption in perspective of Mahatma Gandhi. Gandhi Research Foundation, Jalgaon, Maharashtra, India. Available at http://gandhiking.ning.com/profiles/blogs/corruption-in-perespective-of-mahatma-gandhi-1

6
Attempting a Paradigm Shift

THE BACKDROP

Disappointing Development

Development is a change process for creating a better future. In order to create a better future, the priority is to start from either the bottom or the top of a country. To start from the bottom means to uplift most of the people from the ground putting them on an ascending trajectory that leads to a better collective state and sense of their wellbeing. The assumption is that people constitute the foundation for a solid superstructure of development of a country. And, most of them have to be uplifted for a sound and lasting process of development.

Gandhi wanted the country to adopt this—bottom up-approach. His concept of development was of *sarvodaya* (the rise of all) where "... every individual [is] to become a full-blooded, full-developed member of the society".[1] Many of his ideas were wrapped in religious imageries, were too idealistic, and seemingly unfeasible, but his main contentions have far reaching potential for the wellbeing of all. For example, he wanted the development to focus on the poor and the weaker sections. He emphasized the moral superiority of simplicity over consumerism of the market economy and the medieval values of living a lavish life. He was against concentration of wealth in a few hands. He preferred decentralized decision-making for creating employment opportunities for and hence wellbeing of all.[2] He envisioned building non-coercive communities where individuals and groups were to be governed by self-control, mutual responsibilities, and sense of duties, rather than their rights over each other[3].

His ideas were not given a chance, because Nehru, who had an overwhelming control over the Congress and the State apparatus, was fully committed to socialism. Nehru was keenly aware of the poverty and miserable conditions in which most Indians were living. He was like a philosopher king full of idealism.[4] But he believed in the development from the top. He thought that the country had first to create wealth before giving it to the poor; and for creating wealth, the country needed heavy industries, large dams, elite management and technological institutes, and so on. He believed that "... even cottage industries [Gandhi's priority] cannot develop to any large extent if economic freedom [achieved through heavy industries] is absent".[5] He was an elitist who believed that knowledgeable persons were the best suited to guide the development process.

Nehru's top-to-down approach led to create industrial base, but not enough wealth to alleviate poverty. Whatever wealth was created indeed got more concentrated in a few business houses. The economy grew by what was sarcastically called "the Hindu rate of growth"[6] because of its inefficiency, red tape, and the licence raj. Nehru, of course, had the credit to establish a secular democratic government and contain, at least to some extent, the divisive forces. After Nehru, the politics started rotting from the top and the economy was increasingly stressed compelling it to embrace market reforms, which accelerated economic growth. Between 1991 and 2017, the human development index increased by 50 per cent, life expectancy by nearly 11 years, expected years of schooling by 4.70 years, and per capita income in PPP by 266.60 per cent,[7]—indicating that income increased much faster than other indices of human development. A small number of Indians became disproportionately rich and super rich. The number of billionaires increased—faster than the growth rate of the average Indians. Inequality increased and kept increasing more rapidly than the GDP. India was posed to be 'shining', but only by what the top 10 per cent of the population (about 80 million in 2014) achieved; and in fact, the top one percent grabbed about 22 per cent of the national income.[8] It means 50 per cent Indians remained deprived in many ways. India's hunger was 'alarming'[9] and 42 per cent of all children were suffering from malnutrition and 59 per cent from stunting.[10] Over 25 per cent of Indians remained illiterate.[11]

Box 6.1: The Miserable Indians

India had the highest incidence of tuberculosis ...Three years ago, India accounted for 40 per cent of under—5 diarrheal deaths. Plus, 60 per cent of new leprosy cases globally are in India....India is an environmental disaster. Fourteen out of 15 most polluted cities in the world were in our country. In 2018, two million premature deaths in India were attributed to pollution....Our water situation is perilous. We have the highest freshwater withdrawal in the world.... In 2018, India was ranked 115th out of 158 countries in the World Human Capital Index.... Worse on the Rules of Law Index, democratic India was 62nd out of 113 nations.[12]

The country has now sights and sounds of an affluent nation having high rising buildings and towers, highways, shining malls, super-specialities health care facilities, attractive tourist destinations, and world class educational institutions; but these are the artefacts of the top of the pyramid. A large part of population still lives in unhygienic conditions, with poor health care, and without proper education. The country did not build sound primary institutions, which could have enabled them to acquire basic capabilities to improve the quality of their life. Devoid of the basic capabilities, they cannot avail of the new opportunities. They are caught in failed opportunism that renders them vulnerable to politics. With the rotting politics and their own incapability to improve the conditions of living by fair means, a lot of people find that casteism and communalism are the only open avenues to gain money, power, and privileges.

Castes were already getting politicized since the colonial days. Universal suffrage, granted by the Constitution, let the OBCs (Other Backward Castes) feel empowered in the electoral politics. They had the numerical superiority, although high castes occupied almost all positions in politics and government in the period following Independence (1947). The high caste leaders saw the rising caste consciousness of the OBCs and Dalits as a threat as well as an opportunity. To hedge the threat and exploit the opportunity, they picked up political aspirants from the OBCs and Dalits, and groomed them in order to reach out to them and expand their support base.[13] The upcoming OBC and Dalit aspirants remained submissive to their patrons for a while. but soon developed their own clout. Being bolstered by their numerical superiority in the electoral politics, they got ambitious. Some succeeded their benefactor, others replaced their rivals of high castes, while still others broke away to form their own outfit. As a result, a triangular polarization developed between the high caste, OBC, and Dalit leadership, in which the OBC increasingly got an upper hand over the high caste and Dalit leadership. As political consciousness grew further, the caste groups started getting fragmented. Extremely Backward Castes (EBCs) and Maha-Dalits were carved out of OBCs and Dalits (respectively) in order to create and counteract rival caste leaders. In fact, each caste flaunted its own leader; the major ones had factions with competing leaders claiming to be the only rightful caste leader. Multiple caste-groups and numerous caste leaders, each vying for power, position, and privileges, have now created an attractive ground for manoeuvring for alliance formation in order to grab power positions.[14] They all rally round the ideology of social justice for claiming reservations,[15] although reservations were taken advantage of mostly by the well off among the OBCs and Dalits.[16]

Communalism, which germinated long back in the medieval period and was virulent prior to the Partition, remained subdued for a while after Independence (1947) due to several reasons. Mahatma Gandhi was assassinated by a VHP (*Vishwa Hindu Parishad*) man; the RSS (*Rashtriys Swam Sevak Sangh*) was concerned with the revival of upper caste ideals and wanted its political wing to remain clean of dirty politics;[17] and the Congress occupied most of the political space. As the Congress suffered from internal fractures, the rising OBCs destabilised the high castes' dominance, and politics was infested by corrupt and criminal elements, there was enough chaos and uncertainty for the communal forces to gain strength. *Bharatiya Jan Sangh* was formed (1951) as a political arm of the RSS, joined a non-Congress heterogeneous government that broke down soon, and re-appeared as the BJP (Bhartiya Janata Party) in 1980. The BJP did not mind playing caste cards, igniting communal fire, and embracing winnable corrupt and criminal politicians. It vowed by *Hindutva* and played divisive politics to grow from strength to strength eventually displacing the Congress from the most places in the country.[18]

Go-getter politicians. In this free for all political milieu, ideology has become a sheer rhetoric. Neither *Hindutva,* nor social justice, nor secularism restrains politicians from breaking away from their parties and forming new ones or changing alliances. They freely hop and jump several parties in order to gainfully position themselves. The only asset that they need to possess is a band of personally loyal followers, who blindly believe that all allegations of casteism, crimes, and corruption against their leaders are part of a political conspiracy. They cultivate skills to navigate cleverly and unscrupulously in the political water and to attract enough followers in order to bargain for power positions. Castes are the natural sources for recruiting followers. The BJP has an additional instrument, communalism, which strikes an amicable chord in the minds of fanatic Hindus.

Politicians' strategy works, because there exists in the country a huge stock of ill-educated, unemployed[19] and unemployable, semi-urbanized, idle young and not-so-young ones. They are not fit for any productive work, except for politics that they see as a "lucrative vocation".[20] Of them those who are prone to rowdism, extortions, pretty crimes, and violence perceive better prospect in politics. By these acts, they get noticed by politicians who find them useful for their personal errands and dirty party work. Politicians grant them patronage to hang around them, get government contracts and make large cuts, and take undue advantage of welfare measures. They have a licence to indulge in dubious activities with immunity from law, and still legitimacy to conduct party work. Next step in their progression is to contest and get elected first in local bodies, then in State Assemblies, and finally into the Parliament, and thus become full-fledged politicians, who then patronize new recruits and spread their tentacles into the society at large.

Economic growth has created many opportunities to make quick money by engaging in foul practices that the politicians adopt freely. The ADR (Association for Democratic Reforms) reports a close nexus between political power, wealth, and crime. According to their own submission to the Election Commission, a large percentage of those who are aspiring to get elected, have criminal cases pending against them.[21] An increasing percentage of those who are elected to the Parliament have criminal charges against them.[22] According to own admission, 30 per cent of the MPs (Members of Parliament) had criminal charges against them in the year 2009, which increased to 34 per cent in 2014, and to 43 per cent in 2019. The percentages MPs having *serious* criminal charges in the corresponding years increased from 14 to 21 to 29. "There is an increase of 109 per cent in 2019 in the number of MPs with declared serious criminal cases since 2009". In Bihar, the percentage of criminally charged politicians increased from 70 in 2014 to 82 per cent in 2019. Further, 88 per cent of MPs are crorepati with average asset of Rs. 20.93 crore. In other words, criminalization of politics is increasing fast and now about half of all MPs have criminal charges against them. They are also super rich. The other half is still untainted, and many of them are indeed competent. But they are often hard pressed to compromise and yield space to the criminal politicians and their followers. It is the tainted ones who have over shadowed a large part of the political space in the country.

Box 6.2: Harvard Vs. Hazaribagh
Jayant Sinha and How Educated Politicians Line Up Behind the Mob

IIT and Harvard educated, Union Minister, Jayant Sinha welcomed the convicts of a communal murder with open arms and garlanded them at his residence. "That a Union Minister is forced to garland those associated with events that have fundamentally assaulted India's collective sense of morality and decency, is the tragedy of the lumpenized electoral politics today".[23]

Culture of *baljori* (by force of power). It is these criminal politicians, the go-getters, who are setting the norms for the rest of the society. Most of the people emulate them. As a result, a culture of *baljori* has been created where people believe that power, particularly crude power, matters most. It can override all civic, social, and human considerations. The more powerful ones can, and are entitled to, get what they want, without mindful of their own obligations, other's rights, or public interests. In politics they can shake and move anything or anybody to make space for themselves. In services, they can set any terms and conditions disregarding other's interests. In offices, they delay or sabotage any plan, favour *apane* (family and friends), and discriminate *paraye* (others) unless get in return bribe in some forms. Others in public domains can break any norms. They can adulterate food, sell fake and expired medicines, engage in drug trafficking, run money making institutions, perfunctorily work while demanding full benefits, encroach on public property, block highways on petty issues, form a mob damaging public property and causing violence, and so on. There is hardly any rule or norm that cannot be violated, if one has enough power. There is only one tacit understanding: Not to confront and oppose other's wrong doings unless they directly encroach upon your interests. Let them do what they want and you do what you want. The State is too soft to implement even right decisions, enforce any discipline, regulate people in public, and forcefully punish the culprits.[24] In such a chaotic scenario, the more power you have the more you can gain on many more occasions rendering the less powerful ones lose more and more on many more occasions. That is, the few at the higher up in societal pyramid fare much better than the vast majority of common people, who are mostly losers by the end of the day.

It is not a scenario of development, not of human development, and not at all of a wholesome state and sense of wellbeing of all. We have to start afresh. But we must know what do we intend to build-up and how. That is, what kind of development we want to have that can ensure a state and sense of wellbeing to all.

CONCEPTUALIZING WELLBEING

Material Wellbeing

The GDP (Gross Domestic Product) still reigns over the minds of those who equate development to economic growth and compare nations for their relative affluence and geo-political clout. Policy-makers use it invariably for planning and allocating money to different streams of development. They feel vindicated if the GDP curve rises according to their expectations. Increased GDP yield more taxes to government allowing it to grant subsidies and reliefs in order to help people recover from various deficiencies, distresses, and disasters. The most liquid form of subsidies, money, is preferred to be directly transferred to needy ones in order to help them improve the quality of their life[25] as well as to get their votes in return.

The faith in GDP is rooted in resourcism.[26] Resourcism is defined by its neutrality to the conceptualizations of wellbeing.[27] Hence, the possession of general purpose resources such as income allows people to use them to realize their specific but different constructions of good life. Thus, if a country produces more goods, makes more money, and hence has more resources, the people are believed to be better off and their aggregated welfare is supposed to be maximized. Further, as more resources are utilized, more wealth is created spiralling into the rising GDP. If an economy is free and individuals have equal opportunity to access to resources, they use resources most efficiently to create more wealth. Nobody has to tell them what is in their interest and what is a good life for them. They know how to utilize resources rationally to get the best out of them for their own purpose. Of course, those who are gifted, skilful, motivated, or socio-economically privileged have greater ability to access to more resources. As a result, they create more wealth than those who are not. They are the better performers. The better performers are justifiably entitled to have more wealth and greater power and privileges in the society, which they use to keep creating more wealth. As a result, inequality in their wealth is inevitable. As the wealth keeps multiplying, inequality also keeps accelerating, although some[28] questionably argue that it tapers off eventually. The resourcist, Rawls, maintains that inequality is justifiable so long as the worst performers are better off compared to what they were before. The larger benefits of the high performers trickle down benefitting the worst performers too. Taken together, the wealth is maximized and so does the total welfare of the society. Rationally, the worst performers should feel positive because of their own gains rather than comparing them with that of the high performers. They should pursue their own self-interests rather than envying high achievers.[29] This is contrary to the human disposition to continuously compare with others around them to see how good they are doing and how fairly they are being treated in the society.

This over-reliance on resources to drive development and optimize welfare is faulted on many grounds.[30] Dumping resources does not necessarily lead to development. The failure of foreign aid to the underdeveloped countries is a blatant example. The aid money to African nations led to passive inertia and demoralization of people aggravating their endemic poverty and corruption, and instigating civil wars among them.[31] Further, availability of resources does not necessarily induce countries to enable their people to improve the quality of their life. For example, South Africa having higher gross national income (per capita) than

Philippines, but had lower years of life expectancy and schooling—the two ingredients (besides income) in the human development index.[32]

The assumptions of free economy and equal opportunity are not valid either. No economy is ever so free that it can provide truly equal opportunities to all. Market is invariably tilted in favour of the gifted, skilful, motivated, and socio-economically privileged individuals who corner lion's share of resources. Not only they, but the market manipulators and politically powerful crooks and criminals also distort market mechanisms to grab disproportionately more resources, often depriving more deserving but less manipulative and relatively honest individuals. Resourcism is neutral to traits and dispositions of the high wealth creators. It is also oblivious of *how* they create wealth. Not all wealth creating activities are morally right (such as drug, human trafficking, and prostitution), socially desirable (such as claiming public lands meant for community and fracturing familial harmony), or legally permissible (such as monopolistic manoeuvring). Single minded wealth creating activities ruthlessly exploit natural resources, pollute environment, and degrade climate.[33]

Therefore, many argue that GDP has to be cleansed of immoral activities and adjusted for social and ecological costs. They prefer GPI (Genuine Progress Indicator) to assess the real progress in the development of a country[34]. Simon Kuznets, who first conceived GDP, later on realized that "... the welfare of a nation can scarcely be inferred from a measure of national income.... Distinctions must be kept in mind between quantity and quality of growth, between costs and returns, and between the short and long run. Goals for more growth should specify more growth *of* what and *for* what" (Italics added)[35]. Mindless pursuit of materialism has a high cost[36] such as depletion of natural resources and ozone; pollution of air, water and noise; loss of farm and wet lands; crimes committed for economic gains; and social disruptions such as family breakdowns.[37] Only after adjusting for these and other such costs, the real progress of a country in development can be ascertained.

Even if GDP is purified into a genuine progress index (GPI) of a country's economic growth, many argue, GPI cannot reflect the true wellbeing of people. Income is essential to meet the basic needs and comforts of life. Without the bare minimum of income, people are not only deprived of the essentials of life, but become deficient in skills restricting their access to essential resources and depriving them of the possibility of improving the conditions of their living. They remain depressed and dissatisfied.[38] Increasing income enables them to overcome their deficiencies and attain a better state of the wellbeing. But income helps only to an extent; beyond that point, it loses its salience and the life satisfaction hits a plateau.[39] Life satisfaction yields happiness—how well people feel they are.

Subjective Wellbeing: Happiness

If there is a choice, a common assumption is that people want to be more happy than just rich. Happiness is operationalized through life satisfaction, which is a balance between positive and negative affective experiences.[40] Life satisfaction can be domain-specific such as satisfaction with work, income, social relationships, and neighbourhood or can be indexed as an overall satisfaction with life.[41] Therefore, many argued that happiness is a better yardstick of human wellbeing.

However, people want to be happy not just at a particular time point in their life, but most of their life. So, longevity matters. The total happiness of a person then is the product of satisfaction multiplied by his or her longevity. However, this happiness must not be attained at the cost of other's happiness or the happiness of the future generations. In order to protect their chances of happiness, the shared resources in terms of ecology have to be preserved, protected, and upgraded. If ecology is disregarded and misused, happiness is not going to last long, nor is to be cost-effective. Synthesizing these ideas, the New Economics Foundation (UK) developed the *Happy Planet Index* (HPI) in 2006 for comparing nations for their relative positions in happiness of people.[42] In this formulation, the HPI is the product of life satisfaction multiplied by life expectancy and divided by ecological footprint. Ecological footprint is measured in terms of the natural resources exploited, the carbon emission caused, and so on by a country causing permanent damage to the planet earth, and thereby impacting the happiness of other people and the people of future generations. Because of the rich and unexploited ecology, Bhutan, in one of the assessments, was found to be the happiest country.[43] In 2018,

Bhutan, along with Nepal, had better ranks than India in the HPI.[44] Bhutan's holistic approach in integrating material and spiritual development in terms of Gross National Happiness led the U.N. General Assembly to pass a resolution (2011) for nations to follow the example of Bhutan considering happiness as a "fundamental goal" for human beings.

Happiness is a sense of subjective wellbeing, which indeed should be a fundamental goal of life, but happiness is empty if it is not based on objectively satisfying conditions of life. A subjective sense of wellbeing at best can stir people to start thinking and making efforts for improving the conditions of their life, or to fantasize acting vigorously while remaining passive, or remaining contended with what they are. At worst, it may induce them to resort to defence mechanisms by acting irrationally. In the 1990s, the OBCs in Bihar were empowered by the OBC-led government to treat government officers as they wished. They momentarily felt powerful and good in harassing and humiliating government officers, but their sense of feeling powerful did little to improve their conditions of life and turned out to be a mirage to them and detrimental to the law and order in the society.[45] Further, subjective sense of life satisfaction could also be misleading in understanding how well people really are in the instances where they have to surrender to their circumstances while still consoling themselves to be reasonably happy. Amartya Sen called it "adaptive preferences" where people can be so normalized to their conditions of material deprivation and social injustice that they have to make-believe being happy in order to survive:

> Our mental reactions to what we actually get and what we can sensibly expect to get may frequently involve compromises with a harsh reality. The destitute thrown into beggary, the vulnerable landless labourer precariously surviving at the edge of subsistence, the overworked domestic servant working round the clock, the subdued and subjugated housewife reconciled to her role and her fate, all tend to come to terms with their respective predicaments. The deprivations are suppressed and muffled in the scale of utilities (reflected by desire-fulfilment and happiness) by the necessity of endurance in uneventful survival.[46]

Human Development

Amartya Sen is also critical of the resourcism. He argues that resources do not automatically translate into wellbeing. His example of a bicycle is oft quoted. A bicycle is a resource for transportation and its owner may feel good of its possession, but is useless if he does not have legs. The bicycle would add to his wellbeing only if he were able to *bicycling*—a capability to utilize a resource. Probably, the failure of foreign aid to develop African countries (cited above)[47] was due to the lack of capabilities of the people of the recipient countries to convert aid money into their wellbeing.

Sen considered capabilities as the source of human wellbeing.[48] He argued that individuals' wellbeing depends on living a quality of life that they have reason to value and are capable of achieving it. Following his initiative, it was posited that "Human development is about people, about expanding their choices to lead lives they value.... Fundamental to enlarging human choice is building human capabilities; the range of things that people can do or *be*".[49] Capability, according to Sen, refers to a set of valuable "functionings" that individuals have effective access to. Functionings are states of "being and doing". For example, being healthy and educated and making decent income are the functionings that reflect a person's capability of having a good quality life and a sense of wellbeing. Neither the vision of a good life and wellbeing nor the presence good educational, health, and livelihood facilities can ensure individuals' wellbeing unless they have capabilities to avail of these opportunities through appropriate functionings. Visions are realized only if individuals have the "freedom" to evoke right kind of capabilities. That is, capabilities convert opportunities into wellbeing. That's why human development is conceived as the freedom to expand and acquire valuable capabilities.[50]

How do individuals infer their capabilities from the functionings? How do they know that being educated and healthy and making decent income can be used to make them capable to live a quality of life? The functionings lead individuals to believe that they have self-efficacy. It is this self-efficacy that psychologically helps infer capabilities from functionings:

> Self-efficacy is defined as people's *beliefs about their capabilities* to produce designated levels of performance [functionings] that exercise influence over events that affect their lives. Self-efficacy beliefs determine how people feel, think, motivate themselves and behave. ...A strong sense of efficacy enhances human accomplishment and personal wellbeing in many ways. People with high assurance in their capabilities approach difficult tasks as challenges to be mastered rather than as threats to be avoided. Such an efficacious outlook fosters intrinsic interest and deep engrossment in activities. They set themselves challenging goals and maintain strong commitment to them. They heighten and sustain their efforts in the face of failure.[51]

Individuals' visions of good life could be enormously varied, and could be realized by equally diversified sets of capabilities that individuals can cultivate. However, the United Nations Development Programme (UNDP) viewed that "The most basic capabilities for human development are leading a long and healthy life, being educated, having access to the resources needed for a decent standard of living and being able to participate in the life of one's community".[52] Accordingly, the Human Development Index (HDI) consisting of the years of schooling, longevity, and per capita income was devised which is one of the most frequently employed measures to compare nations. Later on, the HDI was adjusted for the extent of inequality within countries. The countries with greater inequality such as India lost their HDI score more (28.30 per cent) than the ones such as the USA with less of inequalities (15.30 per cent).[53]

Three major indices—GDP (Gross Domestic Product), HPI (Happy Planet Index), and HDI (Human Development Index)—provide different perspectives on development:[54] Economic growth, subjective wellbeing, and capabilities respectively. The latest available evidence showed that none of the five largest economies was among the five happiest people. However, the fourth largest economy, Germany, was also the fourth on the human development index. Probably, income was the common factor leveraging the communality among them. There was much more proximity between the five happiest (HPI) and most humanly developed (HDI) countries. The average rank of the five happiest countries on HDI was 8.00 while the most humanly developed countries had the average rank of 7.00 on the HPI.

In sum, happiness and human development co-vary to some extent and are independent of the economic size of the countries, with probably a few exceptions. It makes sense too—wellbeing has to be closely associated with both happiness and capability. There is apparent overlap between the two. However, there is still an unresolved issue regarding how people who are stuck with their "adaptive preference" can or should be induced to transcend it by acquiring capabilities that can lead to an arguably more "flourishing" life.

Interfacing of Endogenous and Global Models of Development

Sen is right about the "adaptive preference" that some people are so normalized in material deprivation and social injustice that they accept the reality without questioning it. They either do not know or have no hope of any better life. As a psychological defence against the eroding self-esteem, they live in a delusion of being OK. They also find a solace in locating some more miserable people around them giving them a sense of relative wellbeing. As a result, they may not feel as bad as others do about them. They are indeed the victims of an unfair society circumventing their horizon of wellbeing. Such people have to be taken out of the darkness into a sun-shine of better life.

However, there are other more complicated cases where people are not victimized by any recognizable oppressors; they live a modest life at isolated places; but have developed a positive, though restricted, worldview that is apparently neither injurious to themselves nor to others. They are indeed deprived of ever expanding market of variety of products and services, affluence, and an entrepreneurial spirit of competing for more and more. But they are rather contended and happy in their own ways. Should we also consider them the victims of their "adaptive preferences" and, therefore, a fit case to be dragged into the globalized version of a modern state of wellbeing? The complicated issue get further confounded by the stand in Sen's capabilities approach that people must design their own wellbeing as no one else can impose an alien vision of wellbeing on them. At best different perspectives may intersect and negotiate to come up with an agreed model of wellbeing. But, the more power possessed by the holders of a particular perspective often prevails upon the less powerful people.

The case in our focus is of Ladakh.[55] Ladakh is one of the highest, driest, coldest plateaus in the north most part of India. The people, Ladakhis, were not only able to survive since long, but rather prospered. Their terraced fields, irrigated with glacial melt water, yielded enough food for people. Using primitive technologies and scarce resources, and employing shared labour, Ladakhis "established a remarkably rich culture, one that has met not only their material wants but their psychological and spiritual needs as well". They had well-knit family, communal harmony, and cultural activities that included collective activities such as working together in the field, dancing in the evening, celebrating religious occasions, and so on. They were contended. Nobody was perceived to be poor.

Things started changing in the sixties (after the Chinese invasion in 1962). Roads were built connecting Ladakh to the rest of the country. Consumer goods started pouring in. Government made investments in communication, energy, and other infrastructure with an added dose of bureaucratic overview. Foreign tourists were allowed since 1975. They brought modern items of food, fashion, and fun blended with new values about how one should live and entertain new ideas about how many things money can buy. Films and TVS did not only provide images of luxury and power, but also glamorized aggression and violence. Young Ladakhis fantasized to be modern by rushing for sunglasses, walkmans, blue jeans, and other such items. They started chain-smoking cigarettes, relishing driving fast car and racing through the countryside, and shooting people, if an occasion arose. They were desperate to look modern in look, complexion, and possessions; failing which they developed a cultural inferiority complex being ashamed of their cultural roots and state of deprivation.

Newly built schools imparted western education having different themes and symbols which made them denigrate themselves and degrade their traditions. Traditional economy that depended directly on the collective efforts was subjected to government interventions and bureaucratic overview. This disintegrated local inter-dependence depleting social harmony.

As a result, disputes and acrimony increased dramatically not only within close-knit communities, but also within families. Traditionally, there were mutual respect and cooperation between Buddhists and Muslims. But now, there were instances of friction and conflicts. Ladakhis, who did not know what poverty was, now often were found pleading the aid-giving agencies: "We are poor, help us". This was a total transformation of a traditional society at a cost that seems to be unreasonably high.

The case of Ladakh could be an extreme one; but it does highlight a crucial issue involved in imagining a viable form of development at the interface of indigenous culture and global version of development. We no longer live in closed societies at isolated places. Rather, the world has become a flat global village where the juggernaut of globalized version of development is encroaching, overriding, and overrunning cultural boundaries and overwhelming local worldviews without any restraints or limits. We have not been able either to arrest its advance or accommodate it within the local conditions, despite mounting evidence of its conditionality and adverse consequences. Globalization has been shown at best to work only when certain ground level conditions are met; otherwise it can increase instability in economy, make a country more vulnerable to international events and forces, reduce growth rate, and even increase poverty.[56] It has been rightly documented that

> Globalization, which is a consequence of increased human mobility, enhanced communications, greatly increased trade and capital flows, and technological developments, opens new opportunities for sustained economic growth and development of the world economy, particularly in developing countries. Globalization also permits countries to share experiences and to learn from one another's achievements and difficulties, and promotes a cross-fertilization of ideals, cultural values and aspirations. At the same time, the rapid processes of change and adjustment have been accompanied by intensified poverty, unemployment and social disintegration. Threats to human well-being, such as environmental risks, have also been globalized. Furthermore, the global transformations

> of the world economy are profoundly changing the parameters of social development in all countries[57].

On an ethical ground, it is more appropriate to let people think and design their own development by drawing on their own cultural values, traditions, and practices. Endogenous Development is much preferred over the one which is imposed from outside.[58] It is likely to be more enriching, sustainable, and conducive to the people's state and sense of wellbeing. Hence, there has to be an integration rather than assimilation of indigenous culture and economy by the globalized one. It can happen only when a robust design of endogenous development is prepared to interface effectively with the globalized one.

The process of preparing a design for endogenous development can be ideally justified at the most micro level: Individuals. Each individual has unique needs, aspirations, and capabilities to construct an idiographic profile of his life that he has "reasons to value". His development lies in expanding his capabilities to live this valued life.[59] No one else should impose a different view of development on him. However, individuals live not in social vacuum, but with others. They can resist, share, compromise, and yield creating space for designing a common and some unique shades of development that they can pursue individually and collectively. Their collectives, ranging from local to national, too can converge and evolve, through public discourse and democratic procedures, a multiplex of developmental frames that can be held together by inter-locking values, norms, and concerns and guide national efforts for development. Such a multiplex can meaningfully encounter intrusive global forces by a continuous process of give and take in order to sustain a dynamic process of development that would be endogenous at the core but global in their different manifestations.

In order to facilitate this dynamics of designing development, we need to retrieve from the extant literature the critical constituents of "flourishing" life. Philosophers and social scientists, since Aristotle, have advanced a variety of ideas about the unfolding of human growth and the experience of wellbeing. They can serve as referents to individuals and collectives to reflect upon, articulate their own perspectives, and chalk out a broad range of possibilities that they can explore for themselves. The ideas are diverse, but for our convenience can be broadly arranged into a hierarchical order ranging from existential, through social, to psychological wellbeing. They are also found to be culturally conditioned.

Hierarchical Order of Development

Development involves people's deliberate efforts to create a better future for themselves. Better future is often imagined as the one where their needs are satisfied. Thus, development is often equated to the extent that needs are satisfied. Human needs are arranged hierarchically in importance—the most basic ones have the priority, they must be satisfied before the next ones become salient.[60] The most basic are the physiological (e.g., breathing, hunger, thrust, etc.) needs, which have to be satisfied in order for people to survive. They also need *roti, kapara,* and *makan* (enough to eat, wear, and a place to live) for survival. But, surviving now is not enough. They have to be reasonably sure that they will have the essentials of life for having a sense of sustained survival. Only then they would feel safe and secured. Once safe and secured, human beings want to affiliate with others. They look around for people to relate and belong to, share joys and sorrows, and avoid being isolated and left out. Affiliation breeds social comparison, through which human beings self-evaluate their worth in terms of being inferior, equal, or superior to others around them. The inferiors strive to catch up with the equals and the equals try to surpass others while the superior tend to remain ahead of those behind them.

Needs for survival, security, and affiliation are called *deficiency needs,* because those who are not able to meet them are the deprived ones suffering from unhealthy body, low self-esteem, and low capabilities to improve their lot on their own. They accuse either their destiny or the unjust society. They look for any—foul or short cut—ways to make up their deficiencies. They are the ones who are vulnerable to those who manipulate and exploit them. On the other hand, those who have acquired capabilities to satisfy the basic—survival, security, and affiliation—needs, are now motivated to strive for achieving more, improving upon their own performance, excelling others, and actualizing their potentials fully. Urge for achieving, excelling, and self-actualizing are the growth needs, the process of satisfying them puts the people on an ascending trajectory of wellness.[61] In such cases, the deficient needs lose their salience. On the other hand, the growth needs are self-feeding, the more they are met, the more they drive people harder and harder to rise higher and higher. So, the strategy for fostering development is to provide enough for meeting the deficiency needs and then to create opportunities for the growth needs to take over.

Hierarchy is also reflected in the ancient Indian conceptualization of the major goals of life. Indians were prescribed first to seek their material wellbeing (*arth*), then discharge their duties diligently (*dharm*) and indulge in sensuous life (kaam), but finally transcend them to rise on spirituality, attain self-realization, and get free from all previously strived worldly things (*moksh*).[62] In other words, the mundane has to be achieved and lived with, but only as a stepping stone to rise on spirituality, which is conceived to be the ultimate destination of development. Those who are fixated at the mundane, have no chance to rise on spirituality.

Another hierarchical conceptualization of development has a similar three tiers schema :[63] Existential, human, and social. The most basic—existential—concerns with accumulating sufficient material resources in order to meet survival needs, alleviate physical hardship, and get rid of chronic scarcity. This is primarily economic in nature in terms of sustained income and viable livelihood. Once individuals have been able achieve the existential level of development, they are in a position to gain better control over their lives, maintain physical health, live longer, get good education, and acquire better skills for further improving their access to societal resources. In other words, when individuals possess knowledge, are physically able, and are well-informed, they stand a better chance of achieving what they aspire and experiencing a sense of wellbeing. That is, economic growth constitutes the foundation on which individuals build up the second tier of development: Human capabilities (that is, human development), which then enable them to rise to the third tier: Social development. Social development aims at—

> ... promoting social integration by fostering societies that are stable, safe and just and that are based on the promotion and protection of all human rights, as well as

> on non-discrimination, tolerance, respect for diversity, equality of opportunity, solidarity, security, and participation of all people, including disadvantaged and vulnerable groups and persons.[64]

Such a socially developed society can be built only if majority of its people have realized economic and human development. On the other hand, if economic growth is skewed in favour of a few leaving the majority relatively deprived in the basics, the majority would fail to develop capabilities to envision what they can legitimately aspire and endeavour to achieve. Economic deprivation, along with the deficiency in human development, distorts people's vision of what best they can contribute to and get from the society. They often resort to exclusion, conflicts, crime, and other social pathologies for making short term gains.

Journey towards Happiness and Beyond

The underlying concern all along the existential, through human, to social development is to avoid unhappiness and to experience greater and lasting happiness. Happiness is the ultimate goal that people strive to reach. There are two avenues open to them: Hedonism and eudemonism.[65] Those who resort to hedonism seek happiness in the pleasures that they experience in satisfying their needs and desires. It is not only the basic needs that almost all human beings have to satisfy in order to experience a reasonable amount of pleasure. Hedonists continue seeking pleasure by inventing idiosyncratic desires and fantasies to keep chasing pleasure rather mindlessly.[66] Mindless chasing for pleasures by keep inventing new needs becomes an end in itself.

The history of hedonism in the West goes back to the Greek philosopher, Aristippus, in the fourth century B.C. and persisted in the writings of Europeans such as Hobbes and Bentham, who envisioned an ideal society in which people endlessly enjoy pleasure by serving their self-interests.[67] In India, Charvak eulogized hedonism asking people to seek pleasure and more pleasure as long as they live by adopting any—fair or foul—means including stealing and borrowing money. The only goal of life, he insisted, is to indulge in pleasures.

Eudemonia is also about experiencing happiness and it has

an equally long history going back to Aristotle. Aristotle rejected hedonism because it takes human beings for slaves in the service of selfish desires. Getting happiness through pleasures that are experienced by chasing endlessly multiplying selfish desires, according to him, is vulgar and hardly contributes to human wellbeing. Instead, human beings can rise on merit and experience happiness by striving and persistently struggling to cultivate higher order virtues. It is this experience of persistent efforts for self-improvement and becoming righteous that radiates real happiness in the life of human beings.

Eudemonism resonates in Maslow's conceptualization of self-actualization.[68] Self-actualization is defined as the full unfolding of individuals' potentials. Human beings are not always fully aware of their potentials till they satisfy their basic needs and still feel something wanting, and start exploring new possibilities in positive functioning. They strive to devote and work on "something which is very precious to them, ... and aim to realize intrinsic values such as truth, beauty, perfection, simplicity," and ... "re-sacralize whatever they do by seeing the sacred, the eternal, and the symbolic [significance] in them".[69] Such individuals experience unlimited growth—fully, vividly, selflessly, and without being self-conscious or suffering any fear. They listen to their inner voice letting the true self emerge, which they accept and appreciate. They are honest when in doubt; and go through an "arduous and demanding period of preparation in order to realize their potentials, and are open "to be surprised by joy"—the peak experience of actualization.[70] The "joy" and the happiness here are the purest form of wellbeing.

There were a number of other psychologists, particularly in the mental health area, who have advanced a variety of ideas about positive functioning of individuals. The ideas broadly include those of the Maslow's. Integrating them, an attempt has been made to generate a multidimensional model of wellbeing.[71] The model encompasses an acceptance of one's limitations and potentials (Self-Acceptance), an urge for continued growth and development as a person (Personal Growth), a belief that one's life is purposeful and meaningful, not just for seeking earthly pleasures (Purpose in Life), a propensity to relate with others in trusting and supportive ways (Positive Relations with Others), a capacity to regulate effectively one's life in relation to the surrounding milieu (Environmental

Mastery), and a sense of self-determination in realizing the ascending goals of life (Autonomy).

The two—hedonism and eudemonism—have profound implications for the nature of development that people strive for. After having acquired the basic capabilities to meet existential challenges and to live a life of their choice, the hedonists will tend to accumulate wealth selfishly, live lavishly, cause inequality depriving others of their share in resources, and create a social milieu of exclusion and conflicts. The eudemonists, on the other hand, will relate with others empathetically, protect the environment, and grow with others. The former will have much more material affluence than the latter, but the latter will have lasting happiness and a sense of wholesome wellbeing by living in harmony in the community and the environment.

Ancient Indian formulation takes this journey beyond eudemonism. It presents an ideal, like the North Star, which cannot be reached, but can guide human beings to navigate through the mundane to progress towards the highest levels of their growth. The progression is an 'inner transformation' through Yoga, contemplation, reflection, and meditation. It is expected to lead to becoming *sthitaprajna* (steady wisdom), *nirdwandwa* (without doubts and dilemmas), and *trigunatita* (beyond three temperamental orientations).[72] *Sthitaprajna* signifies "a composed state of mind that is not carried away by emotions. It neither gets euphoric in success nor depressed by failures. It is guided by *viveka* (wisdom to decide thoughtfully), which is neither blurred by anger or lust nor fractured by doubts and dilemmas (*nirdwandwa*). Such a mind distinguishes its agency (*karata*) that acts from the one, the observer (*drashta*), who simultaneously and dispassionately analyses the process of acting, as well as from the one, the *bhoagta,* who keeps experiencing the positive and negative consequences of the actions. Separating three—acting, experiencing, and observing—functions of mind can enable a person to balance and counterbalance each other resulting into a composed mind with stable orientations. It is this balancing that renders human beings healthy (*swastha* means 'stable') in body and mind. As a result, they can indulge in worldly affairs but remain un-submerged and detached, can diligently discharge their duties to self as well as to others, and can still rise on a spiritual trajectory ultimately experiencing eternal bliss—the highest level of wellbeing. Not all human beings can reach such a state of inner transformation. However, continuous efforts to progress towards the ideals are likely to make them better and better human beings.

Culture Intervenes

Indian formulation of the inner transformation of human beings is an example of how a culture sets a unique model of growth. In fact, culture conditions discourse at all levels of development. There is greater agreement across nations at the lower (existential and human), compared to the higher, levels of the hierarchy. All nations, for example, agreed to the United Nations' Millennium Goals (2001) to eradicate extreme poverty and hunger, achieve universal primary education, promote gender equality and empower women, reduce child mortality, improve maternal health, combat HIV/AIDS, malaria, and other diseases, ensure environmental sustainability, and develop a global partnership for development. In sum, the universally agreed development has to ensure income, education, health, and gender equity, which have to be realized through global partnership.

However, even the most primary goal—eradicating poverty—is set to be realized differently due to cultural differences. Poverty is defined in terms of a country's wealth and its cultural norms regarding which of the material goods are considered to be a necessity, a comfort, or even a luxury. Poverty in a rich country (such as the USA) has a different profile than it has in a poor country (such as India). Earlier, we saw that the people of Ladakh did not consider themselves poor before its modernization started. Once exposed to the outside world full of new fashion, food, and fun items, Ladakhis perceived themselves as poor in need of an outside bail out. Approaches to poverty alleviation have also been different. The market-oriented approach prioritizes creating wealth, which then is expected to trickle down to the poorest. On the contrary, the welfare-oriented approach is to take comprehensive measures such as subsidies and direct cash transfer to pull the poor above the poverty line.

In fact, cultures make different people learn different beliefs, attitudes, values, and practices that differentially affect how they tend to meet their essential needs in order to improve the conditions of their living.[73] Internally controlled Western people, for example, are conditioned to make efforts directed to overcome barriers and realize the coveted goals while the predominantly externally controlled Indians prefer to appease the powerful ones or solicit the blessings of the supernatural and divine forces to get what they aspire for.[74] In the Western model, the market provides increasingly more variety of products and services that excite people to recognize and invent new desires and fantasies, chasing which stimulate the market to develop new products and services. It is through this reciprocally stimulating process that development occurs. The espoused Indian value, on the contrary, is to contain desires and live in contentment with what one has achieved. Contentment is voluntary, and hence, qualitatively different from the externally constrained "adaptive preference",[75] although there are grey areas where perceived scarcities and compelling needs make a variety of compromises.

Social development is particularly sensitive to cultural differences. Despite a consensus that socially developed society is just, harmonious, and cooperative, there are wide differences in how to get there depending on how human beings and their collectives are conceptualized. Individualist cultures conceive human beings as "autonomous atoms" who are striving to maximize their achievement, compete with others, and excel them. Their aggregated achievements amount to the country's development.[76] Society is conceived as an inter-locking system of networks of contractual roles whereby individuals calculate their profit and costs to relate with others within the parameters of their individual freedom and social contracts without heavy baggage of long term attachment and too much of emotionality. Collectivist cultures, on the other hand, have most people identifying with their collectives, subjugating their needs and aspirations to the collectives, conforming to the collectives' norms and values, taking pride in collectives' achievements, and tending to be embedded in their collectives.[77] Hence, individualists value to live a life characterized by their personal achievements, freedom, and justice. Collectivists are acutely concerned with their public image of "what others will think" if they do not cooperate or meet social obligations or show concern for others. Collectivists opt for social justice through affirmative action over merit and equity for reducing disparity between privileged and deprived. In contrast to the individualist theory of achievement for development, collectivist theory envisions the need for being embedded into own collectives tempered with openness to accept the diversities among various communities.[78]

Cultures, however, are no longer isolated from each other with closed boundaries. They inter-penetrate whereby their influences are segregated and assimilated in varying extent. Some cultures tend to segregate more than assimilate while others prefer to assimilate more than segregate. The Chinese, for example, in the USA acquire an American cultural frame, but also retain their Chinese cultural frame. They switch from one to the other behaving like typical Americans or Chinese in different situations.[79] Indians tend to acquire new cultural ideas and add them to the old ones without replacing the old. So, they assimilate them, as a result of which they are able to draw selectively from the elements from both in order to find hybrid solutions of their choice.[80] For example, they earn money through capitalist entrepreneurship, but use it to live a lavish life like a medieval lord. They serve their individualist interests by collectivist means and collectivist goals by individualist ways. In this way they have a wide range of possibilities by having the best as well as the worse of both—the Western and Indian dispositions.

Putting Pieces Together

State and sense of wellbeing have to be inter-woven in order to constitute a wholesome wellbeing. Separately they are incomplete and inadequate. It is like being rich, but unhappy or feeling happy but not having enough to eat. Subjective sense of wellness, happiness, without an objective base is a delusion or a passing figment of imagination. It is like being at the top of the world after taking a few quick shots of whisky. Such euphoria does last long and ends up with a depressive hangover. Similarly, earning money means having economic affluence to live well and have a sense of satisfaction, but mindlessly accumulating more and more money has the diminishing return. Money is indeed needed to improve living condition, get better education, maintain good health, acquire new skills, and so on. In that case, money becomes an *economic capital* to acquire *valuable capabilities* that are taken for the indices of human development.[81] But these capabilities are themselves the *human capital* that produces self-efficacy, empowerment, and similar other positive self-attributes, which reflect a sense of wellbeing.[82] Being empowered to regulate their own life and capable to achieve their desirables, individuals tend to cast the net beyond their self by reaching out to others, relating with them meaningfully, desiring to live in a civil society which ideally should be free of undue dominance, too many conflicts, gross injustice, blatant discriminations, and other social maladies. Such a civil society is considered to be a developed one, which can be built by *social capital*. Social capital consists of overlapping networks of groups and communities, their shared norms, and trust that facilitate cooperation within and between groups and communities enabling them to act together more effectively to pursue their shared objectives.[83] Their trust and cooperation help them realize 'bonding' among homogenous and 'bridging' across heterogeneous groups.[84] As a result, social capital does not only lead to social development but also to sustainable economic development.[85] Evidence indicates that social capital is positively associated with economic affluence, standard of living, and educational achievements of the family reflecting the quality of interrelationship in terms of cooperation and trust among family members.[86]

In other words, the divide between capital and development (economic, human, and social), which is conceptually the means-goal distinction, becomes fuzzy in reality. Possession of resources (e.g., money) is both an index of economic growth and a capital for its further economic growth as well as for development of human capabilities. The latter are also a capital for a sense of self-efficacy and empowerment that help improve human capabilities to seek meaningfulness in working for and living in a civil society, which is possible only if the members trust and cooperate with each other in their social transactions. The more civil a society gets, the greater is the possibility that its members will cultivate a sense of trust and cooperation. In sum, the state and the sense of wellbeing have to be integrated for a full realization of human wellbeing, and the distinction between capital and development is more conceptual than real.

DESIGN FOR DEVELOPMENT

Earlier in the chapter we described the poor quality of life which most people in India are compelled to live and the caste, communal, corrupt, and criminalized politics that is causing lawlessness and chaotic conditions in the whole society. A radical change in our approach to development that can ensure wellbeing of all is needed earnestly and urgently.

The development that is envisioned here is the one in which most Indians will be adequately educated, generally healthy, and continuously earning enough to live a materially simple but reasonably carefree life relating with others amicably, cultivating humanitarian values, and realizing their potential. Not all will be able to reach to the highest levels of achievement, creativity, innovations, and the deepest levels of inner transformation. But, they will provide the support on which the specially gifted individuals will reach out to the sky in the various domains of the national life: The superstructure will be based on the solid support of the enabled mass.

In such a vision, social, religious, and other forms of diversity will be prized as resources rather than a basis for playing divisive politics. Diversity will mean differentiation rather than discrimination. That is, no groups or communities will be identified for bestowing backdoor favours (e.g., castes and tribes for reservations) or targeted for victimization (e.g., Muslims). Instead of being assimilated or marginalized, diverse castes, and other communities and groups will be integrated in the mainstream. That is, they will neither be totally dissolved losing their identity nor segregated and neglected, but will be enabled to acquire adequate capabilities to compete and excel as well as contribute to the society as equal members and experience success and failures like others, while still retaining their separate—social, religious, or any other—identities.

All individuals are inherently capable of acquiring basic skills to achieve enough to live a modest life of reasonable satisfaction, provided they have access to an appropriate opportunity structure. There are indeed individual differences in capabilities. But they are small and insignificant at the lower than at the higher levels of human functioning. In comparison, the differences in capabilities across castes and communities are large. Some of them have been kept deprived for so long that their members' abilities to acquire necessary capabilities are somewhat blunted constraining them from accessing to the available resources. The welfare-oriented approach in such cases is to compensate for their deficiencies by giving subsidies, cash transfer, and backdoor favours in terms of reservations in jobs. In other instances where the vested interests so demand, the tendency is to hold the deprived people responsible for their plight considering them a fit case for defaming and denigrating. Either—compensating the deficient or derogating the victim—approach perpetuates their incapacities without addressing to the root cause. The appropriate approach is to help them (a) acquire capabilities and (b) to provide an opportunity structure to access to.

Opportunity structure has many layers. The first and foremost layer consists of orderly and stable environment. Orderly means a reasonable degree of certainty of the cause-effect relationship (that is, what is most likely to cause what) and the stable implies that this causal relationship holds over time. In such an environment social norms are clearly defined, rules and laws are strictly followed, people do what they are contracted to do, legitimate right rather than power or connection decides an issue, and disruptive and violent acts do not result into positive outcome. In sum, life goes on smoothly with least of uncertainty, friction and disruption. Such an opportunity structure can be put in place by an authority that proactively meets legitimate demands and genuine grievances of people, but firmly rejects those advances and demands which are spurious and outlandish. It creates awareness among people of their rights as well as obligations, commits to maintain law and order judiciously, shares its pro-people stance, and puts in place a strong apparatus to isolate and sanction anti-social elements. This part of the opportunity structure is initially authority-centric, but people quickly sense its superiority over a chaotic condition and accept it as a predictable social environment that spares their energy for putting it to a positive purpose.

Once certainty is assured, people need more. They have an built in impulse to aspire for a good life, free from the anxieties of living in scarcities, sound health and good education, and then opportunities and challenges to keep achieving, excelling, exploring new avenues, and accomplishing something extraordinary in order to stand out amidst others. They need to build up variety of basic to specialized capabilities to avail of existing opportunities and to create new ones. Increasingly specialized capabilities and expanding opportunity structure are mutually reinforcing—stimulating each other, co-evolving, and leading the people and the society to higher and higher levels of development. The authority such as the State in such a scenario is expected to shift from controlling and regulating to a facilitating role where as the people assume leading role in rising on the development trajectory.

The root of all capabilities, however, lies in *the most basic process of learning how to scan opportunities and make a right effort persistently enough to reach the coveted goal*. As the effort leads to success, it tends to be repeated, set in the mindset, and is readily available as a capability whenever it is called for. All attractive goals elicit efforts, although not necessarily either right or persistent enough to crystallize into capabilities. People often take short cuts, adopt dubious ways, double cross, or make half hearted efforts and blame others for their failure. The right kind of efforts are those which are directed straight to the goal, are socially acceptable, and do not infringe upon the rights and dues of others. That is, they are task oriented and socially tempered. Once individuals acquire them, they function accordingly. They tend to acquire the basics of capabilities, that is, when and what for to compete and when and what for to cooperate in order to optimize their own as well as collective gains. The underlying motive is to grow together, not at the cost of others.

The best time and context to acquire the rules for employing capabilities for optimizing own and collective gains are the early socialization in the family and learning in schools. Socialization in the family, compared to the school system, however, is less amenable to interventions. Hence, schools are a more appropriate vehicle for cultivating capabilities based on the effort-outcome expectancy moderated by social concerns. Both—school system and family—are embedded in social institutions that regulate how people should relate and interact, how family should function, what and how schools should reach, and so on. Therefore, institutions are the appropriate place to plan a design for development.

UNDERSTANDING INSTITUTIONS

In his Nobel Prize lecturse on December 19, 1993, North defined institutions as "the rules of the game: the humanly devised constraints that structure human interaction".[87] By 'constraints', he actually meant 'regulators', for institutions do not only constrain, but also enable people to perform and achieve what they cannot do without institutional support.[88] A more inclusive view is to conceptualize institutions as *"social rule-systems"*—systems that are durable and consist of social *rules* prescribing what to do in particular conditions, *conventions* which are particular instances of how rules are followed, and *norms* which are shared social standards to judge what is appropriate or inappropriate in specific situations.[89] Rules, conventions, and norms enable people to organize their thoughts and navigate socially in orderly ways. Without them, people will be left in a social vacuum unable to decide how to relate and act with others. So, society evolves and maintains institutions.

People in a society naturally interact with each other, identify their compatible preferences, and converge on common goals or purposes that, they think, can be served only through institutions. Institutions thus are social constructions reflecting collective choice where individuals' interests and biases play an instrumental role in shaping them, but once they are crystallized, individuals subjugate their individual options to them. That is how institutions constrain human interactions and become lasting, stable, and self-perpetuating framework, which individuals inherit from their predecessors and follow for their advantage. Language is a typical example.

There are certain basic functions that every society must perform. Hence, they are the foremost that have to be invariably addressed by the members of the society. Naturally, they become the priorities for interactions leading to develop institutions such as family, government, economy, education, and religion (among a few others), which are *primary* in importance and are found in every society.[90] However, societies differ in their forms, historical experience, internal dynamics, and external milieu causing people to experience different sets of strengths, weaknesses, threats, and opportunities. So, the primary institutions do not only unfold differently, but also proliferate to generate variety of specific institutions providing guidance on diverse issues. Social issues are interrelated and appear in overlapping clusters. Hence, corresponding institutions also overlap. As a result, a number of institutions may pertain to one social issue and a specific institution may be salient for several issues. Therefore, clusters of overlapping institutions pertaining to several interrelated social issues render the society as an interlocking and intersecting network of institutions of varied forms and reach—conflating and making cooperative, competitive, and conflicting demands on people. Familial rules, for example, are more elaborate in traditional than modern societies and clash as well as collaborate in a number of social spheres. In fact, most of institutions also contain contradictory elements within themselves. Rituals and beliefs in Hinduism, for example, are incongruent in many ways and are often contradictory to its philosophy.

Presence of supportive as well as conflicting elements between and within institutions enable institutions to self-perpetuate, while simultaneously being susceptible to changes and re-interpretations. If parts of an institution become irrelevant, the other ones assume greater salience and centrality. For example, if rituals and pollution-purity part of the caste system have become redundant, opportunism has taken over making up and still perpetuating caste system as a powerful institution.[91] Incongruent elements in institutions indeed open the possibility of naturally happening or inducing changes[92]—the formal if the incongruence becomes untenable and the latter if the changes promise some tangible gains. The process of *sanskritization* and *westernization* are the examples.[93] Similarly, politics has displaced the core element, faith, in Hinduism by restructuring it in terms of the ideology of Hindutva.[94] The main frame of institutions (e.g., caste and religion) remains intact in salience, but the rules, conventions, and norms within them undergo minor to major changes. Some changes occur overtime out of spontaneous human interactions, others are deliberately introduced with specific purposes.

Institutions which evolve out of spontaneous human interactions are called *organic*, compared to the *pragmatic* ones which are deliberately devised and socially engineered as special instruments for explicit purposes by motivated individuals, groups, or authority.[95] Pragmatic ones appear as organizations that serve as tools from which the progress in a society can be crafted.[96]

They could be large governance related institutions that aim to make macro changes in the system (for example, *NITI Ayog*) or small non-government organizations (NGOs) in remote parts of the country struggling to improve the life of marginalized people. However, the distinction between organic and pragmatic institutions is more conceptual and of relative emphasis than immutable. Human interactions are never free of the footprints of the more powerful players, who adopt a number of ways to channelize human interactions in order to shape institutions according to their interest. Familial institutions, for example, are biased in favour of men, who seem to manipulate interactions intuitively. Hinduism unfolded under Brahmins' worldview. Many economic institutions are implicitly or explicitly engineered by the rich and powerful individuals and groups in business and government. On the other hand, pragmatic institutions become viable and attain legitimacy only when individuals within them own the rules, conventions, and norms, which they do only when they get chance to interact and align their own needs, expectations, and goals with those of organizations.

Organizations are special forms of institution as they draw boundaries to distinguish their members from non-members, set principles of sovereignty concerning who is in charge, and delineate roles and positions to specify members' rights and obligations.[97] Social organizations such as family, caste, and religion are largely organic while work organizations such as companies, schools, and hospitals are primarily pragmatic. The latter are founded and run by individuals, their teams, or authorities with an explicit purpose to achieve specific goals and objectives. Work organizations, compared to social organizations, have more clearly demarcated boundaries, formalized authority structure, and well defined roles and positions enforced by rewards and sanctions for compliance and violations (respectively). As a result, work organizations have a great deal of influence on their members. When individuals join a work organization, they are willing to yield to organizational demands and expectations. If there are disparities between what they want to do and what the organization demands them to do, they are likely to suppress their inclinations and comply with organizational demands. However, more often than not, individuals keep nursing their inclinations, even secretly, that condition *how*, if not *what*, organizational injunction they comply with. Nevertheless, so long as they comply with, their compliance backlash on them and dent their intentions. Organizations eventually change their members' thoughts and behaviour, except when outside influences are stronger than those of the organization.

Organizational boundaries are never totally closed. An organization is always embedded in a network of organizations allowing influences to flow both ways through its porous boundaries. There is massive evidence,[98] for example, that the authority relationship learnt in the family resonates in work organizations. Autocratic parents, for example, are also autocratic executives. Similarly, new ways of handling co-workers learnt at job come handy in dealing with people outside. Earlier in the chapter, we saw how amoral politics of the 1980s spilled into society and then increased crimes and corruption in the society were ploughed back into politics. For an organization, the most critical consideration is whether it is able to regulate the inflow and outflow of influences in such a way and to such an extent that they facilitate its own and societal development.

There are indeed organizations, which are able to regulate inflow and outflow of influences so as to integrate their members' needs and expectations with organizational aims and objectives and position themselves in the society so as to contribute significantly to its development. Being able to be integrated internally and proactive externally, they set rules, conventions, and norms that spread out into the society. Such organizations become the fountains from which positive changes may flow out for development and wellbeing of people. They become institutions in the best sense of the term. They are the ones which are proposed here for interventions.

Nodal Institutions for Intervention

If the vision is to see the most Indians sufficiently educated and healthy to earn enough for living at least a modest life in harmony with others and the environment, the top priority for interventions have to be given to educational, health care, and income generating institutions, particularly primary and secondary schools, public health care system, and skills developing ones that can lead to sustainable income generating activities. They are the primary institutions, the importance of which is widely acknowledged. In fact, the country is committed to them. The commitment is reflected in the various Commissions, Acts, schemes, and rhetoric right from the days of Independence (1947). The new ones are the Right to Education (RTE), *Kaushal Vikas* (Skill Development) *Yojana*, Mid Day Meal Scheme, *Sarva Shiksha Abhiyan*, Health for All, and National Health Protection Scheme (NHPS) including *Ayushman Bharat* and Wellness Centres, and Mahatma Gandhi National Rural Employment Guarantee Act (MGNREGA), among many others[99]. For the privileged ones, there already exist world class schools, colleges and universities, super-speciality hospitals, and numerous other opportunities.[100] Despite all those high sounding missions and schemes for the common people, the institutions that are responsible for enabling them to acquire basic capabilities are extremely crippled and disappointing.

For example, there indeed exists a public health care system. It has 3-tiers: Sub Centres (SCs), Primary Health Centres (PHCs), and Community Health Centres (CHCs) for providing both promoting and curative health care. However, they are grossly deprived of the doctors. A latest report of the Ministry of Health (Government of India) conceded a shortage of about 82 per cent surgeons, gynaecologists, physicians, and paediatricians in the primary health centres, and the shortfall exceeded 90 per cent in seven States.[101] Only 10 per cent doctors join the public health service, and worse they do not want to be posted in rural areas even when they are given attractive incentives. Those who are posted in a rural area, remain largely absent affecting the morale and behaviour the allied personnel. Very often they do not have medicines and equipment for essential procedures. No wonder in the year 2014-15, only 28 per cent outdoor patients availed of the facilities of SCs, PHCs and CHCs leaving the rest 72 per cent on the mercy of private providers such as quacks, faith healers, and private doctors and hospitals. Majority of the in-patients (58%) in rural areas reported going to private hospitals. Even among the poorest 20 per cent rural households, 42.5 per cent of the in-patients got treated in private hospitals. Private hospitals are exploitative. They prescribe expensive medicines or brands often from the sources in which they have vested interests and force patients to go through expensive or unnecessary procedures. The Chief of the NITI (National Institution for Transforming India) Aayog (which has replaced the *Planning Commission*), summarises the situation: "More than five decades worth of experience with the provision of primary, secondary and tertiary healthcare by the government have been deeply disappointing".[102]

Similar is the state of school education. Government schools teach about 113 million (65%) school going children in 20 States. However, their enrolment between the years 2010-11 and 2017-18 fell by 2.40 crore while the private schools added 2.10 crore new students,[103] although many of the private schools are more like money-making shops than educational institutions. Parents still prefer them, though they have to pay rather than to get their wards enrolled in free government schools, because the public schools "do not have learning environment".[104] Only 6.40 per cent of government schools fulfilled the norms of the RTE (Right to Education) regarding the minimum required infrastructure.[105] In 2017-2018, the government paid Rs. 51,917 per pupil on teacher salary alone that is equivalent to 45 per cent of the per capita income of Indians.[106] Teachers take the most part of the government budget allocation. But they too are frequently absent minding their personal errands or hanging around the State educational functionaries. They are incapable or are hardly interested in teaching. No wonder, they are disappointing in terms of their students' learning indices. Indian students ranked last but one among 74th countries.[107] A recent nation-wide survey of 5.5 lakh students in the age range of 3 to 16 drawn from 596 rural districts disclosed the poor levels of their learning.[108] Naturally, government schools are losing their relevance. In 2015-16, Rajasthan, Maharashtra and Chhattisgarh alone closed about 24,000 government schools because their total enrolment had fallen below 10 students. In sum, the existing education policy must be thoroughly revised to put in place "better accountability" and "monitoring mechanisms".[109]

Of various government schemes, the MGNREGA (Mahatma Gandhi National Rural Employment Guarantee Act) is the most visible. It aims to provide at least 100 days of employment to one adult in the poor households. But it is crippled by many factors. An evaluation[110] revealed that many non-poor got job-cards made in their name, others got them in their children's name. There were instances of rampant corruption and delays in payment, faulty measurement of work, and manipulation of records in collusion with government functionaries and *panchayat* members. The worse, there was no provision to build up new capabilities and skills for future.

The common factors that ail all three kinds of institutions are their inadequate infrastructure, untrained and/or unmotivated personnel, and above all extremely deficient governance. Necessary resources have to be mobilized and rationally allocated for creating and maintaining adequate infrastructure. For examples, rural health centres do not only need buildings and beds, but also medicines and equipment, and residential facilities for non-local doctors and para-medical staff. Schools need classrooms, textbooks, furniture, toilets, drinking water, playground, and reading and learning materials. Sufficient fund for income generating schemes along with streamlined procedures and adequate administrative arrangements are must. Obviously, liberal and rational allocation in the country's budget is essential.

Similarly, human resources involved in these activities have to be developed adequately. Doctors must have compulsory rural posting for certain years in their career, preferably during their initial years. They must stay at the place where they are posted. Besides treating patients, they have to be trained and oriented to participate in the community in order to provide health promoting and disease preventing services. Teachers have to be properly screened and thoroughly trained not only in pedagogy and participative teaching, but also in inspiriting their students and becoming their role models. It means that educational, health care, and livelihood institutions need to be linked backward to the institutions that produce teachers, doctors, and administrative functionaries. They too have to be renovated re-fashioned adequately to supply enabled and energized personnel for the nodal institutions.

Childhood is the best period to inculcate an appropriate perspective on life and a wholesome view of wellbeing, which means encompassing as well as balancing materialist, social, and spiritual orientations in light of their potentials and limitations. In order to do so, reading and learning materials must be locally relevant within a broader framework of knowledge about sciences (natural, social, and earth), religion and culture, and so on calibrated for levels ranging from first grade to high school. Children must be made to realize that money is important, but only as a means to build up capabilities to live values based and socially integrated life. Experiential learning through group projects and sports of not only individual excellence, but also of social values of justice, tolerance, empathy, cooperation, harmony, and so on has to be woven into the school textbooks and taught as an indispensable part into the curriculum. Those involved in income generating schemes have to follow the streamlined procedure of allocating work, evaluating performance, and making payments promptly and correctly. More important, they have to change their mindset from being "privileged providers" to becoming the "instruments of change" by leveraging poor people's quality of life as well as their skill.

Of the three, governance is the most critical factor, the laxity in which compromises the efforts of vitalizing the other two: Infrastructure and personnel. The governance policies regarding educational, health, and income generating institutions have to be clearly articulated, independent and IT-enabled mechanisms for monitoring and evaluation have to be put in place, and a system for generously rewarding and promptly sanctioning for graded role functions and dysfunctions must be established. All three—roles definition, monitoring, and evaluation—have to be highly regulated for the basic role functions of teaching, heath care, and employment providing—with zero tolerance for deviation and negligence. Technology such as biometric attendance, CCTV cameras, and allied accessories now are available and can be employed adequately for the purpose. Those teachers, doctors, government officers, and their allied persons, who are found incapable or negligent have to be eased out and those who perform their roles diligently and are creative and innovating must be duly recognized, well-appreciated, and amply rewarded. The ground level functionaries in all three segments—education, health, and employment—have to have adequate autonomy, though duly monitored and evaluated, to function freely from the exploitative overview of bureaucrats and the interference of politicians.

While the systems for the ground level are proposed to be clearly defined, highly regulated, meticulously monitored and evaluated, and duly rewarded and strictly sanctioned, the higher levels of institutions of learning, health care, and wealth creation have to be open, flexible, and innovative so that the participants can strive to excel and reach unprecedented heights of achievements. It is expected that once people acquire basic capabilities through primary institutions, many of them will ascend on the development trajectory by driving themselves hard, overriding obstacles, and creating new opportunities.

AN ACTION PLAN

Is it utopian? No, not really; but it is indeed idealistic and a long drawn process demanding enormous and sustained efforts. We know where we want to go, but there are formidable obstacles in our way. We have to keep our eyes fixed on the goals and overcome the obstacles.

No action plan will work, which will not involve the State in a major way. The Governments (Central and States) control most of the resources, take policy decisions, and have the administrative establishment to implement them. Like most other governments elsewhere in the world, they subscribe to the GDP-centric elitist approach to development, which benefits mostly a few while throwing crumb to the rest in the name of welfare. *We are not thinking of welfare, but of an enabling State that gives the top priority to building primary institutions at the grassroot levels.* It is a radical change in the approach. The most serious problem in making this change is a large percentage of corrupt and medieval minded bureaucrats and politicians in power who are least inclined to embrace such a radical change. They can be made to change only if strong public pressure is mounted on them. The pressure will also trigger the sleeping conscience of the honest and competent bureaucrats and politicians, who will wake up to own the call for a radical change in our approach to development.

From where will this public pressure emanate? The best promise is held by the activists and their organizations who are already engaged in the efforts for uplifting marginalized people. Some of them are professionals who have left their lucrative career for working to energize the marginalized people. Others are fired by their idealism. They have the dedication, skills, and mass contact to take up the challenge of making this radical change. However, they are mostly constrained by their limited vision, sporadic activities, and isolation from each other. Some of them have indeed gone beyond distributing reliefs by helping the distressed in getting redress by organizing self-help groups for income generating activities. Some run schools and health camps, but on small scales. Now, they are envisaged to play much more critical roles in promoting the new design of development.

They can play their roles in three ways. First, they can mobilize people and create a movement to press policy makers to think and act afresh and plan a wholesome development for all. They can cooperate with them to make concrete action plans for establishing primary institutions taking local conditions in account. Second, once the institutions get going, they can assume the responsibility of providing unbiased monitoring and evaluation of them. Third, they can coordinate the private players and those in the public domains so that the primary institutions establish a solid foundation of enabled people, from which the more gifted will reach the new heights of excellence in the various national domains.

The professionals and their organizations are indeed private players. It means the action plan incorporates the idea of private-public partnership in development. The State is designed to have a major role in building primary level institutions and maintaining an orderly and stable environment. However, at the upper end of institutions for building more specialized capabilities, the State needs to allow the private players a greater role while creating supportive infrastructure and putting in place regulatory mechanisms for them.

There is a more critical role that the activists and their collectives can play in facilitating development. Having the intimate knowledge of the minds of the people and the local dynamics, they can mobilize people to elect honest and competent persons who can take up more enthusiastically the mission of a wholesome wellbeing of all Indians. It means the activists and their collectives have to play politics. Why not? If the root causes of disappointing development are located in politics, the uprooting of them must also be done politically, of course tempered by the fervour for a wholesome development of all.

CONCLUSIONS

The country has indeed emerged as one of the largest economies in the world. It has now artefacts, signs, and symbols of a great nation: Growing cities, high rising buildings and towers, new highways, shining malls, super-specialities health care facilities, world class educational institutions, space research, blooming IT companies, markets overflowing with variety of goods and services, free market offering new opportunities, growing number of billionaires, and so on.

But, a closer look reveals that the vast majority of people are still living a miserable life in unhygienic conditions with poor health, too many children, serious malnutrition, little or no education, and unemployment or unemployablity. Per person income of Indians is still very low by any international comparison, so is the human capital[111] or any other index of international comparison in development. In other words, we have built a shining bright and impressive superstructure, but have failed to provide it with a solid foundation. The superstructure is precariously suspended up by a few bright and cleaver individuals and groups, who are harvesting most of the benefits of development. They are engaged in mindless money making, a capitalist a *mantra* that the common people tend to emulate, fail, get deprived, and impatient. That makes them vulnerable to corrupt politics, which exploits them by fanning cateism and communalism for short term gains.

Superstructure will collapse unless it is supported by a solid foundation. The solid foundation is conceptualized to consist of the masses who are educated, skilful, healthy, and productive; who have capabilities and confidence that they can create a desirable future by their own efforts; who are disposed to create and live in just, cooperative, and harmonious communities; and who strive to attain peace of mind and lasting happiness.

We need institutions that can foster such people. We need them particularly at the grassroot levels for primary and secondary education, public heath care, and inculcating skills that can prepare people for stable income generating activities. They are the top priorities to which concentrated national energy should be directed. There are existing institutions in these domains, but are in deplorable condition. They have to be renovated and the new ones have to be established. Their basic functions have to be defined clearly, strictly performed, and fully accountable with due rewards and prompt sanctions. Beyond the primary ones, the institutions of higher education, special health care, and wealth generation need to have full autonomy as well as exact accountability to promote higher learning, innovations, creative experimentation, excellence, and proactive stances. What is envisaged is pervasive governance at the grassroot with increasing flexibility, openness, and autonomy at the top level institutions. It is by such a design that the country as a whole will develop a viable superstructure on a solid foundation.

The present bureaucrats and politicians in power are unlikely to be inclined for such a radical change in the approach to development. They have the vested interest in the existing system. Hence, the State policy can change only if powerful public pressure is built up. The best way to do so is to call upon the activists and their collectives to get involved. However, they have to get better organized, form networks for enhancing their clout, and enlarge their roles to put pressure on the policy-makers for this radical change, offer to provide independent and unbiased monitoring and evaluation of the institutions once they get going, and most important mobilize the people to elect honest and competent persons to the policy making bodies.

Notes

1. *Harijan* , 28 January 1939, p. 438.1.
2. Nadkarni, 2014, pp. 45 –54; Nadkarni, 2015, pp. 90-103.
3. Easwaran, 2011.
4. Gopal, 1982.
5. *National Herald*, 1939.
6. https://en.wikipedia.org/wiki/Hindu_rate_of_growth
7. Human Development Indices and Indicators Statistical Update, 2018.
8. Piketty, & Chanel, 2017.
9. IFPRI 2012, p. 42.
10. Hungama (Hunger & Malnutrition Report, Prime Minister office, in January, 2012; Saxena, 2012.
11. The Census, 2011.
12. Bajpai, 2018.
13. Roy, 1995.

14. See details in Chapter 5.
15. Lohia, 1964.
16. Prakash, 2007.
17. Hansen, 1999.
18. See Chapter 5 for details.
19. Youth unemployment rate ranged from 12.90 percent (2013) to 18.10 percent (2018), average being 15.50 percent. https://tradingeconomics.com/india/youth-unemployment-rate.
20. Jha & Pushpendra, 2012.
21. The ADR (Association for Democratic Reforms) Report, May 13, 2013. http://adrindia.org / content/nexus-between-elections-crime-and-money-ten-years-election-watch
22. The ADR (Association for Democratic Reforms) Report, May 26 , 2019.
23. Sagarika Ghose, 2018, pp . 20.
24. See Gunnar Myrdal,1968, *On India being a Soft State.*
25. See Chapter 1 for details.
26. In Rawls ' formulation (1971).
27. Wells, Undated.
28. Kuznets,1955 among others.
29. http://web.nmsu.edu/~dscoccia/320web/320RawlsDP.pdf
30. Pilling , 2018 among others, see details in Chapter 1.
31. Diaz-Guerrero, 2000, Maathai, 2009; MacLachlan, Carr & McAuliffe, 2010; Moyo, 2009.
32. The UNDP Human Development Report, 2010.
33. See details in Chapter 1.
34. https://en.wikipedia.org/wiki/Genuine_progress_indicator .
35. Simon Kuznets, 2014.
36. Kasser, 2002.
37. Lawn, 2003.
38. See review of literature in Sinha, 2013, p. 60.
39. Diener, 2013; Diener, Tay, & Oishi, 2013.
40. Bradburn,1969.
41. Andrews, 1991; Diener, 1984.
42. Marks, et al. , 2006.
43. https://www.oneworldeducation.org/bhutan-worlds-happiest-country
44. https://www.atlasandboots.com/happiest-countries-in-the-world-ranked/
45. Jha, & Pushpendra, 2012.
46. Sen, 1985, pp, 21-22.
47. Diaz-Guerrero, 2000, Maathai, 2009; MacLachlan, Carr & McAuliffe, 2010; Moyo, 2009.
48. Sen, 1999.
49. *The Human Development Report* 2002, p. 13.

50. Sen, 1999.
51. Bandura, 1994/1998, p. 1.
52. *The Human Development Report* 2002, p. 13.
53. http://en.wikipedia.org/wiki/List_of_countries_by_inequality-adjusted_HDI, accessed on May 11, 2014.
54. See Appendix 1.
55. Norberg-Hodge, 1997.
56. Stiglitz, 2002.
57. *Copenhagen Declaration on Social Development,* March 14, 1995.
58. Alechina, 1982.
59. A highly individualistic perspective advocated by Sen, 1999.
60. Maslow, 1971.
61. Alderfer, 1972.
62. See Sinha, 2014, p. 10.
63. Foa, undated.
64. *Copenhagen Declaration on Social Development,* Commitment 4, 1995.
65. Waterman, 1993.
66. Kahneman, Diener, & Schwartz, 1999.
67. Ryan & Deci, 2001.
68. Hudson, 1996.
69. Maslow,1971, p. 50.
70. Maslow,1971, p. 47.
71. Ryff, 1989; Ryff, & Keyes, 1995.
72. Chakraborty, 1987, p.107.
73. Berry, 2010.
74. Sinha, 2014.
75. Sen, 1985, pp, 21-22.
76. McClelland, 1961.
77. Triandis, 1994.
78. Tripathi, 1988.
79. Hong et al. 2000.
80. Sinha, 2014.
81. Sen, 1999.
82. Foa, undated.
83. Putnam, 1996, p. 56; Cote & Healy, 2001, p. 41.
84. Putnam, 2007, p. 106.
85. The World Bank, 2000.
86. Sinha, R.B. N., 2016.
87. North, 1994, p. 360. See also North, 1990.
88. Bardhan, 2010.
89. Hodgson, 2006, p. 13.
90. Hodgson, 2006.
91. Kothari, 1995, p. 7.
92. Chang, Ha-Joon, 2005.
93. Srinivas, 1956.

94. Nandy, 1998.
95. Menger, 1871 / 1981 / cited by Hodgson, 2006.
96. Reinert, 2006, p. 8.
97. Hodgson, 2006.
98. Sinha, 1990 for details.
99. Such as Commissions for higher education: Ambani-Birla (2000), Sam Pitroda's Knowledge Commission (2009) and Narayan Murthy Committee (2012).
100. Misra, & Bal, 2014.
101. Dey, 2019.
102. Statistics and quote from A rvind Panagariya, 2018.
103. Kingdon, 2019.
104. Saha, 2017, April.
105. HRD Minister's reply to Parliament in August 2016.
106. Kingdon, 2019.
107. Programme for International Student Assessment (PISA) test in 2009.
108. Annual Status of Education , 2018.
109. Kingdon, 2017; 2018.
110. Sushmita, 2015.
111. India ranked 105 of 130 countries in human capital. http://reports.weforum.org/human-capital-report-2016/

REFERENCES

Alderfer, C.P. (1972). *Existence, relatedness, and growth: Human needs in organizational settings.* New York: Free Press.

Alechina, I. (1982). The contribution of the United Nations System to formulating development concepts. In *Different theories and practices of development.* Paris: UNESCO Publications.

Andrews, F.M. (1991). Stability and change in levels and structure of subjective well-being. *Social Indicators Research,* 25, 1-30.

Annual Status of Education (2018). A survey conducted by the NGO: Pratham https://www.classiciasacademy.com/blog/annual-status-of-education-report-aser-2018/

Bajpai, K. (2018). Our real ranking. *The Times of India,* Patna, November 3.

Bandura, A. (1994/1998). Self-efficacy. In V.S. Ramachandran (Ed.), *Encyclopedia of human behaviour* (Vol. 4, pp. 71-81). New York: Academic Press. (Reprinted in H. Friedman [Ed.], *Encyclopedia of mental health.* San Diego: Academic Press, 1998).

Bardhan, Pranab (2010). Institutional economics of development: Some general reflections (pp. 15-40). In Timothy Besley and Rajshri Jayaraman (Eds.), *Institutional microeconomics of development.* Cambridge, Massachusetts: MIT Press.

Berry, J.W. (2010). *Culture and societal development.* Lecture delivered at the Central University of South Bihar, Patna, November 6.

Bradburn, N.M. (1969). *The structure of psychological well-being.* Chicago: Aldine.

Chakraborty, S.K. (1987). *Managerial effectiveness and quality of work life: Indian insights.* New Delhi: Tata McGraw Hill.

Chang, Ha-Joon (2005). *Institutional change and economic development.* United Nations University Press (Anthem Press. Tokyo, New York, Paris).

Copenhagen Declaration on Social Development (1995). World Summit for Social Development, Copenhagen, March 14.

Cote, S. and Healy, T. (2001). *The well-being of nations: The role of human and social capital.* Organisation for Economic Co-operation and Development, Paris.

Dey, S. (2019). Shortfall of 82 per cent specialists in primary health centres. *The Times of India,* Patna, July 1, 2019, p. 8. Full Report available on www.toi.in

Diaz-Guerrero, R. (2000). Is abnegation a basic experiential trait in traditional societies? The case of Mexico. In. J.W. Berry, R.C. Mishra and R.C. Tripathi (Eds.), *Psychology in human and social development: A Festschrift for Durganand Sinha* (pp. 68-85). Delhi: Sage.

Diener, E. (1984). Subjective well-being. *Psychological Bulletin,* 95, 542-575.

Diener, E. (2013). The remarkable changes in the science of subjective well-being. *Perspectives on Psychological Science,* 8, 591-612.

Diener, E., Tay, L. and Oishi, S. (2013). Rising income and the subjective well-being of nations. *Journal of Personality and Social Psychology,* 104 (2), 267-276.

Easwaran, E. (2011). *Gandhi: The man.* Tomales, CA: Nilgiri Press.

Foa, R. (undated). Indices of Social Development: Handbook. Cambridge, MA: Harvard University. file:///C:/Users/Jai/Documents/Social%20Development.pdf

Ghose, Sagarika (2018). *The Times of India, Patna,* July, 18

Gopal, S. (1982) (E.d). Selected works of Jawaharlal Nehru (Volume 9) (pp. 386-387). New Delhi: Orient Longman.

Hansen, T.B. (1999). *The saffron wave. Democracy and Hindu nationalism in modern India.* Priceton: Princeton University Press.

Hodgson, G.M. (2006). What are institutions? *Journal of Economic Issues,* 15 (1), 1-25.

Hong, Y., Morris, M., Chiu, C. and Bennet-Martinez, V. (2000). Multicultural minds: A dynamic constructivist approach to culture and cognition. *American Psychologist,* 35, 709–720.

Hudson, D.W. (1996). *Happiness and the limits of satisfaction.* Lahnam, MD: Rowman Littlefield.

Human Development Indices and Indicators Statistical Update (2018). United Nations Development Programme.

Hungama (2012) 'Fighting Hunger and Malnutrition', at http://www.naandi.org/CP/HungamaBKDec11LR.pdf; Accessed on 7 July 2014.

IFPRI (2012). Global Hunger Index Report: The Challenge of Hunger. International Food Policy Research Institute (IFPRI), Bonn, Germany.

Jha, M.K. and Pushpendra (2012). Governing caste and managing conflicts: Bihar, 1990-2011. *Policies and Practices,* No. 48. Kolkata.

Kahneman, D., Diener, E. and Schwartz, N. (1999). *Wellbeing: The foundation of hedonistic psychology.* New York: Russell Sage Foundation.

Kingdon, Geeta Gandhi (2017). In 5 years, private schools gain 17 million students, government schools lose 13 million. *Hindustan Times,* April, 17.

Kingdon, Geeta Gandhi (2018). When ideology overcame sense: RTE imposes a bureaucratic, grotesquely inefficient regime starving our children of good education. *The Times of India,* Patna, March 13, p. 14.

Kingdon, Geeta Gandhi (2019). Poor remedies to learning crisis. *The Times of India, Patna,* June 24, p. 14.

Kothari, Rajani (1995) (Ed.), *Caste in Indian politics.* New Delhi: Orient BlackSwan.

Kuznets, Simon (1955). Economic growth and income inequality. *The American Economic Review,* 25 (1), 1-26.

Kuznets, Simon (2014). Beyond GDP International Conference. *OECD.* Organisation for Economic Cooperation and Development.

Lawn, P.A. (2003). A theoretical foundation to support the Index of Sustainable Economic Welfare (ISEW), Genuine Progress Indicator (GPI), and other related indexes. *Ecological Economics.* 44 (1): 105-118.

Lohia, Ram Manohar (1964a). *The Caste system.* Hyderabad: Rammanohar Lohia Samata Vidyalaya.

Maathai, W. (2009). *The challenge for Africa: A new vision.* London: Heinemann.

MacLachlan, M., Carr, S.C. and McAuliffe, E. (2010). The aid triangle: *Recognizing the human dynamics of dominance, justice and identity.* London and New York: Zed Books.

Marks, N., Abdallah, S., Simms, A., Thompson, S. et al. (2006). *The Happy Planet Index.* London: New Economics Foundation.

Maslow, A.H. (1971). *The farther reaches of human nature* (posthumously edited by B.G. Maslow). New York: Viking Press

McClelland, D.C. (1961). *The achieving society.* New York: Van Nostrand.

Menger, Carl. (1871). *Grundsätze der Volkwirtschaftslehre.* Tübingen: J.C.B. Mohr. Published in English as *Principles of Economics,* Edited by J. Dingwall and translated by B.F. Hoselitz. New York: New York University Press, 1981.

Misra, S.N. and Bal, Monalisa (2014). Growth, development, and elitism: An insight into Commissions on higher education. *International Journal of Educational Research and Technology,* 5 (3), 29-35.

Moyo, D. (2009). *Dead aid: Why aid is not working and how there is a better way for Africa.* London: Penguin.

Myrdal, Gunnar (1968). *Asian drama: An Inquiry into the poverty of nations* (Three Volumes). New York: Twentieth Century Fund.

Nadkarni, M.V. (2014). *Ethics for our times: Essays in Gandhian perspective.* New Delhi: Oxford University Press, 2014. pp. 45–54.

Nadkarni, M.V. (2015). Gandhi's civilizational alternative and dealing with climate change. *Journal of Social and Economic Development, June, 90-103.*

Nandy, Ashis (1998). The politics of secularism and the recovery of religious tolerance. In Rajeev Bhargava (Ed.), *Secularism and its critics.* Delhi: Oxford University Press (pp. 321-344).

National Herald, June 21, 1939. In S. Gopal (ed.), *Selected works of Jawaharlal Nehru* (Volume 9), pp. 386-387. New Delhi: Orient Longman.

Norberg-Hodge, Helena (1997). To raze a village: The modernization of a thousand year old culture. In Jerry Mander and Edward Goldsmith (Eds.), *The case against the global economy: And for a turn toward the local.* San Francisco: Sierra Club Books.

North, D.C. (1990). *Institutions, Institutional Change and Economic Performance.* Cambridge University Press, Cambridge.

North, D.C. (1994). Economic performance through time (Nobel Prize lecture given on December 19, 1993). *American Economic Review,* 84(3): 359-68.

Panagariya, Arvind (2018). It's all in the design: Ayushman Bharat can be transformational if governance of public health care is altered. *The Times of India,* Patna, March 7, p. 6.

Piketty, T. and Chanel, L. (2017). Indian income inequality, 1922-2014: From British Raj to Billionaire Raj? Paper Series, No. 11. In Alvaredo, F., Chancel, L., Piketty, T., Saez, E. and Zucman, G. (Eds.), *World Inequality Report, 2018.* Paris School of Economics, Paris.

Pilling, D. (2018). *The growth delusion: The wealth and well-being of nations.* London: Bloomsbury.

Prakash, N. (2007). Impact of reserving jobs for minorities on labour market outcomes: Evidence from India. Department of Economics, University of Houston, Houston, USA.

Putnam, R (1996). Who killed civic America. *Prospect,* March, pp. 66-72.

Putnam, R. (2007). In Lynda Lee Kaid and Christina Holtz-Bacha (Eds.), *Encyclopedia of Political Communication.* Thousand Oaks: SAGE Publications.

Rawis (1971). A theory of justice. Cambridge; Havard Universiy Press.

Reinert, E.S. (2006). Institutionalism—ancient, old and new: A historical perspective on institutions and uneven development. Research Paper No. 2006/77, World Institute of Development Economics, Helsinki, Finland.

Roy, R. (1995). Caste and political recruitment in Bihar. In Rajni Kothari (Ed.), *Caste in Indian politics* (p. 215-244). New Delhi: Sage.

Ryan, R.N. and Deci, E.L. (2001). On happiness and human potential: A review of research on hedonic and eudemonic well being. *Annual Review of Psychology, 52*, 141-166.

Ryff, C.D. (1989). Happiness is everything, or is it? Explorations on the meaning of psychological well being. *Journal of Personality and Social Psychology*, 57, 1069–1081.

Ryff, C.D. and Keyes, C.L.M. (1995). The structure of psychological well-being revisited. *Journal of Personality and Social Psychology,*. 69 (4), 719-727.

Saha, D. (2017, April). India Spend, May, 2016. http://archive.indiaspend.com/cover-story/in-5-years-private-schools-gain-17-mn-students-govt-schools-lose-13-mn-26146

Saxena, N.C. (2012). *Governance challenges to reducing hunger and malnutrition in India.* United Nations Development Programme.

School Education in India (2016). National University of Educational Planning and Administration and Department of School Education and Literacy, Ministry of Human Resource Development Government of India, New Delhi. http://www.dise.in/Downloads/Publications/Documents/U-DISE-SchoolEducationInIndia-2015-16.pdf.

Schumacher, E.F. (1973). *Small is beautiful: A study of economics as if people mattered.* London: Blond & Briggs.

Sen, Amartya (1985). *Commodities and capabilities.* New York: North-Holland.

Sen, Amartya (1999). *Development as freedom.* New York: Oxford University Press.

Sinha, J.B.P. (1990). *Work culture in the Indian context.* New Delhi: Sage.

Sinha, J.B.P. (2013). Human development: Concept and strategy. In R.C. Tripathi and Y. Sinha (Eds.), *Psychology, development, and social policy* (pp. 59-80). New Delhi: Springer.

Sinha, J.B.P. (2014). *Psycho-social analysis of the Indian mindset.* New Delhi: Springer.

Sinha, R.B.N. (2016). Social capital and collectivism as predictors of development. *Indian Journal of Psychology*, Centennial Issue, 79-89.

Srinivas, M.N. (1956). A note on sanskritization and westernization. *The Far Eastern Quarterly*, 15 (4), 481-496.

Stiglitz, J.E. (2002). *Globalization and its discontents.* New York: Norton.

Sushmita (2015). Mahatma Gandhi National Rural Employment Guarantee Act: A Review. *International Journal of Arts, Humanities, and Management*, 1 (7), 18-26).

The ADR (Association for Democratic Reforms) Report, May 13, 2013

The Human Development Report (2002). United Nations Development Programme (UNDP).

The *Human Development Report* (2018). Human Development Indices and Indicators. United Nations Development Programme (UNDP). September, 14.

The World Bank (2000). Discussion Paper. Measuring Social Capital; Current Collection and Future Directions. Australian Bureau of Statistics. Blaxter, M. Poland, F. Curran, M. http://www.oecd.org/unitedkingdom/2382339.pdf

Triandis, H.C. (1994). Theoretical and methodological approaches to the study of collectivism individualism. In U. Kim, H.C. Triandis, C. Kagitcibasi, S.C. Choi, and G. Yoon (Eds.), *Individualism and collectivism: Theory, method, and application* (pp. 41–51). Thousand Oaks: Sage.

Tripathi, R.C. (1988). Aligning development to values. In D. Sinha and H.S.R. Kao (Eds.), *Social values and development*. New Delhi: Sage.

Waterman, A.S. (1993). Two conceptions of happiness: Contrasts of personal expressiveness (eudaimonia) and hedonic enjoyment. *Journal of Personality and Social Psychology*, 64, 678-691

Wells, T. (Undated). Amartya Sen: Capability Approach. *Internet Encyclopedia of Philosophy*. Available at http://www.iep.utm.edu/sen-cap/. Retrieved on June 23, 2018.

Appendix 6.1

Highest Ranking Countries on GDP, HPI & HDI

Countries having Highest GDP	Ranks		
	Gross Domestic Product[a]	Happy Planet Index[b]	Human Development Index[c]
United States of America	1	18	10
China	2	86	90
Japan	3	54	17
Germany	4	15	4
United Kingdom	5	19	16
Average Ranks		38.40	27.40
Having Happiest People			
Finland	42	1	23
Norway	28	2	1
Denmark	35	3	5
Iceland	-	4	9
Switzerland	20	5	2
Average Ranks	31.25		8.00
Having Highest Levels of Human Development			
Norway	28	2	1
Australia	14	10	2
Switzerland	20	5	3
Germany	4	15	4
Denmark	35	3	5
Average Ranks	20.20	7.00	

[a] Projected GDP Ranking (2018-2023). Source: International Monetary Fund, *Economic Outlook*, April, 2018. Released on June 9, 2018. http://www.statisticstimes.com/economy/projected-world-gdp-ranking.php

[b] https://www.atlasandboots.com/happiest-countries-in-the-world-ranked/

[c] https://en.wikipedia.org/wiki/List_of_countries_by_Human_Development_Index, Estimated for 2016

To Recapitulate

Since Independence (1947), India's economic growth has been remarkable. It is now the fifth largest economy and is the third in purchasing power parity in the world. The economic growth has resulted into all the artifacts, signs, and sounds that an affluent nation has. However, they hide the fact that the development so far has been contributed by a small minority of gifted and privileged individuals and their companies, who have harvested a disproportionately larger share of benefits. Inequality has been increasingly alarmingly.

Vast majority of Indians still live in miserable conditions with hardly any opportunity to get good education and skills, proper health care and nutrition, and stable gainful employment. Most of them do not have even a toilet and access to uncontaminated drinking water. They are unable to avail of the opportunities created by the economic growth, but fantasize to have a slice of the pie. This makes them vulnerable. Politics exploit them. Politics in India started rotting from the top since 1970s. It got increasingly more corrupt and criminalized, taking into its fold the vulnerable majority, and thus corrupting and criminalizing them too. With no ideology as the overriding force, politics politicized castes and religion, and itself got deeply embedded in casteism and communalism. Thus, while a minority of Indians created wealth for the nation, though mostly for themselves, the development of the vast majority of Indians was thwarted by caste politics, communalism, corruption, and crimes.

Caste system and religion did not originate as evil forces. Castes emerged out of occupational differentiation and specialization leading along the growth in science, technology, commerce, and trade. Competitive interactions among religions (Brahminism, Buddhism, and Jainism) led to the unimaginable heights of philosophical thoughts. Particularly, Buddhism spread Indian culture to a large part of Asia. However, they were also misused whenever the rulers so designed. The British politicized castes and religions and the State politics since the 1980s further exploited them for electoral gains.

Thus, casteism, communalism, corruption, and crimes are the symptoms of bad politics and lack of adequate development of people. So, the remedy lays in people's development, which can immune them from bad politics and disruptive forces. The development so far has relied solely on the aggregated indices, irrespective of who and how many created wealth and its artefacts. It tends to stimulate insatiable urge for money making, exclude the majority, beget elitism, and accentuate inequality leaving the most dependent on its crumbs.

An alternative design aims to shift the focus from solely materialistic and elitist to wholesome development of all. It means enabling most Indians to have education, skills, and health to earn stable income in order to live a modest life in harmony with others and the nature, and to attain lasting peace and happiness. It is on this solid foundation of the wholesome wellbeing of the most that the superstructure of excellence by the gifted few can be viably erected.

In order to realize the aims, the top priority in planning development has to be given to establish sound institutions for foundational learning, primary and public health care, and skills based stable income generation. Despite Constitutional commitment, political rhetoric, and numerous schemes, the existing institutions are in shamble. They have to be completely overhauled and the new ones have to be established with adequate infrastructure, well trained and motivated personnel, and efficient governance characterized by fairness in forming them, their meticulous monitoring and evaluation, dispensation of due rewards for performance, and prompt sanctions for negligence.

The Central and State governments control most of the resources and have been the custodian of development. Naturally, they have to play a leading role. However, the policy makers and the administrative establishment are unlikely to be genuinely inclined for this radical change, unless public pressure is built on them.

The people, even the poor and deprived, are now aware of the importance of good education and adequate health care. A few from them have overcome obstacles to rise at the height of excellence. But the people still need a movement that can build pressure on policy makers to make a radical change in the planning and on the administrative establishment to implement it in a mission mode. The best chance for initiating the movement comes from the activists and their organizations who are already engaged in improving the lot of the marginalized people. They have the dedication, skills, and public contact. They need to get better organized, network with other individuals and organizations, and mobilize people to create the movement. Then, they can cooperate with the policy makers in making areas-specific concrete plans. They also have to enlarge their roles by providing monitoring and evaluations once the institutions get going. Ultimately, they have to mobilize people to elect honest and competent law makers.

It is a long drawn process, but a beginning has to be made, and the sooner the better.

Index